Life's a Stitch
The Best of Contemporary Women's Humor

Edited by
Anne Safran Dalin

RANDOM HOUSE
REFERENCE

This book is based on *Creme de la Femme,* 1997, 0-375-70056-0
Concept developed by Anne Dalin
Edited by Nancy Davis

Interior cover illustration and chapter openers by Flash Rosenberg.

This book is available for special purchases in bulk by organizations
and institutions, not for resale, at special discounts. Please direct
your inquiries to Random House Premium Sales,
toll-free 800-800-3246 or fax 212-572-4961.

Please address inquiries about electronic licensing of reference
products, for use on a network or in software or on CD-ROM, to
the Subsidiary Rights Department, Random House Reference, fax
212-940-7352.

Visit the Random House Reference Web site at
www.randomwords.com

Library of Congress Cataloging-in Publication data is available.

Typeset and Printed in the United States of America

9 8 7 6 5 4 3 2
September 2002
ISBN 0-375-71970-9

New York   Toronto   London   Sydney   Auckland

Editor's Note

Life is made up of firsts: first step, first day of school, first kiss, first big job, . . . an unending list. In 1997 I experienced one of the most important firsts of my life, the publication of *Creme de la Femme: The Best of Women's Contemporary Humor,* a fundraiser for three charities.

Although I had done many different kinds of fundraising, putting together a book of humor was a notable first for me. So what made me think I could do such a thing? In a word, naiveté. Then, of course, I had to actually *do* it. We've all heard the saying, "Act as if," and that's what I did. I acted as if I had put together many books and knew exactly what to do.

Happily, the Muse of Funny Women smiled kindly! The pieces of the project fell into place and I started to receive packets of material—songs, poems, musings, cartoons, plays, short stories, shorter stories—in the mail. Who could ask for anything better than being sent mountains of funny material to pick and chose from? I wound up with more than 90 talented and generous women contributing their work to this very worthwhile cause. This project also introduced the voices of many new writers and afforded them the opportunity to become published authors. This was *their* first, and I am delighted to have been instrumental in making it happen.

Creme de la Femme went on to sell out three printings!

Now, we have the opportunity to present a new and updated version, *Life's a Stitch,* which will continue earning money for the charities involved. Women's writing helping women! And we have the opportunity to provide firsts for *new* hitherto-unpublished women with something special—and specially funny—to say.

Laughter truly is the best medicine. I have heard from so many people telling me how much *Creme de la Femme* has meant to them, in good times and bad. One woman told me she had received more than a dozen inspirational books when she was diagnosed with a serious medical condition, and as much as she may have gotten out of them, *Creme de la Femme* helped her the most: It took her mind off her problems, and more than that, it made her laugh. Those were powerful words to me. I hope that *Life's a Stitch* will do the same thing, and provide an always-needed smile or giggle, or a real belly laugh.

I want to start my thank you's with Wendalyn Nichols, Editorial Director of Reference at Random House, who helped give a jump-start to *Life's a Stitch*. She has nurtured this new version with tremendous fairness and determination. Time and again she has proven herself to be a woman of great insight and generosity. I couldn't have asked for more. I must also thank Wendi for teaming me with Debbie Posner, whose e-mails kept me laughing through a tight schedule and who has become a valued friend.

My unending gratitude goes out to everyone who has donated their work to *Life's a Stitch* and *Creme de la Femme*. There are too many people to thank individually in this limited space, but I will keep thanking each of you every time we speak. Without your constant support and generosity, I would never have accomplished this fabulous dream.

To my mother, Celia Safran—I love you and I know you're kvelling as you read this.

Finally, I want everyone to know that my husband, Jim, and our children, Nancy and Josh, are the most special people in the world. They shared me with this project for many months at a time . . . and now I'm back.

Anne Safran Dalin

Contributor's Page

Amy Krouse Rosenthal is not in this book. Had she been in this book, she may have written about lingerie, porcelain frogs, or the gourmet tortilla wrap trend. Ms. Rosenthal—again, had she been in this book—may have written an essay which began with the word "recently" and ended with the word "shame," "solipsism," or "betcha." Perhaps she would have written a poem (rhyming) about a dinner guest who takes too much extra sauce. It is just as likely however, that Ms. Rosenthal would have contributed a sonnet about bedspreads, or Robitussin®. You may have found a piece titled "Confession" in which she spoke of never writing down the order number when ordering from a catalog, even though she pretends to do so when the sales person says, "Do you have a pen handy? I'm going to give you your order number now." Had she written for this book—which again, she did not—she may have reflected on the human ability to eat at seemingly inappropriate times, like after a funeral, or at a charity luncheon featuring a Holocaust survivor flown in from Paris. One would not be wrong in presuming Ms. Rosenthal would have concocted some sort of chart, James Joyce to J.J. Walker. She may have pondered the curious "two first names" configuration of certain writers (Steve Martin, Jon Stewart, Woody Allen) and concluded with the heavy-handed joke that she will officially be changing her name to Amy Susie. She may have posted the results of a survey ranking the expletives most often used in highly annoying (but not life-threatening) situations, e.g. after burning a hand on a hot skillet or in the frustrating throes of trying to untangle a computer cord. (Top Three: #1: S---! #2. Jesus F------- Christ! #3. F---!) Ms. Rosenthal may have tried her hand at a piece of serious reporting, only to abandon the assigned worldly issue in favor of talking about a lumber truck she spotted with the sign "WE ARE LUMBER ONE." In this book, Ms. Rosenthal will not report on a study which found that everyone's favorite word is their own name; that there is an actual physiological response; that hearing your name releases some "happy hormone"; that when you were a kid and they did roll call, didn't you feel kind of good when they got to your name . . . "Amy?" "Here!"; that when you pass someone in the hall at work, don't you feel a certain tingle when the colleague says "Hi, Mike," instead of just "Hi." That whole article is not here. Something else you will not find here: a short story about how she was working at a coffeehouse one afternoon and when she got up to go to the bathroom she debated whether or not to take her wallet and that she decided to leave it when she spotted a priest a couple of tables away. Nowhere on these pages will you find: Ms. Rosenthal's brave and masterful exposé on the growing Lebanese Lesbian community; a transcript of everything she said last Tuesday; a charming thing her kid said; a three-page, run-on sentence ("creative non-fiction") about feeling chronically distracted, always just a shade away from *being present.* If you were looking for her piece called "Monday"—the one written entirely on a Post-it note about her habit of jotting down little notes all weekend so when Monday rolls around and she is in the position to get out and write for a few hours, she will take these key notes and finally write the thing she imagines she can write or should write, the thing that always seems so clear and possible and startlingly original from the vantage point of Sunday, this idea of Monday and all those hours, but of course the promise of Monday is more exciting than the reality of it—this would not be the place. Again, Ms. Rosenthal is not in this book.

Amy Krouse Rosenthal

Authors' Acknowledgments

Janette Barber: To Barry Brown.

Francesca Blumenthal: I thank the singers, musicians, critics, and other members of the New York cabaret community for turning my mere flirtation with songwriting into a passionate and rewarding love affair.

Michele Brourman and **Robin Brourman Munson:** We are especially grateful for the opportunity to support the National Alliance of Breast Cancer Organizations. Our mother, Liz Brourman, has fought successfully against breast cancer for these past twenty years. We're so proud of her spirit and courage, and wish to dedicate this contribution to her.

Fran Capo and **Anna Collins:** Thanks to all our loyal fans, friends and families for making "The Estrogen Files" so successful. Thanks. No really, thanks. THANKS!!!

Elisa DeCarlo: Many thanks to *Ms.* magazine for turning down "Intimacy" for being "too funny."

Sally Fingerett: To my editor Ted Field, to the kind and generous Anne Dalin, and to my girlfriends—Use your purse, use your wings, alpaca shells, . . . anything! Save me a seat!

Julie Halston: All my friends (you know who you are), Caroline's Comedy Club, Erv Raible and Ralph Howard, Thank You!!

Madeleine Begun Kane: I have some wonderful, loving people in my life, most notably my parents, Ernest and Beatrice Begun, and my husband Mark Kane. I want to thank them all, especially Mark, who inspires me, makes me laugh, and who taught me how to have fun.

Jane Read Martin: Neil Leifer, Caroline Aaron, Susan Greenhill, and Anne Dalin.

Heather McAdams: Chris Ligon—Loving Husband. John Mullen—Secret Agent. *The Chicago Reader*—First Break.

Amanda McBroom: Jerry Sternbach, whose music made the words sing. George Ball, my husband and constant inspiration. The women of Texas, who taught me how to really laugh.

Susan Murray: For Joan Murray, who taught me how to fight the good fight using laughter and cookies.

Mary Jo Pehl: To my beloved family and friends: thanks for making me laugh and letting me make you laugh.

Karen Rizzo: "Don't I Know You?" is for Bea Rizzo, who had a great loud laugh.

AUTHORS' ACKNOWLEDGMENTS

Flash Rosenberg: Exuberant thanks to the indefatigable Anne Safran Dalin, who so generously collects and connects us all—in humor and in health. Irridescent swoons to Robert "write-that-down" Peanutbutter Woodward. And love to my parents, Marilyn and David, who gave me the keys to the fun house of the interior.

Amy Krouse Rosenthal: The author wishes to thank *The New York Review of Poetry* for first publishing "Contributor's Page" (then titled "Gravy, Gravy, Please Pass the Gravy) in their annual Sauce Issue, volume 1, non-rhyming.

Kate Shein: Much thanks to Richard LaGravenese who brought me to Joan Micklin Silver. Thanks to Joan Micklin Silver and Julianne Boyd who brought me to *A. . . . My Name Is Still Alice.* And thanks to Lisa Loomer for giving my phone number to Anne Dalin.

Debi Smith: The other three of The Four Bitchin' Babes (Christine Lavin, Sally Fingerett, and Megon McDonough), through whom my contribution to this book was made possible.

M. Sweeney Lawless: Thanks to Andrea Jayne Lucard, Catherine & Keith, Valhalla—patron of the arts!, Tom Peyer, Young Survival Coalition (www.youngsurvival.org), Jim Torok, Robert Prichard/Surf Reality, the fabulous babes of Wellesley College, Pete Meinke, and all the smart, brave, funny women in my extended family who made me both a Sweeney and a Lawless.

Jackie Tice: Thanks to Tom Walz for his quick wit and alliteration!

Martha Trachtenberg: Many thanks to Anne Dalin, for creating this project and letting me be a part of it; to Tom Griffith, for providing both inspiration and exquisite vegetable sound effects for the song; and to Michael Griffith, for being himself.

Riggin Waugh: For My Therapist, the one who finally passed the audition. See you on Tuesday. Love, Six-Thirty.

Camille West: Thanks to my husband, Scott, for his exhaustive research and assistance on the song "Viagra® in the Waters."

Anne Dalin: Thank you to Flash Rosenberg for her magnanimous, unstinting, and open-hearted work on this edition's chapter openers and end papers. Thanks to Estelle Parsons and Joan Micklin Silver for supporting this project from its very beginnings. And a very special thank you to my daughter, Nancy Eve Dalin, truly my "in-house" editor. Your editorial expertise was invaluable in helping me with this project.

Contents

CONTENTS

CONTENTS

CONTENTS

CONTENTS

I Can See Clearly Now

Botero

(The speaker is SANDRA, an overweight woman in her 30s)

So I'm catching the new spring display—depressing
as usual—in the window of The Ample Woman's
Shop on 5th and 32nd

And I become aware of a man standing next to me.

His reflection in the glass is staring at my reflection
in the glass.

His eyes move slowly and carefully over every bulge
and billow of my size 22-X image.

I am about to get my image out of there, when he
turns to me and says, with a slight foreign accent:

"You have surely a pretty face,

"But your body—she is beautiful. Do you model?"

"Sure," I reply, "I model bikinis on Baywatch."

"No, no," he cries, "That is not much beautiful.

"Beautiful is *there* . . ."

He outlines the acreage of my reflection with his
hands.

"Your body is beautiful, sumptuous, joyous. I am
Botero the painter. I want to paint your body."

"All right, wise guy, paint it orange. It'll take two
gallons of Benjamin Moore, not counting the
primer."

He apparently took this as a "yes"

—a language problem—

And before I could scream "Jack Sprat" he had me
by the hand and was gently but firmly wedging
me into a cab.

"No way!"

"Trust me," he said. And for some reason, I did

His studio was an enormous loft—the whole top
    floor of a cast iron building in SoHo.

In the center of the studio was an immense easel
    and a banquet-sized table covered with pots of
    paint

Like buttercream in every imaginable flavor

And jars of brushes.

Rows of clean canvases, ranging from huge to
    humongous, stood against the whitewashed walls.

Beneath the skylight was a platform draped with
    luscious velvet the color of ripe seedless grapes

On which stood a large armchair, a plump chaise
    lounge, and an open trunk overflowing with
    costumes of all kinds. He asked me please to help
    myself—"You will see. They are much
    accommodating." I rummaged through them.
    They were wonderful. Nothing like the Ample
    Woman's "tummy tuckers." These were soft,
    yielding, expansive . . . "Yes," he said, making a
    wide circle with his arms, "Built to embrace
    realms of flesh measureless to man."

Botero painted me

Hour after hour

Stopping only to bring me great platters

Of fruit, cheese and pastry.

He painted me in a short pearl gray silken tunic, a
    ruffled amethyst-colored dress light as air, a gown
    of shimmering yellow with balloon sleeves—and
    many, many others.

He directed my poses with beautiful images

That carried me through the long sessions:
I was the Venus of the chaise . . .
A wood-nymph reclining on a bank of velvet . . .
The armchair became a horse
For me to ride
Bareback,
Side-saddle,
My gauzy bodice
Open to the wind . . .
The chaise lifted me
Like a huge pink orchid,
My body a honeyed chalice . . .

Holy Grail!

Botero painted me
Day after day after day . . .
The canvases got bigger and bigger.
He painted me
Larger than life itself
Fat and sleek—and beautiful
Measureless to man.

When he was done
There were 23 paintings of 22-X
Beautiful beyond all hopes and dreams.
I cried, "I love you Botero!"
He smiled,
"No more to model bikinis on Baywatch?"
"No, no," I laughed. "That is not much beautiful."

He didn't pay me with money.

Instead he let me choose 2 of the paintings.

"Take them to MOMA."

"Who?"

"Museum of Modern Art."

I couldn't bear to part with both.

I sold the smaller one to MOMA—for $350,000.

Me, with my certificate in dental hygiene from St.
  John's,

Who didn't know Da Vinci from d'Amato

Who didn't even know Botero's first name

Who thought maybe "Botero" *was* his first name

Me—who could only find a job in a very ample
  dentist's office

$350,000 for my sumptuous, joyous body!

Crowds of slim sophisticated people

Flocking to museums

To gaze in wonder and awe

At this 22-X filling 23 canvases

As easily, as perfectly

As Dr. Kleinman's beautiful crowns fill the
  emptiness between ordinary molars . . .

Botero's last words to me were "Stay far from
  Giacometti."

Jacka who?

I checked it out—had a great laugh!

Every day now I laugh

I am a nymph, a Venus

Riding bareback open to the wind

My clothes embracing realms of flesh

Measureless to man.

Make way for me!

I step from the canvas

Fat and sleek,

Warm and alive

And full of attitude.

I am my own Botero.

June Sigler Siegel

You

(WOMAN on telephone)

> But Fred, I can't get home for dinner. The meeting
> of Women in Advertising is tonight and . . . They
> are not all ball-busters . . . well, so Mary is but . . .
> No, Liz is not pushy—aggressive, maybe, but not
> pushy . . .
> It's not the same thing . . . You're aggressive, Fred
> . . . No I am not comparing you to Liz I only mean
> . . .
> Oh, Fred . . . I'm sorry . . . Fred?

Please do not think I am strident
Humorless, whiny, or shrill
It's true that I voted for E.R.A.

But you give me a thrill
I admit that I joined a committee
It was something my mom made me do
I signed a petition for equal pay
But I love *you*

Fred, you remember

I went to that beauty pageant
But you know I didn't protest
Some of the girls say those things arc unfair
But I said that *you* know best
Now and then I may go to a luncheon
Where women can speak entre nous
But I swear I would never burn underwear
And I love *you*

We are post-all-that-nonsense people
Designing our life style neatly
Sharing the bed and the chores
And the rent
(You spend half your salary
I spend every cent)
The equality of our commitment
Fulfills me completely

You've got to look at history, Fred

Gramps dominated my grandma
He made her stay home with a child
Alimony still keeps my mother in chains
But you let me run wild
Free to be a new-century woman
Who can paddle her own canoe
I am grateful for all my political gains
I recently heard we can fly combat planes
Where are you now, Nancy Drew?

Oh Fred, I insist
I'm feminine not feminist

I perfume, I powder, I shave, and I tweeze
I hated "Thelma and Louise"

Fred . . . I'll be home for dinner

And Fred
I *LOVE YOU*

Georgia Bogardus Holof

I Think, Therefore I am

Anne Gibbons

Let's Party

About once a year it occurs to me that I owe a lot of people a social debt and really ought to have some kind of party to try and pay them back. I'm not saying I act on this impulse. I'm just saying it occurs to me. And when it does, it is followed immediately by a sense of panic that makes me feel like one of the members of that Chilean soccer team that survived an air crash and had to contemplate eating a former teammate. In other words, I freak. The next thing I do is begin paging compulsively through books on the subject of "entertaining at home."

Of all the volumes in print on this topic, none fill me to overflowing with as much simultaneous loathing and secret envy as the combined oeuvre of Martha Stewart. Each one of these intimidating tomes is expensively bound and bursting with many, many beautiful color photographs featuring captions such as "a dramatic croquembouche surrounded by fresh flowers makes a spectacular centerpiece on the table in the library" or "Hepplewhite chairs, grandmother's plates, old silver, and long-stemmed Italian poppies grace the dining table set on our porch."

The author is a pretty blond woman with good bone structure and an uncanny ability to make whoever is her closest competitor for the title of Little Miss Perfect appear to have a learning disability. Her chapters have titles such as "Cocktails for 50—a festive occasion!" or "Summer Omelette Brunch Outdoors for 60!" I didn't even scan that one, since it is nearly impossible for me to get even one omelette out of a pan not looking like something I found at the bottom of my purse. But these are not the kinds of problems that plague Martha Stewart. "I always have baskets everywhere filled with fresh eggs," she tells us, perhaps while relaxing on the veranda of one of her summer homes in the mountain region of Neptune where I believe she spends a good deal of her time. Why? Because she simply gathers "eggs of all shapes, sizes, and hues from our

9

Turkey Hill hens." She has her own hens. She has her own bees. She probably has a trout stream and a cranberry bog. She's always somewhere picturesque ladling something steaming into something gleaming.

The most pernicious thing about her is the way she makes the thing she recommends appear somehow vaguely doable. "To entertain at home is both a relief and a rediscovery," she says offhandedly, perhaps while seated pertly in the spacious living room of her weekend place on one of the moons of Jupiter. "It provides a good excuse to put things in order. Polish your silver. Wash forgotten dishes. Wax floors. Paint a flaking window sill." Of course it does. Especially during those long Jupiterian winters that I understand can go on for decades. Nothing puts me less in the mood for thankless chores than the swelling sense of panic that comes from planning a party.

So here at last is advice for people such as myself, busy, frazzled, with no innate hosting abilities or graces.

Merrill Markoe's Home Entertaining Guide for the Panicky Social Debtor

Chapter One: Planning the Event

1. The Guest List. Martha Stewart says, "When you meet someone interesting at a party it is a natural reaction to think of all the other people who would like to meet him too. Sometimes I do this years in advance—putting people together in my mind." And I say to her, "Have a licensed professional sit you down and tell you all about lithium." I begin by inviting only those people I am so sure like me that virtually nothing I could say or do would sway their opinion. If this total does not get you beyond the fingers of one hand, add a select number of others who you know suffer from weight problems and/or eating disorders. These are people for whom heavy calorie consumption is always a problem so if you screw up the food it won't matter. If it does happen, your guests will be secretly relieved.

2. The Menu. Checking back in with Martha Stewart we learn that "a dramatic spicy taste is an inappropriate way to begin dinner." Therefore, it only makes good sense to begin by offering each and every arriving guest an enormous peppery bean burrito. "Cocktails that last much longer than an hour jeopardize the shape and momentum of the evening," Martha cautions. Since these are the very things that are most terrifying, figure on a two-hour cocktail period minimum. Now you've got everyone right where you want them: feeling fat and sleepy with a limited desire or ability to eat anything.

3. The Theme. Martha Stewart says, "Your own dishes, possessions, and personality will determine the style and tone of the occasion." That is why I like to use as my theme "the breakup of the Soviet Union," my table settings and decorations reflecting with amazing accuracy the chaos, poverty, and desperation of a culture in the throes of disintegration.

Chapter Two: Day of the Party Preparations

1. As soon as you awake, begin your futile attempt to remove the vast quantities of pet hair that have settled over everything in your house like a gentle dusting of snow on a wintry morning. Pick up as many of the saliva-coated pet toys as you can find and hide them somewhere. Anywhere. Especially the squeaking vinyl turkey leg with a face.

2. Martha Stewart thoughtfully reminds us to "Remember to empty a coat closet" to accommodate the outerwear of your guests. So, take all the stuff you have in there and move it to the . . . no, the garage is full. So is the bedroom closet. And the hall closet. Which is why I recommend that you just put everything back into the coat closet and lower the heat in the house so that your guests will not be inclined to take off their coats or sweaters.

3. Begin to anesthetize yourself. It may be politically incorrect in this day and age, but as much as you might like to, you aren't going to be driving anywhere. So isn't it worth it just this once to provide yourself with an impenetrable smokescreen between your problems and anxieties and your own ability to perceive them?

4. Don't forget that "music can establish and sustain an easy mood." I prefer a simple loop tape of AC/DC singing "Highway to Hell." But select your own favorites, depending on your theme.

5. Clean the pet hair off everything again, making sure to notice that there is just as much this time as there was before you spent all those previous hours removing it. But this time, if you are sufficiently sedated, you may enjoy taking all the saliva-coated pet toys and assembling them into a colorful centerpiece surrounded by fresh flowers and grandmother's old silver. Place the squeaking vinyl turkey leg with a face proudly in the front. Or go directly to

Plan B

Turn out all the lights in your house and greet arriving guests in your bathrobe and pajamas. Wearing an expression of sympathetic, quizzical bemusement, say to them, "Geez—this is kind of embarrassing. The party was last night. But hey—come on in. Can I get you a cup of tea?" They will probably stay only a few minutes—just long enough to get angry about already getting pet hair all over some cherished item of clothing. But because the error will seem to be theirs, your social obligations will be paid in full!!

Merrill Markoe

Hostess with the Mostest

SHE WAS AMAZING

SHE WAS THE HOSTESS
AND YET SHE HAD MANAGED
TO HAVE A DEEP, MEANINGFUL
CHAT WITH EVERY SINGLE
PERSON AT HER PARTY

Mary Lawton

Blank Canvas

... AND HERE IS AN EXAMPLE OF CULTURAL LIFE AFTER FUNDING CUTS TO THE ARTS !

Bulbul

Typical Japanese Woman

I am the typical Japanese woman," my neighbor, Mrs. Okano, insists a few mornings after the newspaper interview comes out. It's been at least two or three weeks since we've seen each other. I'm coming back from shopping and she's at the foot of the apartment stairway waiting, she tells me, for the mail carrier.

"I'm serious," my neighbor says, "if you want to know anything about typical Japanese women, you can ask me."

Ted calls Mrs. Okano "the mayor" of Maison Shōwa, our apartment complex. She's there at the mailboxes at eleven o'clock most mornings, exchanging gossip, news, and information with the other women in fifties-style housedresses and slip-on plastic street sandals. I am the outsider in this group, the only foreign woman in Maison Shōwa, but she makes a point of including me in their conversations. She tells me when a neighbor has twins, an event for Maison Shōwa, and is delighted when I respond that I have stepsisters who are twins. She says she will make sure to tell the neighbor and perhaps we can talk together sometime about twins, in America and in Japan. ("Do you know," she asks me, "that twins are twice as common in America? Some scientists think it is because of our diet. Maybe too much soy sauce," she jokes.) Often, Mrs. Okano passes along more mundane information: she warns me of an upcoming earthquake drill one day and another time, tells me that a woman from NHK (the national public television station) will be by to collect a "voluntary but required" user fee.

Twice she's invited me into her apartment for afternoon tea. It's 2DK just like ours but seems smaller. It is crammed with furniture, including several large, freestanding wardrobes that hold clothes for herself and her husband, their two children, and Mr. Okano's mother, who has just moved in with them. Their housing situation is not atypical, even for this affluent suburb. I have gathered that Mr. Okano is an executive at a major corporation; they drive an Audi and own state-of-the-art electronic equipment. But housing costs are astronomical here. A new apartment in the Kansai area can be hard to find and often requires exorbitant "key money," sometimes up to a year's rent paid in cash in advance. Mrs. Okano occasionally hints that they will be moving soon but always abruptly switches to some more immediate topic, so we never discuss the new home.

I've never seen her husband or children. From our conversations, I've learned that her son is in junior high and her daughter in high school. Both are enrolled in *juku* five nights a week.

"It's necessary" is all she says, putting an end to any further questions I might have about her children spending so much time in school, studying so hard. "Besides," she laughs self-consciously, gesturing around the crowded living room, "at *juku* they can stretch their legs."

Over tea, she tells me I am the first *gaijin* she's ever had in her apartment. She taught high school English briefly before she got married but this is the first chance she's had to practice her English in years. She is one of the few Japanese in our apartment complex to put out a Japanese flag on national holidays, so I assume her politics must be fairly conservative, but it's not a subject we discuss. We talk about our town, Japan, children, America, and anything else that happens to come up. Since neither of us is fluent in the other's language, we spend a lot of time riffling through dictionaries, gesturing, pointing. We speak a strange language, somewhere between English and Japanese, and sometimes find ourselves frustrated that we each know exactly the same words in each other's language.

"Interesting," she'll say.

"*Omoshiroii,*" I respond.

"*Muzukashii,*" I'll say.

"That's difficult, complicated," she'll translate.

She's been to tea in my apartment too, and has told all of the neighbors how I hang old kimonos on my walls like art and use soba to make spaghetti. We have learned from one another, enjoyed each other's company.

"Why do you consider yourself 'typical'?" I ask her.

"Because I am," she laughs. "There's nothing unusual about me at all!"

"I think it's unusual," I say admiringly, "for someone to admit she is typical. Most people think they are pretty special."

"Oh, maybe in America," she laughs. "But in Japan, every woman thinks that she is typical."

As we are laughing, the mailwoman zooms up on her red motorbike. Mrs. Okano excuses herself and goes out to meet her.

She reminds the mailwoman that she will be moving today and that from now on her mail should be delivered to her new address.

"You're moving *today*?" I ask, surprised at how disappointed I feel.

"*Gomen nasai, gomen nasai,*" she apologizes, realizing that I'm outside the information loop. Probably everyone else at Maison Shōwa has known for weeks.

I tell her I'm sorry to hear that she is moving, but that I hope she will enjoy her new apartment.

"It's a *house,*" she says, unable to conceal her pride.

She is expecting the movers this afternoon but insists on inviting me in so she can give me a copy of a map she has neatly drawn, marking the way to her new house.

"Now you can come visit me," she beams, handing it to me. "I gave my husband a map this morning so he can find his way to our new house tonight after work." She says this casually, as we start to make our formal goodbye bows.

"I don't understand. You mean, he doesn't remember the way?"

"He's never been there."

"I don't understand," I repeat, this time in Japanese. "He's never been there?"

Now she's confused by my confusion, and repeats again, in her best English, that she's drawn him a map because he's never been to the house itself.

"Excuse me, please," I say, upping the politeness level of my Japanese. "I do not understand how he could have bought a house without seeing it?"

"He didn't buy the house, I did."

"And he never saw it before you bought it?"

"Of course not. That's woman's work. I told you I'm a typical Japanese woman. Isn't this how women do it in America?"

Mrs. Okano is shocked when I tell her that few American married women make major financial decisions without consulting their husbands and that I don't know any married woman who would go out and buy a house on her own. There might be some, but I don't know any.

"Really?" She's as incredulous as I am.

"Never."

"What about a car?" she asks me.

I shake my head no.

"Appliances—refrigerator, television?"

"Not usually."

"Furniture?"

"Probably not. Most American husbands would be mad, I think, to come home and discover their wife had just bought a new couch or dining room set without consulting them."

"I thought all American women work, earn their own money?" She knows me well enough to know I wouldn't lie about this but she's finding the whole conversation bizarre.

"It's true many American women work outside the home," I begin again, slowly. "But even the ones who earn their own money often consult their husbands about big purchases."

"This is what Americans call 'women's lib'?" Mrs. Okano laughs out loud, then covers her mouth with her hand. She apologizes for her rudeness, but cannot stop laughing.

By noon, everyone in our apartment complex will have heard about how the poor *gaijin* woman works full-time as a college teacher, but wouldn't even buy a measly sofa without first asking her husband's permission.

"*Kawais!*" she says finally, exchanging her laughter for the ritual expression of sympathy (How pathetic, how pitiful!). Mrs. Okano reaches out and pats my arm encouragingly, as if I'm a small child badly in need of comforting.

"No wonder you like Japan so much!" she says.

Cathy N. Davidson

Brain Lint

Brain Lint by Amy K.R.

When leaving a tip at, say, Starbucks or Caribou, i often do so with exaggerated gestures or take a bit longer than necessary to place the doller in the dish, just to make sure they know what a nice and generous customer i am.

'clunk! ≣ shuffle, shuffle...

Brain Lint by Amy Krouse Rosenthal

Can you be a feminist but still do a double take when you see a female UPS driver?

hmm... weird...

scratch scratch

UPS Worldwide Delivery

amy@suba.com

Brain Lint by Amy K.R.

I want it because:

- i used to have it and lost it.
- you have it
- it's something i should not have.
- it is pretty.
- i want everything.
- i imagine it will make a difference.

amy@suba.com

Brain Lint by Amy Krouse Rosenthal

When someone gives you directions to their house, there is always a point where you realize, "I think they are giving me way more detail than I need." They think they are helping you by saying, "You'll turn left at the first light — there's an Arby's on the corner and a church with white shutters and this funny dolphin sculpture, if you pass a Blockbuster, then you've gone too far, oh and there's this red...

Amy Krouse Rosenthal

19

Don't I Know You?

It will be cold at work, the air conditioner perpetually conditioning. My work. Where I work. My twenty-second job in half as many years. Eeny meeny miney moe catch a job by the toe . . .

I drive down Hollywood Boulevard past tourists in Disneyland sweatshirts taking videos of each other in front of Ripley's Believe It Or Not. Sometimes I honk and wave and they turn their cameras on me in my twelve-year-old Honda. The sweet scent of jasmine stains the air this time of year, overpowering all other olfactory sensations. If you suck in air through your nose too hard or too fast at any given moment or place in Los Angeles you could almost fall in love. Smells like paradise feels like Times Square. Left on La Brea, right on Sunset Boulevard. I arrive. Sunset Plaza. One city block of pricey boutiques and crowded outdoor cafés visited at lunch by living dolls with large collagen lips, the eminently sun-glassed, tourists in Toon Town T-shirts, old ladies with Divas' faces sewn into place, young men in Sundance caps and *Hair*. Hair gone from home to car to destination. Strands lying obediently next to each other, coaxed, willed into place. I watch everyone eat lunch from the doorway of where I work.

I work at Boutique Morgana on the Plaza. Emily, the manager, is an acquaintance of mine. We met in yoga class where I was trying to rid myself of the angst I'd experienced in my last job . . . my twenty-first. I needed a new job. She had just fired a salesgirl for screaming in the dressing room at a naked customer. That's how it happens.

"Clients, not Customers." Emily reminds me.

I never actually touch any money. No dirty green bills. Just plastic. And no dollar signs next to the three and four figures on each price tag. And that is not a short wool jacket, that's the DALAI. All the clothes have names. Longer wool jacket—LAMA, longest—HIMALAYA. Long jersey tee—AIR, short sleeved—VALERIAN. There's APOLLO and ATHENA, MERLIN, and

GAIA. And ATLANTIS and SUN and MOON and VENUS and the History of the World in silk chiffon. The FRIDA KAHLOS—diaphanous medieval velvet gowns—slip off their hangers (trying to run away?). I feel a special bond with them.

Ten-oh-two. My day begins.

SHE enters. She with well-trained hair of gold streaks perfectly haphazardly spaced, aubergine wool pant suit, matching pumps. Emily nudges me, "Sarah Lynn Gold, very good client."

I squint as I walk towards Ms. Gold. "Hello, let me know if I can be of help today." Haven't dropped the squint, now I am staring at her. In my head I add twenty pounds, color the hair mousy brown and frizzy, tie-dyed shirt, hooded zipper sweatshirt, earth shoes.

Emily whispers into the back of my head. "You heard of her? She's a big producer."

I drop my squint and watch she-with-aubergine-armor in profile. I casually circle her. She smiles. I smile back. The Doctor Diamond nose. I recognize it. Doctor Diamond, nose doctor plastic surgeon to entire neighborhoods of a certain well-to-do New York suburb. Girls, my friends, a cousin, all owing their eighteenth birthday present to Doctor Diamond. Dr. D., known for a signature diamond tipped nose. A generation of girls with the same secret cousin nose. Girls with names like Sharon Berg and Missy Feinstein and Janet Levy.

Sarah Lynn Gold is stuck in her smile. I'm stuck in my squint. She says, "Gee you look familiar."

Sarah Lynn Gold. Drop the Sarah, bump the nose. Twenty years and no longer tying lengths of incorrigible hair around empty orange juice cans. No longer a baby fat princess proudly revealing a sixteenth calico patch on threadbare bellbottoms. Lynn Gold. Sat next to me. We shared a lab table in Al the Frogman Fishbine's sixth-period eighth-grade Biology class. Al the Frogman specialized in magic tricks with vital pig organs and Borscht Belt stand-up while he showed the class how to pin a lizard to a cork board. Al the Frogman . . . smelled of Wrigley's spearmint and Southern Comfort. Killed the lizards with his breath. Hit poor Amy Funicello over the head with a goat bladder when she couldn't commit the table of elements to memory. No one came near Amy for months after that. Word spreads quickly in eighth grade as do cooties. Lynn and I started a petition to get Al Fishbine's tenure revoked. We whispered together. Got nearly the whole eighth-grade class to sign . . . and some ninth graders. Lynn was well connected even back then. She knew ninth and tenth graders.

Ms. Sarah Lynn Gold holds a GUINEVERE to her chin. "I LOVE this. This is a great dress."

I nod. Never saw her or spoke to Lynn after eighth grade. I moved. She made new friends . . . eleventh graders, TV producers, movie directors.

She hangs up the GUINEVERE. "I know you. Didn't you work at Luma Café?"

"No."

"The one in New York?"

"Sorry."

"The Brooks project. The one that got canceled? You cut your hair."

"No, I don't think so. I'm . . . uh, a biologist. Normally, I am."

Emily stands nearby making the hangers equidistant on the silk rack. She coughs. Sarah Lynn and I watch Emily cough. Emily could be coughing up light bulbs considering how intently we stare at her.

"I could have sworn . . ." Sarah continues. "I'm very good with faces."

Inside I'm shouting. Remember how we organized the class? I was smart. Made you laugh. Introduced you to Bette Midler and Three Dog Night. Aloud, "Oh well." I begin to make the hangers equidistant on the tropical wool rack.

Sarah Lynn Gold leaves the store and crashes into Blythe Danner. They hug noisily.

Al the Frogman still has tenure although I heard he died a few years back.

Karen Rizzo

Fly Me

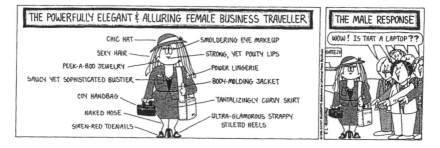

Cathy Guisewite

Broad Comedy

Somewhere out there in the universe is a very funny woman named Kerry O'Brien. Actually, I'm assuming she's still funny. The last time I saw her we were three and best friends at All Souls nursery school. My report cards attest to our joint comedy prowess: we appear to have spent most of our time rolling around on the floor cracking each other up. Or putting on "movie shows" where we would make the rest of the class sit quietly in neat rows and watch as we performed our shtick in the block corner (trying out the show in the sticks, as it were).

At four we split up the act and I went solo to an all-girls school. There, with a drama department devoid of boys, I was able to sink my teeth into the choicest comedy roles, and on a real stage no less. My gravedigger in *Hamlet* was rivaled only by my bad drunk in a bad fedora in *Ten Little Indians*. We were such smart girls. But we were so naive: no one ever bothered to tell us women weren't meant to be funny.

Not surprisingly, ten years later I found myself on a shrink's couch uttering these fateful words: "If I could just be a comedy writer I'd be so happy." I am now a Hollywood sitcom writer. Studios, on an alarmingly regular basis, pay me to be funny. I'm pretty sure they know I'm a woman. And I wouldn't necessarily say I'm happy. Call me bemused.

My first hint that I wasn't in comedy Kansas anymore came when my agent phoned me to tell me about my first break. "*Mango Man,*" (all sitcom titles have been changed to protect the innocent and the guilty) she said, "is very interested in you. You're the best woman they've read." "The best woman?" I asked. "Sure," she said, exasperated. "They had to hire a woman. You're the best. (Pause) What. You're not happy." "No," I explain in my best girls'-school logic. "I'm not a funny woman. I'm just funny. Period." "Welcome to Hollywood," said my agent. "Go to the gym. We'll do lunch tomorrow and talk."

What I learned that day has stuck with me. The female writer quota, like male waxing, is a lot more prevalent in Hollywood than you'd care to know. What's fascinating is that while sitcoms will fight over a handful of women writers, once hired they rarely know what to do with us. We're like that goldfish you diligently tossed rings to win at the school fair: once you got it home you realized you have nothing to put it in and you have no idea what it eats.

There is an unwritten understanding in sitcoms. Women are very good at coming up with stories and writing "treacle scenes" (that ubiquitous part of any bad sitcom, usually act 2, scene 3, when someone says "I think we need to talk.") They are also good to have around to answer general questions about the female anatomy and to field fashion questions. ("No, Amanda can't wear linen in that dinner scene. It's December.") What women, in general, are not hired for is the real stuff of comedy: jokes.

For the most part, writer's rooms are still the denizens of young male writers practicing what I call the Stooges Principle: if you like the Three Stooges, you're funny and can bring in your toys and play. If you don't, you're probably a girl and have cooties. Since appreciation of the Three Stooges does, I'm scared to admit, alarmingly often divide down gender lines, this rule has been quite effective at keeping most women at the comedy water cooler. (By the way: note how many times a Three Stooges joke makes it into your favorite sitcom. They're stealthy.)

Recently I had a (male) boss tell me, point blank, that women aren't funny. When I pointed out to him that he hired me to be funny and, last time I checked, I was a woman, he thought for a moment and then answered with bosslike aplomb: "Yeah, but you're not a woman." With that he turned on his heels and exited, off to make his next executive decision. On more than one occasion I have had the following "compliment" from a fellow male writer: "You're good. You write like a guy." What they mean is: I'm confused. You're actually funny and you have breasts.

Male writers apparently aren't the only ones I'm confusing. While comedy has done wonders for my checkbook, it has been hell on my dance card. As my friend Karen likes to point out, being a woman in this business is like playing the children's game Careers. You get sixty points and you get to decide between a family and career. Unfortunately, the guys still get both.

I have a friend here in L.A. He is neurotic. He is losing his hair. He wears bad clothes. He is a classic nebbish. He is also a TV producer. And women flock to him like swallows to Capistrano. On any given day he is entertaining another would-be model, or struggling actress. His position and paycheck shriek "big break" to these girls. In Hollywood, a guy's producing credit on *Seinfeld* is better than any Spanish Fly.

Now when you're a female comedy writer, it doesn't exactly work the same way. Here's the scenario. You enter a bar. You think you look pretty good. A man with a goatee approaches you. (In Hollywood, a goatee is a necessity. Like milk or toilet paper.) You trade meaningful glances. He approaches. You flirt madly. He asks what you do. Women writers have learned to answer this question as if discussing the very ill: "I write (hushed whisper) comedy."

There is a long pause. During this pause he is thinking the following: "She's probably gay. She's too smart. She won't laugh at my jokes. Oh God, she probably makes more money than me. Hey, maybe she has another gay friend and the three of us could . . . Whoa, is that Michelle Pfeiffer?" He exits quickly to the opposite end of the bar. Really. This happens.

Don't get me wrong, I don't just blame the men of Tinseltown. There are plenty of women happy to uphold the stereotype. Why, right now, there are two very successful comediennes with hit shows who are very vocal about not wanting women writers on their staffs. Both have been victims of bad men throughout their lives. One speaks out against domestic violence. Ironically, while society has come to uncomfortable terms with the image of women being punched, women doing the punch lines still scare them.

Conversely, not all men are scared of funny women. God bless them. In fact, my first benefactor was a man of some stature. It was Robert Lowell, the famous poet. I was five. He was judging a smart writing contest I entered with a touching poem in verse about a crab with a weight problem. He found my piece joyous and effervescent and funny. And better than the boys'. I won. But then again, he was clinically crazy at the time and I had a pageboy haircut so it probably doesn't count.

I have a recurring dream. Kerry O'Brien and I are running a show. I enter the writer's room and it is full of bright, funny women. (Okay, and some enlightened men.) We don't spend hours writing jokes about PMS. We don't talk endlessly about our sexual conquests. We write brilliant, witty repartee for a brilliant, witty sitcom that wins many brilliant shiny awards. Then we go home to our husbands who have spent all day polishing our Emmys. And we make them laugh till they cry.

Jenny Bicks

Two By Two

"YOU MEAN NOAH DISCRIMINATED ON THE BASIS OF MARITAL STATUS?"

Martha Campbell

Therapy Audition

I quit therapy a few years ago because, financially, I had to choose between my therapist of eight years and my cleaning boys of six months. I loved my therapist, but, frankly, my cleaning boys were cheaper and, truth be known, they made me feel better about myself.

But now, my lover and I are having problems, so we're auditioning therapists. Trying to be optimistic, I say we're going to therapy "to get fixed." My lover thinks this makes us sound like cocker spaniels on our way to the vet.

So, what are we looking for in a therapist? Well, she must be kind, she must be witty, very sweet and fairly pretty, take us on outings, give us treats, play games—Oh, wait a minute, that's Mary Poppins. We'll settle for a dyke who doesn't get on our last nerve or charge us an arm and a leg.

When my lover schedules the first audition, she tells our prospective shrink that we're looking for a lesbian or lesbian-friendly therapist. My lover's the diplomatic one. I want a dyke.

It's a spacious office uptown—across from the zoo. The audition is free.

"How are you?" she greets us.

Oh, we're fucking great. That's why we're here—because life is fucking wonderful. "Fine, thank you," I respond, "and you?"

She asks us each to talk a little about ourselves, our family history, our relationship history, and THE PROBLEM. The problem is that my lover's 15-year-old daughter has moved in with her, and our time alone together has been cut drastically. For reasons too numerous to mention, we can't move in together.

The therapist says, "You have a unique problem. Most couples come to see me because they're having problems communicating. You two seem to communicate very well. You just have this 'given' with no apparent solution."

"Well, we were kind of hoping her daughter could come live with you," I say. My lover and the therapist laugh. They think I'm kidding.

As the session nears its end, the therapist asks if we have any questions for her.

I look at my lover. My lover looks at me. We both know the question. We got this therapist's name out of the gay newspaper, but we don't know if she's queer. I know my lover will not ask. "Are you a lesbian?" I blurt out.

"I was afraid you were going to ask that." The therapist proceeds to beat around the bush. "What I usually tell people is—Does it matter? Some of my clients are gay and lesbian, and some aren't. So, does it really matter?"

Well, hell yes, it matters. It's a fair question. Not too personal under the circumstances. After all, she advertised in the queer paper, and she expects us to tell her the most intimate details of our lives. It's not like I asked her if she's a top or a bottom, for chrissake.

I look at my lover and joke, "Write that down, honey. Not comfortable with own sexuality." My lover, I can tell, wants to disappear on the spot.

The therapist offers to see us for, say, six sessions, but has already said that she doesn't know what she can do for us. In other words, we're no more encouraged than we were 50 minutes ago. Would we go to a dentist on those terms? I think not. We thank her for her time and leave. Needless to say, she does not pass the audition.

Next?

Riggin Waugh

She Loves Me

I love men.
But I figure I've had more potential mothers and sisters-in-law
. . . than potential husbands.
Once in Queens, after I gave a comic lecture about my work,
an elderly woman in the audience tenderly clasped my wrist,
pressed her son's business card into my hand,
and urged me to contact him.
The fact that he's an organic banana farmer in Hawaii,
while I happen to live in New York City, wasn't really the issue.
An artist in New Jersey still confides how she wishes
I had married her son, years and two children after
I was the photographer at his very happy wedding.
And a television reporter who came to do a news story about me
whipped out a wallet photo of her 39-year-old son
in hopes of introducing us.
And of course, all of these were the real thing. *TRUE LOVE!*
When a woman offers you her son (or a brother),
you know *SHE loves YOU.*
To offer a son! This is how straight women
seriously flirt with each other. I know.
Oh how I ached to fix up my own dear brother with my best friend.
Not that they would be such a perfect match . . .
but because I would love to be related to her.

Flash Rosenberg

Ida Mae Cole Takes a Stance

—————

(IDA MAE COLE stands at the bus stop counting the change in her purse. SHE snaps her gum furiously, then sucks her teeth when she realizes that she is twenty-five cents short. Ida stops abruptly to gaze at the passersby, cutting her eyes as SHE meets unwelcome stares. Her clothing is overstated, though clearly color coordinated.)

Go on, look! Go on! *(Resumes counting her change.)* Does anybody know if this is the bus that go downtown, 'cause if it is I need another quarter. Anybody got an extra quarter? *(Places her hand on her hip and steps forward.)* Well? WELL? CAN'T ANYBODY HEAR ME? *(Freezes in her pose for a few seconds.)* I'm one of those loud-speaking women you walk around and say excuse me to at least three times . . . *(Raises her eyebrows.)* I dare any of you to tell me otherwise . . . Yeah! 'cause you see . . . I'm the loud-speaking woman who pushes her way forward and always grabs the last potato . . . peel it, slice it, and eat it right there so that everybody knows that it's mine . . . Ain't no trace of attitude here, 'cause attitude is passé. What I got is Posture! *(Hits a pose.)* Punctuated! *(Rolls her neck.)* PERIOD! There are three postures that I'm known to assume . . . Numero Uno. Head cocked, eyebrows arched, lips pursed, hand on hip, finger pointed and a waving. *(Assumes posture number one. Without taking a pause.)* This is the tell me why I was docked a day's pay for coming in an hour late 'cause my daughter had a fever. This is the get off my stoop and go on home position. This is the try me stance, the tell me stance, the why don't you take your fingers off me muthafucka stance. *(A moment.)* Lawd, I stepped on into this posture just the other day. I'd pulled number twelve down at the health clinic, and then had to wait eight hours for the doctor to tell me he . . . ain't . . . gonna . . . see . . . me . . . Well, I marched on in his office. I stripped down to the paper robe, oh yes, which covered everything but the bootie. MMM! . . . You have to leave, he said, like he'd just been served the last pig's foot in the jar, and you know how that taste after it been sitting in the sun for a few months. *(Moves into position number one.)* Try me! I said . . . And he did, he tried me . . . And you know what happened . . . *(Takes two definitive steps forward.)* I GOT EXAMINED! The first time in four years too, and waited eight hours for the doctor to feel my ti . . . toddlytutus *(Touches her breast.)* and ask me how come I hadn't come in sooner, sooner? Sooner! Only day off in the last year and he's going to ask me how come I didn't come in sooner . . . Shoot . . . *(Stares, then releases posture number one, eases into posture number two, a more relaxed position.)* Posture number two. Legs spread, smile taut, head swaying . . . The go 'head ask me girl, I won't tell. The oh really, the oh no, oh but it ain't true that he wears her panties beneath his suit. That's what I told her, least five times that he was no good, 'cause I know his type. He gonna make you clean up then won't show. He gonna make you full up, then won't stay, make you pay out, then won't go. And I know what I'm talking about 'cause if you shift the posture on just one foot it becomes a welcoming posture, a thank you posture, the yes I will marry you, the no, I love only you . . . The where were you, the what do you want looking at me that way? I need you, I'm sorry, I'm here stance . . . The one that receives the drunken blows and the casual insults, that took an extra shift in the factory to pay for his new suede coat from Vim's, that prayed the siren wasn't going to bring me no bad news about my child, that . . . *(Counts her change again.)* Shucks . . . that don't forget, no punctuation needed . . . Not even that time on the bus when . . . when . . . *(Smiles, then laughs.)* I turned my head, and here comes one of them big-thighed women traveling in my direction, and I'm not in the mood to move . . . bump! She slaps one of her thighs up against mine and the vibration sends a tremor on through my body. *(Shakes her body.)* Excuse me! We say in unison. I strike posture number one. *(Assumes posture number one.)*

She don't move. I don't move. Her finger starts a waving, *(Begins to move her finger to emphasize her words.)* my finger starts a waving. Her head starts a moving, my head starts a moving. You going to let me by? she says, deep like Barry White. No place to go! I say smooth like Anita Baker. I eased on into posture number two to let her know that I'm flexible. Then she had the nerve to pull a posture on me I'd never seen before. So I tried all variations. *(Explores a range of positions.)* And she kept throwing them back at me. *(Gives a long penetrating stare.)* We locked eyes, and I thought oh lawd we're gonna throw down right here on the bus heading out to Kings Highway. Then I saw her eyes the night she'd gotten drunk, the vacationless year, the death of her youngest child, the *(Touches her side.)* mammogram results she hadn't told anybody about, and the new suede coat she bought at Vim's for her man . . . I turned away quick, damn if we didn't have the same posture, damn if we didn't. *(A moment.)* I took two steps to the side, and said GO ON SISTER! GO ON! And that big-thighed sister shoved on down to the back, until she disappeared behind a bus full of attitude. *(Assumes her final position.)* And it all leads to head tilted, muscles relaxed, arms crossed, and feet firmly planted, this is the just so position. It's the just so position you see on the bus . . . Yes, I'm the loud-speaking woman you avoid on the bus, with the steadfast posture you can't get around. *(Counts her change again.)* Anyone got a quarter? I don't have change . . . *(Assumes posture number one.)* I said does anyone got a quarter?

Lynn Nottage

I Can See Clearly Now

Martha Gradisher

You Can Dress a Dyke Up, But You Can't Take Her Out

J ust when you think the world is no longer providing humor column material, a dyke puts on pantyhose and goes out in public and the comedy goddess smiles again.

The dyke of mention was me. And the auspicious pantyhose-appropriate occasion was an annual dinner at the Grey Poupon League put on by some very nice folks. Not only do these folks give full scholarships to nursing school (which makes me admire them), they gave one such scholarship to me (which makes me love them). Each year they have a dinner and invite all the past and present recipients of these scholarships. They call it a "collegial exchange." I don't know what a "collegial exchange" is. I do, however, know that if it weren't for the scholarship I would be scrounging around in Dumpsters looking for aluminum to sell for tuition money. So, pantyhose or not, I go.

As I mentioned, these dinners are held at a certain club for old, white, straight men who still carry their forefathers' money around in their hip pocket. We'll call this club the "Grey Poupon League," because: a) I don't want to be sued, and b) it's the kind of place where you are tempted to say "Pardon me but do you have any Grey Poupon?" to everyone you see, but you don't because you figure they probably won't get it anyway. So, the evening began with a man reading from his holy bible and talking about how the particular bible he was reading from was special because Mother Teresa signed it. He passed it around and I did the spit test to see if the signature was real. He then launched into a long, loud prayer and I started praying myself, namely "Don't let him sit with me don't let him sit with me don't let him sit with me." But faster than you can say "republicans on corporate welfare" he sat down at our table, all the while continuing his scripture-quoting frenzy. He then proceeded to ask all the female scholarship recipients what their husbands do for a living. Inexplicably, he skipped me.

Jesusman's star shone most brightly however, when he tried to make conversation with a student seated to his left. This particular student met her husband in Sierra Leone and had taken her husband's name. Reading the student's name tag, Jesusman mused "Mbassa . . . Mbassa . . . hmmm . . . is that Italian?"

Mrs. Mbassa glanced up, gave Jesusman a slightly quizzical look, said "no" and kept on eating.

After the dinner was over, I made a stop at the bathroom before my short trek home. As I walked in the door marked "ladies" I passed by a blue-haired lady who was grooming herself at the sink.

As I entered the stall and began a protracted struggle with my pantyhose, I heard a loud sniff from Blue Hair. In a voice just loud enough for me to hear, she said, "I don't know what's happening to this club. Transvestites do not belong in the Grey Poupon League."

I looked at my reflection in the shiny toilet paper dispenser. I saw myself with short haircut, no makeup, skirt askew and prolific leg hair showing through my hose. I started giggling so hard I couldn't even finish what I had started. I thought "Oh lady, don't you think I'd try a little harder to look like something other than a dyke in a dress if I were an actual transvestite?"

But then it occurred to me. Transvestite. Hmmm . . .
Isn't that Italian?

Kelli Dunham

Mixed Meditation

Heather McAdams

Pisser

It never changes. Yet still you forget, particularly if you are an infrequent theater-goer, as you finish wolfing down your "pretheater" meal, throw your money on the table and say, "Oh, I won't take the time to use the restaurant bathroom here, I'll wait till I get to the theater." Then you get to the theater and you realize that the line of tight-lipped women spilling into the lobby isn't for will-call. And you can't believe, as you take your place in line by a continuously used water fountain whose flowing stream relentlessly reminds you of your calling, that you forgot again. That rule, ironically golden, that in any public gathering place, despite their differences in anatomy and under attire, despite the fact that society doesn't treat them equally, there are always an equal amount of bathroom stalls for men and women. You watch men walk past no line, return in twenty seconds, buy a drink, furtively have a smoke, buy some candy, read the whole fucking playbill, and you've moved up three feet. You wonder if maybe (and with increasing fear) the women in front of you have somehow cosmically started their periods the same time as you, something to ponder, and also something that would add at least fifty seconds to each woman's bathroom time (BT). In fact, you start calculating the amount of time it will take each woman ahead of you, given their age, layering of their attire, size of their purse, and connecting children. A kind of BT profile. So a ninety-year-old woman in a jump suit with a poncho treating her six-year-old grandchild in tights and petticoat to an afternoon of culture is off the charts. While waiting for what could only be such a duo (who've tauntingly flushed the toilet about an hour ago, but who still have not emerged from the stall), you silently design the perfect theater, with one stall for the men, just to show 'em, and fifteen hundred stalls for the women—no, no—a catheter with every playbill—no, no—twenty-minute intermissions—no, no—each theater seat is actually a porta-potty. You start wondering if the women in the other three stalls (for a thousand-seat house) are all pregnant. You wonder if you're pregnant. You start thinking pregnant women shouldn't be allowed to experience the wonder of theater, they embody wonder. You start thinking, from now on, no fluids for three days prior to show time. And then, suddenly, it's your turn for a stall and you're so overcome with opportunity, you can't go. The house lights start flashing, the bell starts dinging and you go to your seat, dissatisfied with your output, and you spend the whole first act plotting your intermission exit. Sure, I'm three seats away from the aisle, but those three people are, again, old, and even though you remind yourself you'll be old someday and have some empathy for what is in your future (no matter how well you take care of yourself), the seven shopping bags at their feet is not encouraging. You study the playbill every time the lights come up on stage to see, first, if there's going to be an intermission, and if it's a musical, if there's a production number big enough to cover your exit before curtain. Of course, if it's a play, and it's *Death of a Salesman,* you're dead. You start avoiding tragedies altogether, knowing any attempt to leave for the restroom will become part of the show. *Oklahoma* is a very good play for weak bladders.

It's not enough that we don't have equal pay, that we age faster, that we have to go through childbirth, that we're missing the gene for computer literacy, that we're ultimately responsible for birth control, that we can't have it all no matter how many articles tell us we can, these same people who are writing those articles are designing public bathroom facilities. They either have a false sense or absolutely no sense of our needs. They don't realize that women tend to pee in pairs, one going along with the other for company. That they often are busy giving the babysitter last minute instructions, or helping their husband find his keys or doing any one of the myriad things required to just get out of the house, and often their bodily needs are left to the last minute. That they don't know what it is to do only one thing at a time, so it just doesn't seem natural not to make fuller use of an evening of theater. In short, women need more porcelain when they've paid for a ticket. No doubt this tradition got started on the *Titanic*. It wasn't just lifeboats they ran out of.

Lissa Levin

Reality Check

"It's our new Reality Check.
No matter how many we issue, it will never cover your expenses."

*Carol*Simpson*

CHAPTER 2

The Estrogen Files

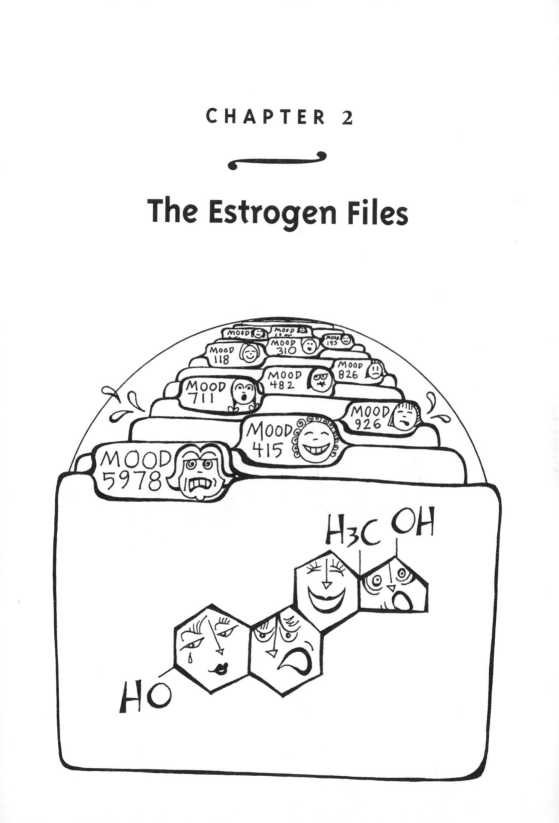

CHAPTER 2

The Estrogen Files

The Estrogen Files covers the lives of two single women, FRAN TAS-
TICA and ANNA LITICAL, as they e-mail each other their crazy adventures. Unbeknownst to them, two hunky government agents, JOE
TUESDAY and SAM SATURDAY, are secretly confiscating their e-mails to
try to figure out the minds of women. Of course they are men, so
they can never do it. *"It's a voyeuristic diary of comedy, mayhem, and
male misinterpretation."*

Episode 1: The Cat & The Mattress

The Cat

Dear Anna,

I feel like I am living in a Stephen King novel! My cat was missing
for two days. I heard a meow but couldn't tell whether it was coming from inside or outside the house. I'm yelling "Zookie, Zookie!"
My new neighbors think I'm doing some ancient Zulu war chant. I
was worried because my kid Quinn reminded me our wacko neighbor Jimmy kills cats AND he has a motive. The other day, Jimmy
came banging at my door and yelling in broken English, "Your son
scratched my car while he was flinging THIS stick. My 46-year-old
tenant saw him and she wouldn't lie." Yeah, like being the magic
age of 46 prevents a person from lying. Tell Clinton that! Quinn
swears he didn't do it. I'm just nodding my head, trying to calm
this wacko down.

If a bird crapped on his head, he'd go out and shoot the whole
species? The guy's a nut. He had a live rooster in his backyard for
a month, then killed it. Said it was cocking too loud. What the hell
did he want him to do, moooo? I didn't know a certain cocking
level meant death.

Anyway, he tells me he kills cats. I'm thinking he kidnapped Zookie
from our attached balconies to revenge the scratch. Zookmeister
is dining with the Jeffrey Dahmer of cats!

I'm searching the house, hoping Zookie's just into a game of feline
hide-and-seek. I enroll my sister Gigi into the cat hunt. We hear no
meows. Figures! Maybe the cat's dead and Jimmy has made him
into an old-world pâté.

42

While we are searching, my phone rings. I answer the phone and out my window I see Jimmy with a sack, looking suspicious. I think Zookie is in the bag. I panic.

Jimmy spots me in the window and zooms out his driveway. I hop his fence, and run into his backyard looking for evidence . . . cat blood, anything. I spot a bowl of fresh milk. The maniac lured our cat. Probably poisoned him.

I don't want to get caught for trespassing. I try to climb back over with the bowl of milk in my hands, so I can lift fingerprints for proof. Do cats even have paw prints? Who the hell knows?

Gigi sees me and yells, "What are you doing in Jimmy's yard?" AHHHH. I jump and drop the milk! I look up and see some idiot guy in a gray raincoat watching me. Great! This pervert has been hanging around my neighborhood for a while. Actually he's really cute, looks a little like Antonio Banderas.

I get back to our yard and Gigi says she found Zookie in the base-ment wall. Great! When the idiot plumber came, he broke a hole in the wall and now the cat decided to use it as an escape hatch. I guess he didn't like the brand of cat chow we were serving.

We try to get Zookie out of the wall by using water and a broom . . . nothing. He growls a low guttural growl. I'm thinking, *You better stop this; I'm the one who cleans your cat litter.* I swear the cat was cursing in Swahili. Then he disappears. Now for sure he's stuck in a pipe or drain somewhere. I'll be flushing the toilet and the damn cat's paw will rise up and scratch my ass.

So, I do the only logical thing, I make a bigger hole . . . no cat. He sneaked out and ran up the stairs back into my house. Upstairs the cat is looking at me like, *You idiot, what took you so long?* I wasn't sure if I should hit him or kiss him. Kind of like some men I know. Overactive imagination or were my hormones just acting up?

Tell me what's up with you and Highwater Moon and then I will tell you about the karate pilot I met through the Internet. Off to the monthly estrogen festival tomorrow . . . should be fun . . . a TV crew is coming.

Fran

The Mattress

Dear Frannie:

What is it with cats? They disappear, give you heart failure, and then look at you like, "Helloooo—where's my Kibbles 'n Bits? How about a little service, here? Garfield wouldn't put up with this kind of attitude."

What a day! I was out trying to find a mattress because Highwater Moon is coming this weekend. I'm sleeping on two twin mattresses pushed together. Every time I turn over, I fall into that oh-so-lovely gap in the middle.

Anyway, some putz tried to pick me up in the mattress store. The salesman no less. Get this: I was lying down on a mattress, you know, testing it out, and I closed my eyes for two seconds and when I opened them, there was this guy's big greasy face staring down at me; he had on glasses that literately took up half his head, and they were like the thickness of the Hubbell telescope, so it made him look like he had those giganto eyeballs. And you could tell his hair was permed. Permed! Didn't that go out with Nik-Nik shirts and disco?

So he goes, "I just wanted to tell you, in order to really test a mattress, you gotta take off your shoes and stretch out on it, to really get *the feel.*"

I said, "Really? I thought for sure in you had to observe a mattress from a distance and try to *imagine* what it felt like. You know, that new Zen way of testing mattresses."

Whoosh. Right over his head. He goes, "Oh right . . . so then, how about having dinner with me?"

The look on my face must have been like the look on Shelley Duvall's face when Jack Nicholson axed the bathroom door in *The Shining* and went "Heeeere's Johnny!"

I guess he thinks that since he works in a mattress store he can get anyone he wants into bed, like maybe by osmosis or something.

Fran, I think Highwater Moon may be "the one." Not only is he nice, but that fellow is the sexiest man in the land! Yes, yes I know —there's more to a relationship than sex. But as far as I'm concerned, if the sex stinks, what's the point? I may be considered base and shallow; but baseness and shallowness are highly underrated. (Especially by people who aren't gettin' any.)

Besides, I prefer to be a hedonist. Hedonists have fun. Life is too short not to. You never hear a hedonist say, "Sorry I have to leave the party but I must go home and cross-reference last year's annual tax reports—I'll check out the nude tap-dancer some other time."

I believe you can have a meaningful, yet hedonistic relationship with someone. You can discuss social issues and world hunger and whether or not it's PC to wear a faux-fur coat with a real fur collar, you just discuss them with your clothes off.

How's your love life? Are you still doing that online personal ad thing? I tried that once. I got 700 letters in my P.O. box. First thing I did was eliminate the ones that had the words pasted in from magazines. I found a common thread; they always lie with the pictures. Yeah, it's them, but like 15 years ago when they had hair and a waistline and their nose hair was an inch shorter. How was that last guy you met?

I'm working the Chuckle Factory in Miami tomorrow. Last time I was there someone in the audience had a nervous breakdown. The guy had like 12 champagne cocktails and suddenly in the middle of the headliner's act he stood up and started shouting, "Fight the power! Fight the power!" Then he passed out face down into a bowl of creamed spinach and artichoke dip. ("I only work the best places," she said, wagging her pinky finger in the air.)

Oh, I ended up going to Mattress Mania and getting something there. A woman waited on me.

Love ya,
Annie

(In a nearby van we hear the correspondence of the two rookie agents, one in Florida and one in New York, observing Litical and Tastica.)

JOE TUESDAY: Saturday? This is Tuesday.

SAM SATURDAY: Tuesday, this is Saturday.

JOE TUESDAY: What day is it anyway?

SAM SATURDAY: It's Thursday.

JOE TUESDAY: Tell me. How do two good-looking guys like us get stuck with a job analyzing women? We were never married, don't have kids—what was the government thinking?

SAM SATURDAY: Probably that we were the only two men left on the earth not jaded.

JOE TUESDAY: You're right! We know women are all the same.

SAM SATURDAY: NEVER let them hear you say that!

JOE TUESDAY: Why? They think the same about us. Enough, let's get this report done.

SAM SATURDAY: Tuesday, you still wearing that stupid gray raincoat?

JOE TUESDAY: Yeah, part of the official government spy issue wardrobe. And you?

SAM SATURDAY: I'm busy playing with my toys. Today I'm talking to you via my necktie. Pretty cool James Bond stuff.

JOE TUESDAY: Okay, let's put in our "expert" reports on these two and call it a night.

SAM SATURDAY: Okay. Roger.

JOE TUESDAY: Who's Roger? *(pause and gets it)* Very funny. Over and Out.

TOP SECRET ANALYSIS
JOE TUESDAY'S ANALYSIS OF FRAN TASTICA
Time: 10:00 PM
Code Name: The Cat & The Mattress

Tastica is obviously in love with Jimmy or she wouldn't hop a fence to get closer to him. Her cover-up is her obsession with her cat. Zookie is some code name that she and her sister have worked out. She obviously has good taste in men if she thinks the "man in the gray coat is cute" (that's me) . . . but really . . . Antonio Banderas!

SAM SATURDAY'S ANALYSIS OF ANNA LITICAL
Time: 10:00 PM
Code Name: The Cat & The Mattress

Subject Litical is picky about what she lays down on and who she lays down on it with. Mentioned someone with the code name "the one." Also known as Highwater Moon. So many aliases. Possible KGB agent. Suspicious. Will keep a close watch. Has a psychological fear of men with glasses. Perhaps memories of a nearsighted father who, because of his myopia thought she was somebody else? Subject also mentioned hedonism. Isn't that a Club Med thing? Conclude subject could be colluding with spies in a tropical resort.

Fran Capo and Anna Collins

The Estrogen Files: Money, Men and Motherhood is a weekly cybersitcom that can be read on the Web at www.theestrogenfiles. net. It has won four awards, was written up in the *LA Times, Newsday,* and *Yahoo Internet Life.* It can be heard live on Internet radio as well.

A Human Side?

*"I'd love to show the world my human side...
could you create one for me?"*

Carol*Simpson

Dear Kenny Rogers

*"Lady . . . I'm your knight in shining armor,
and I love you. You have made me what I am,
and I am yours . . ."*

Dear Kenny Rogers, or anybody like that: I want to be exactly what you want. And after I am, I want you to promise me, and mean it, that you'll love me forever. I'll be strong . . . in an attractive, weak sort of way . . . and independent, without crossing that line of unappealing, and sweet with genuine niceness to everyone. And you watch me decorate the tree and you notice I look great . . . in a subtle, I have no idea I look great kind of way. And you pick me up and carry me off to the bedroom that I have decorated in classy yet folk artsy colors and calico. And we make passionate love, with me exuding just enough need but being careful to be distant enough for you to wonder about. And you brush the hair from my forehead, and I weep faintly into your chest . . for no reason, other than how fragile and sincere I am.

I want to be a Mrs. Kenny Rogers kind of woman. You know . . . the kind of lady he sings about: "Oh, Lady, I was just scum in the sewer until you came along and made me a man." With hair that's light, but not really blonde, that would be too cheap. Instead, sort of a wheat-and-sunstreaked affair with not a lot of hairspray. A ninety-five-dollar cut that looks like your hair just naturally grows out of your head like that. The kind of woman who always, no matter what, has that I-understand-and-am-knowing-without-being-threatening kind of always smile.

I don't need a lot of makeup or jewelry. I was born with diamond studs permanently pierced in my ears. Fun, yet mature; spiritual, but never kooky or culty; and always understanding, yet firm and moral. I am equally comfortable on Walton's mountain or in a Rolls Royce. My legs are long . . . like the horse I ride every morning. And sometimes . . . sometimes, when I'm reading an old classic that I've had rebound in light leather, I glance over at Kenny and chuckle, 'cause he's still such a little boy. Last night I wept when I heard his grandmother's neighbor's sister died. But quietly, on the bed, until he came in and held me for hours, admiring my natural foallike beauty.

I never gossip or talk about Kenny to anyone. I just smile knowingly, and hang that handmade ornament on the Christmas tree. While Kenny admires my ass.

Kathy Najimy

Lowest Common Denominator

Jennifer Berman

Ode to a Love As Strong As an Emery Board

I knew we were right for each other the moment we met. And for five years we had a wonderful relationship—talking for hours, laughing, and yes, at times, crying.

Now it's over.

I'm not making excuses, but I was fragile, vulnerable. A once-vibrant woman, I'd grown haggard and hostile, each day a rerun of kids, cooking, and cleaning. I hungered for attention, understanding, and, perhaps, just a hint of excitement.

I had tried talking to my husband. Tearfully I told him: "My life is meaningless."

He picked up his head, having been intently examining the plant growth on the bottom of his tennis shoe, and asked, "What? You're going to enlist?"

"That's right babe," I replied. "I think the military could really use me. I've been practicing with the kids' remote-control helicopter, and I'm sure I could handle one of those Apaches. What do you think?"

"Sure, I'll take a drink," he said.

With that, our conversation ended, and I walked out the door.

It wasn't as if I was looking for someone. It just happened. Actually, a friend had innocently introduced us. But that's all it took. From then on, we had a standing appointment of sorts. We'd see each other every week or two, usually just for a couple of hours unless it was a special occasion. Then we'd take longer.

But that's all in the past.

My manicurist has gone on to a career in banking, and I'm left with a heavy heart, hangnails, and cuticles that are completely out-of-control.

Oh, I know what you're thinking: "Geez, she was just your manicurist, get over it."

Well, you couldn't be more wrong. No, this was not a simple she-has-a-file-I-have-fingernails relationship. We truly enjoyed each other's company. Granted, she was getting paid, not to mention a big fat tip. Nevertheless, I think we had something special.

Who else would give me their undivided attention for a couple of hours—truly listening, allowing me to share my innermost thoughts, my deepest concerns? More importantly, my manicurist never disagreed with me. She was the first person who recognized what had been obvious to me for years: I'm always right.

She was also insightful. I'm convinced that if you have a good manicurist you'll never need a therapist. And, unlike many of-course-this-is-completely-confidential shrinks, manicurists can actually be trusted.

How often do you hear of a manicurist speed dialing "Hard Copy" the minute her client leaves, or splashing their sordid secrets all over the tabloids? Admittedly, the fact that the details of my life are about as compelling as your average toaster-oven manual probably limited such opportunities.

And did I mention I got to leave the house? For two hours every other week, I entered a world where people addressed me by my first name? This initially took me by surprise, having assumed that immediately after giving birth, the state automatically changed your name to Mom, which is most frequently pronounced M-high pitched scream-O-even higher pitched scream-M!

In this dream world, other odd things happened. I was able to sit down. For many consecutive minutes. I almost fell off my chair the first time I was asked, "Would you like a cup of coffee?"

"You're a saint," I replied, throwing my arms around her, weeping. "I have never experienced such kindness." (In time I learned a simple "thank-you" would suffice.)

And when I left this other world? I felt renewed, invigorated. And, my nails looked darned nice too.

So please, don't even show me an orange stick. The pain is still too fresh. The mere sight of an emery board can send me reeling. And I will never again look at a bottle of Moscow Red the same way.

It was, after all, our color.

Carrie St. Michel

Rosebud

Rosebud was originally written as a short film with subtitles—but please don't let that discourage you. First of all, only the first couple of pages are hard. And second of all, if you're old enough to see a movie with subtitles, you're old enough to read one. It was produced and directed by Neil Leifer, starred Caroline Aaron as Carol and Susan Greenhill as Jane, and was selected for the 1992 Edinburgh Film Festival.

The Place: One of New York's many nail salons.
The Time: The 1990s
The Characters (in order of appearance):

PEDICURIST TINA: a Korean pedicurist in her early twenties.
MANICURIST CHRIS: a Korean manicurist in her early twenties.
JANE: a regular salon customer in her late thirties. Married.
CAROL: Jane's friend. Also a regular salon customer in her late thirties. Has never been married.
PEDICURIST PATTY: a Korean pedicurist in her early twenties.
NOSY OLD WOMAN: a regular customer who passes her time in the salon eavesdropping.
SONNY: a regular customer who could easily be confused with John Gotti. Dapper. Italian.
VARIOUS EXTRA CUSTOMERS AND SALON WORKERS

(We open in a New York City nail salon. There is a row of small tables with relaxed customers on one side and stone-faced name-tag-

bearing Korean manicurists working diligently on the other. At the pedicure thrones—two chairs, each sitting above a small sink—we meet TINA *and* PATTY, *pedicurists who sit hunched on impossibly small and very uncomfortable-looking stools. They are waiting to perform their magic on yet another pair of tired, calloused feet. Manicurist* CHRIS *has carved out a little niche for herself near the thrones. As they wait for their regulars,* JANE *and* CAROL, *to come in for their weekly appointments, they pass the time chatting in their native Korean tongue.)*

PEDICURIST TINA: *(in her native Korean . . . so this part is subtitled)* He even has a special little nickname for me when we're in bed . . . *(then in English . . . and in a gravelly whisper à la Citizen Kane)* Rosebud.

MANICURIST CHRIS: *(in Korean and subtitled)* He calls you . . . *(in English and incredulous)* . . . Rosebud?

PEDICURIST TINA: *(reaffirming in the same whisper)* ROSEBUD!!! (and the three giggle uncontrollably for a moment)

*(*JANE, *who is just getting settled in her chair, has been listening but doesn't understand anything, obviously, except for the word "Rosebud."*

CAROL *bursts into the salon and up onto the throne next to* JANE. *They exchange ad-libbed greetings with one another as well as with* CHRIS, TINA, *and* PATTY. *Then the manicurists and pedicurists get to work.)*

CAROL: Jesus, Mary, and Joseph!

JANE: What?

CAROL: God!

JANE: What?

CAROL: *(rubbing her thighs and indicating something "over there" with her head)* I should have taken a Valium. Followed with a Prozac chaser.

JANE: What? Tell me.

CAROL *(indicates "over there" with her head again):* I'm not kidding! Do they serve alcohol here? I need one of those new martinis I'm always reading about.

JANE: What happened?

CAROL: I just had a . . . you know . . . *(still being secretive)* "Bik Wak."

JANE: Huh?

CAROL: *(more deliberate)* A "BIK. WAK."

JANE: What the hell is a "Bik. Wak"? *(then . . .)* Oh . . . a BIKINI WAX!?

CAROL: Oh, thank you! Now the whole city knows. Did you make sure my cousins in Brooklyn heard you?

JANE: Did it hurt?

CAROL: *(still whispering)* Are you nuts? It's like sex with a sand-blaster.

JANE: Why are you whispering? *(gesturing towards the manicurists and pedicurists)* They can't understand you. They only speak four words of English; "What color?" and "Cut cuticles?"

PEDICURIST TINA: *(in Korean and subtitled)* Four? Try four thousand. And what are the other customers? Deaf? Pass me the pumice. *(PATTY passes the pumice without ever looking up)*

JANE: Anyway, where were you last week? I missed you.

CAROL: Oh, I threw my back out so I went to a healer.

JANE: A healer?

CAROL: This very spiritualistic woman who cures physical, mental, emotional, and attitudinal illnesses with common household rice. It costs a fortune, but it's worth every penny.

PEDICURIST PATTY: *(in Korean and subtitled)* Someone's making money off of rice? Why didn't I think of that?

JANE: Rice? Like in the kind you throw at a wedding?

CAROL: Exactly. Except she's a vegetarian so this is brown rice.

PEDICURIST PATTY: *(in Korean and subtitled)* Oh. Brown rice? Forget it.

JANE: What does she do? Put you on a rice diet?

CAROL: No. No. No. It's not like that at all. First you explain your problem to her—mine happens to be a bad back from sleeping funny. Then, she pokes and prods you a bit, bounces a quarter off your stomach, makes you repeat an ancient holistic chant, and massages lavender oil into your ears.

JANE: You're kidding.

CAROL: I've never been more serious.

JANE: So where does the rice come in?

CAROL: When she's finished, she tapes nine pieces of rice in an upside down "Y" on your diaphragm.

PEDICURIST TINA: *(horrified, in Korean and subtitled)* And she thinks a bikini wax hurts?

JANE: *(in disbelief)* Your diaphragm?!

CAROL: Not that diaphragm. Here. *(indicating her chest)*

JANE: What the hell does that do?

CAROL: It relaxes your skeletal muscles, enabling your red blood cells to flow more evenly, with a greater awareness of their space. This then allows your white blood cells to prioritize themselves thus discarding any "bad seed" cells. And finally, it reoxygenates your lungs while filtering out the evils of city living. I'm surprised you haven't heard about it. Everybody's doing it.

JANE: *(in disbelief)* Not this everybody. *(pause)* Back problem, huh?

CAROL: Uh-huh.

JANE: Sleeping funny?

CAROL: Yeah.

JANE: Gimme a break, Carol. I wasn't born yesterday. Who is he?

CAROL: Well . . .

JANE: I knew it! Why didn't you tell me?

CAROL: Because every time I start to say I have a new boyfriend, we break up before the words are even out of my mouth. It's my own customized jinx.

JANE: Details. I want details.

NOSY OLD WOMAN: *(drying her nails in front of a fan and eavesdropping on everybody)* Excuse me. But aren't you a little old to be dating?

CAROL: *(stunned by the woman's rudeness)* If I'm old enough to periodically stop having sex, I'm old enough to date.

(Clearly, neither CAROL nor JANE want this woman to enter into their conversation. They do not encourage her.)

NOSY OLD WOMAN: You were never married?

CAROL: No. *(then specifically to JANE—because she is still appalled that the woman is trying to join in)* And could she possibly say that a little louder? I'm not sure they heard it in the skin peeling room. The one in Beverly Hills.

JANE: Where'd you meet him?

CAROL: In my aerobics class. He's very fit.

JANE: Go on.

CAROL: Romantic.

JANE: Nice.

CAROL: I-talian.

JANE: Weo!

CAROL: Rich.

JANE: Okay!

CAROL: Oh, and thoughtful!

JANE: Sure sounds like "Mr. Right!" What's his name?

CAROL: Tony. And if he's not "Mr. Right" he's at least "Mr. Right Enough For Now, Even Though Lord Knows I'm Not Making Any Predictions Because I've Done That Before And Look Where It Got Me."

(TINA shoots a glance at CAROL for one split second, then quickly resumes working.)

PEDICURIST TINA: *(in Korean and subtitled)* Are all Italian men named Tony?

PEDICURIST PATTY: *(in Korean and subtitled, gesturing toward the very dapper SONNY, who is having a manicure)* Not Sonny.

(SONNY smugly smokes his cigar, blowing the smoke in the direction of the NOSY OLD WOMAN.)

PEDICURIST TINA: *(in Korean and subtitled)* Sonny doesn't count. He's a thug. All regular Italians are named Tony, and all thug Italians are named Sonny. Didn't you see *The Godfather?*

JANE: So . . . how long have you been seeing this Mystery Man?

CAROL: Two months today. And he sends me flowers at least once a week. You know how I have this thing about fidelity? Well, this guy is f-a-i-t-h-f-u-l.

PEDICURIST TINA: *(in Korean and subtitled)* Ten bucks says he's married.

JANE: You said that about Max . . .

CAROL: Max was a psychotic, insincere cradle robber. This guy's forty-one and his head is screwed on straight. He wants to have a baby, not date one.

JANE: So . . .

CAROL: Who knows. My track record is pretty . . .

JANE: Lousy?

CAROL: Jane! What are you? My friend or my mother? I'm telling you—this guy's different. He surprised me after work last night and took me dancing.

PEDICURIST PATTY: *(in Korean and subtitled)* Where does your boyfriend take you?

PEDICURIST TINA: *(in Korean and subtitled)* The park, the movies, Japanese restaurants.

(SONNY gets up to leave. He gallantly tips every manicurist in the salon. In unison, they all bid him goodbye.)

JANE: How many nights a week do you see him?

CAROL: Three. Sometimes four. He never cancels unless it's a work thing. Although he did last Saturday.

PEDICURIST TINA: *(in Korean and subtitled)* Haven't we heard this before? She'll find out he's cheating in a month. My guy never cancels.

JANE: Well, then maybe this is it. I know when I met Ed, I had completely given up on men. I was thirty-four and getting wedding invitations from kids I used to baby-sit.

CAROL: Tell me about it. I'm still getting shoved out onto the dance floor to catch the bouquet.

JANE: But this sounds serious.

CAROL: It is. Otherwise, I wouldn't subject my thighs to such torture.

JANE: Remember—the way to a man's heart, even in the 90s—is still through his stomach . . .

PEDICURIST TINA: *(simultaneously, in Korean and subtitled).* . . . Through the bedroom door.

JANE: *(con't)* Fill him up so much he can't move . . . and then jump on him. (Pause) What's his favorite restaurant?

CAROL: Come to think of it, I don't know. We never eat out.

JANE: What is he? A cheapskate?

CAROL: Worse. A health nut. He cooks for me at his place.

JANE: That's an impressive switch. A man saying the way to a woman's heart is through her stomach. A green light to eat!

CAROL: It's not as great as you think.

JANE: What do you mean?

CAROL: Well, he cooks, but it's not exactly human food . . .

JANE: What is it?

CAROL: *(pausing, as if really trying to figure out what it is)* Hay, maybe? Straw? . . . It's all this weird-ass, macrobiotic, low-fat, high-fiber, vegetarian . . . cruciferous . . . Alpha Beta . . . High-Octane . . . Retin-A'd . . . triglyceride . . . shit.

JANE: So then look at it this way. You have a boyfriend and a personal trainer all rolled into one.

CAROL: I guess. But frankly, I'd kill for a huge plate of linguine with clam sauce, an eggplant parmigiana hero with extra cheese, and a dozen bottles of cheap Chianti.

JANE: Oh, no. He doesn't drink, either?

CAROL: Oh, he drinks. His bar features several beautiful decanters of . . . Perrier, Evian, seltzer, and Pellegrino.

(A woman gets up to leave the salon. Her freshly painted toenails have cotton wedged between them and Saran Wrap covering them. Her fingernails are still wet, too, so she holds her hands in the air as if someone has just yelled, "Stick 'em up!" One of the other manicurists piles her coat, purse, and a shopping bag over one shoulder.)

CAROL: *(looking at the woman—who is truly a sight to behold)* Will you look at what we women go through just to try and look like Murphy Brown?

JANE: Hell, I do this for Ed, not me. He has a foot fetish—thus my weekly pedicures. And because of this . . . fetish . . . he likes to, you know hmmmm, hmmmm, hmmmm my toes.

CAROL: What?

JANE: You know . . . da-da-da . . . my toes.

CAROL: *(loudly and in disbelief)* SUCK YOUR TOES? Edward J. Regent likes to suck your toes? I couldn't be more stunned if you said Prince Philip.

JANE: SSSHH!!!

CAROL: Well, my, my, my. I have a whole new respect for Ed.

JANE: What finally hooked him was, I dipped my toes in different flavored liqueurs every night. Champagne one night, peach Schnapps the next—I even mixed up a little pail of Old Fashioneds one night which I kept right next to the bed. Dip. Dip. Kiss. Dip. Dip. Kiss. The next thing you know he's on bended knee proposing.

CAROL: Wow! Really?

JANE: Dating is like fishing. It's all in the bait.

CAROL: I don't know. You think if I dipped my toes in sparkling water Tony would automatically propose?

PEDICURIST TINA: *(in Korean and subtitled)* Are you catching any of this?

PEDICURIST PATTY *(in Korean and subtitled):* Unbelievable.

PEDICURIST TINA: *(in Korean and subtitled)* I wouldn't suck these toes if my life depended on it. And I'm their grounds-keeper.

MANICURIST CHRIS: *(in Korean and subtitled)* Maybe I should try it on my husband. A nice, subtle arsenic.

PEDICURIST TINA: *(in Korean and subtitled)* Forget that! Let's market it! Liqueur-flavored nail polish. We'll make a fortune. *(in English)* Rinse please, Carol.

JANE: The trick is to pamper him. All men really want is a mother.

PEDICURIST TINA: *(in Korean and subtitled)* Mother by day. Hooker by night.

CAROL: I *do* pamper him. I gave him a back rub the other night . . .

JANE: Good.

CAROL: It was great if I do say so myself. The rub that broke the bachelor's back.

JANE: What's your hurry? It's only been two months.

CAROL: Two months may be nothing to an old married broad like yourself. But once a woman hits thirty and she's still single, her body and her ovaries start to age the way cats do. You know, where one human year really equals seven ovary years?

(CAROL pauses to calculate—for the first time—just how old her ovaries would be according to the equation. She is clearly horrified at the result.)

CAROL: *(continues)* Oh my God, Jane! My ovaries are almost three hundred years old! I'll give birth to my own great-great-great grandchildren!

JANE: That's nothing. I had one kid and my ovaries went on Social Security.

PEDICURIST TINA: *(in Korean and subtitled)* Sounds like she's starting to panic. Me, too.

PEDICURIST PATTY: *(in Korean and subtitled)* You? You're only twenty. She's got fifteen years on you. Pass me the lotion.

PEDICURIST TINA: *(in Korean and subtitled)* But I'm not married.

MANICURIST CHRIS: *(in Korean and subtitled)* You're dating someone—that's a start.

PEDICURIST TINA: *(in Korean and subtitled)* No one I could bring home. He's not Korean. He's not even Asian. Can I have the cuticle cream?

JANE: So, are you doing something special for your two-month anniversary?

CAROL: He wanted to go for a 10-mile run. I wanted champagne and caviar in bed. So we compromised man-style . . . we're going to a Knicks game.

JANE: Remember your six-month anniversary with Gerry? You and I spent it at my house eating frozen pizza and watching *Love Story* while Gerry and his buddies kept company with Boom Boom La Fleur.

CAROL: Men. You can't live with 'em . . .

JANE and **CAROL:** *(simultaneously and to each other)* . . . And you can't kill 'em.

JANE: So . . . is your *(mouths the word, "sex")* life good?

CAROL: JANE!

JANE: Come on! Good as Ed is, after six years of marriage, I'd like to know if there's anything new out there I need to know about.

CAROL: Well, yes, your honor, it's great.

PEDICURIST PATTY: *(in Korean and subtitled)* Of course. It's only been two months. *(then, in English)* What color?

JANE: Hot Tomato, please, Patty. *(and then)* How great?

CAROL: He takes top honors. Considering all my other relationships have been like Tours of Duty.

JANE: A true Italian Stallion?

CAROL: A true Italian Stallion.

(CHRIS, TINA, and PATTY's interest has been piqued.)

JANE: Really? No weird quirks?

CAROL: No. No weird quirks. Well, he does do one rather strange thing.

JANE: Yes?

CAROL: But it's not life-threatening.

JANE: Yes?

CAROL: Or even relationship-threatening.

JANE: Go on.

CAROL: It really isn't that big a deal.

JANE: Tell me.

CAROL: I feel funny saying it.

JANE: Carol! Tell me!

CAROL: But since you asked . . .

JANE: TELL ME!

PEDICURIST TINA: *(in Korean and subtitled)* SAY IT ALREADY!

CAROL: During . . . you know . . . sex . . . he has this little nickname for me.

(At this point, EVERYBODY in the salon is riveted.)

JANE: Yeah?

CAROL: He calls me . . . *(in a gravelly whisper).* . . "Rosebud."

PEDICURIST PATTY: *(incredulously)* ROSEBUD?!

(Pop-cut to stunned faces and fade out.)

The End

Jane Read Martin

Talking Want Ad

___

In a casual, free, off-handed manner of speaking

> I'm looking for a man to wash my clothes
> Iron my shirt and blow my nose,
> Sweep the floor and wax the kitchen
> While I sit around playing guitar and bitchin'.

>> Mud all over my boots,
>> Cigar butts on the rug
>> Beer cans lined up around the wall
>> . . . That kind of thing.

> I'm looking for a man to cook my meals,
> Wash my dishes and take the peels
> Off my bananas with a grin,
> And ask me how my work day's been;

>> Insufferable
>> As usual;
>> Playing the guitar
>> Is such a struggle.

I'm looking for a man with curly hair,
Great big muscles and a nice derrière;
To get up nights and feed the baby,
And have my coffee when I'm ready.

> I've got to feel good in the
> Morning
> That's when I make my best
> Music.

So if you feel you'd like to apply,
Just send a photo or drop on by;
And you can shine my shoes today
And if you do that good, I'll let you stay

> And cook my supper;
> And after you've finished the dishes,
> If you're lucky, I might let you listen to me
> Practice my guitar.

Janet Smith

Travel Diary

Iceland: Land of Ice

**Friday, the 1st of February 3:00 p.m.
Eastern Daylight Time**

My fiancé and I are very much in love. We book two tickets for Icelandair's Valentine's Day excursion for Reykjavik. Not everyone gets the idea to visit a cold climate in the winter, but air fare to Iceland is $399.00 round-trip and you can bring a friend for free, so that if you live in a place with high rents like New York City, you are actually losing money by staying at home. I have always wanted to become better with finances, so Iceland makes a lot of sense.

The travel agent's doctor advises that people traveling to Iceland undergo a regimen of sleep cycles and melatonin tablets to combat the combination of jet lag and the long arctic nights that disturb natural circadian rhythms and result in seasonal affective disorder—even acute depression. My fiancé and I discuss this but decide to make the most of our trip by keeping awake the entire four days. We plan to do this mostly through will-power.

**Friday, the 8th of February 9:20 a.m.
Greenwich Mean Time**

It is a four-and-a-half-hour flight and we spend it enjoying complimentary beverages, reading travel brochures and watching in-flight movies featuring Hollywood movie stars like Ben Stiller and Eddie Murphy. As we make our final approach to land, it's 8:20 a.m. but the sun has not risen. We touch down at Keflavik International Airport in a hailstorm.

Keflavik, as an airport, rhymes with nothing in English. Here, everyone—reservation clerks, concession stand cashiers, baggage handlers—all of them are statuesque, blonde, and have pronounced cheekbones. If it is true that all people are carbon-based and made in the image of God, it is also true that Icelanders have the best-looking carbon and the rest of us are made in the image of God's morning face.

At the duty-free shop, my fiancé and I discover that the conversion of Icelandic currency is not possible, as it does not go into U.S. dollars evenly. We spend 9,000 or 900 "króna," which is the Icelandic word for money. We buy 40 "Brennivin," which is their word for little bottles of clear liquor.

On board the bus to town, it begins to snow sideways. From a distance, Reykjavik appears to be a white expanse of land with buildings on it and some sort of government.

Friday, the 8th of February 9:30 a.m.
Greenwich Mean Time

There is still no sun and we feel sleepy. My fiancé and I check into the Hotel Lokisve and the concierge, whose name is "Thorra"—which is a real name in Iceland—gives us coffee and tells us to think of her as "Mrs. Recommend." We tell her we will and we wait patiently for daylight.

While we're waiting, we consult our travel book, *Let's Go to Lonely Iceland*. The guide says you can make any trip more enjoyable by setting little goals for each day—for instance, a sojourn to a local point of interest or the discovery of a little out-of-the-way restaurant or a visit to a house of worship where you wouldn't be caught dead at home. We decide to make our quest the search for ice, reasoning that since we are in Iceland, we should be able to find not just ice, but the *perfect* ice. We have breakfast and plan to find the perfect ice once the sun rises. This happens in a few hours and by this time several more cups of strong coffee have made us both shaky and weepy.

Friday, the 8th of February 3:30 p.m.
Greenwich Mean Time

From the window of our hotel room, we can see in the hazy light that the inhabitants of Reykjavik have fashioned their houses—and even their roofs—of heart-breaking cheerful colors: union suit red, forest green, robin's egg blue. Their little city crouches bravely under ever-present clouds, which bring the unceasing punishment of rain, freezing rain, sleet, icy rain, snow, and rain which later freezes. My fiancé and I decide to stay in our hotel and eat packages of crackers and cheese you spread on them with little red plastic sticks. We find these in the mini bar and they only cost 90 "króna"—which is the Icelandic word for money.

Friday, the 8th of February 5:00 p.m. Greenwich Mean Time

The sun is going down already but none of the hotel staff seems to notice. The concierge, whose name is "Thorra"—which is a real name in Iceland—suggests that we go to dinner at a restaurant called Útlendinguron Freyjugata. We thank her very much and strike out for the center of town.

On the way to the restaurant, we begin our search for perfect ice, reasoning that it must be easy to find ice in Iceland: all we have to do is find water whose movement is almost too slow for the naked eye to capture and almost too painful for the naked eye to melt. It has begun to hail and the hailstones are the size of Milk Duds; they hit you coming down, then bounce on the pavement and hit you coming up. My fiancé and I stand in a doorway until the hailstorm is over.

For the first time, we become aware of the city's eerie post-apocalyptic atmosphere. We consult our guidebook, which tells us that no dogs are allowed in Reykjavik because Icelanders believe it is cruel to keep a dog in the city. When we get to the restaurant, we order a couple glasses of the local specialty. When she comes with another round of drinks, we tell the waitress that Reyjavik feels like the setting of the plague that killed all the dogs and cats and left earth wide open to become the Planet of the Apes. The waitress says she is happy without dogs around, as her hand was bitten when she was young. My fiancé and I order another round of the local specialty without bothering to explain that dogs only bite because they know your hand is full of bones.

Friday, the 8th of February 8:00 p.m.
Greenwich Mean Time

The sun has been down for hours now and we are restless. It seems as if the restaurant almost hurried us through our dinner. Evidently, Icelanders do not enjoy singing show tunes or hearing anyone else sing them. Meanwhile, my fiancé and I decide to put off the romantic part of the weekend until we get used to the light and spend the rest of the night bar-hopping— eating small portions of traditional Icelandic foods as we go— and then drinking glasses of the local specialty to get rid of the taste of the small portions of traditional Icelandic foods.

It turns out that the local specialty we have been drinking is Brennivin, the same clear liquor that comes in tiny bottles at the duty-free shop. It is a traditional 190-proof drink that Icelanders have nicknamed "Black Death." The bartender advises us to drink Brennivin to cleanse the palate after eating rotten shark—which it does not do because the rotten shark was not first set on fire.

We drink a big bottle of Brennivin and by closing time, we have sampled all their traditional Icelandic cuisine, such as whale meat, reindeer, puffin, a sheep's head boiled with the eyes in, and something's testicles.

Back at the hotel, we drink some of our little bottles of Brennivin—which are not as strong because they are smaller— and we play cards until the restaurant opens for breakfast. I cannot stop thinking about how many people before me have thought of eating testicles, and it makes me feel small.

Saturday, the 9th of February 10:00 a.m.
Greenwich Mean Time

It is still pitch black outside.

The concierge, whose name is "Thorra"—which is a real name in Iceland—suggests that we eat at the restaurant Kaffitír Dónalegur on Laugavegur. We thank her very much and go there for a breakfast of eggs without any traditional Icelandic foods. We board a tourist excursion bus bound for local attractions. The first of these is the side of the road. There, we see a herd of small, stocky Icelandic ponies, their long hair blowing like fringe from their flanks and manes and stoic shanks. On the plains, there are no hills to shield them from the incessant icy winds. The ponies tear sustenance from the ground in the form of stubble and the tufts of lifeless grass. They are fed hay from carts which amble out from shelter—shelter where the ponies dare not go. They stand in fields day after day, their gentle muzzles chapping in the wind.

I board the tour bus in shame.

Next, the tour bus passes 80 miles of black and barren lava fields and we pay a visit to the extinct volcanic crater Hagid, that lifeless eye shut against the sight of billowing thunderclouds overhead. When I can no longer bear to witness the volcano's retiring defeat, I go back to the bus and stay on board for the rest of the trip.

My fiancé tries to convince me that I should come out for a few minutes when we are at the geysers, or to come out and climb a small hill to see Gulfoss, the gigantic 5-tiered waterfall. However, there's a bathroom on the bus, so I stay there and drink some of the little bottles of Brennivin from the duty-free and I am fine.

Saturday, the 9th of February, 5:00 p.m.
Greenwich Mean Time

The sun is setting and there's nothing we can do about it.

The concierge, whose name is "Thorra"—which is a real name in Iceland—suggests that we sample the fish menu at the Andstyggilegur restaurant on Kringlumyrarbraut. She also suggests that we wear gloves, as the weather forecast is for precipitation and the sleet is known to draw blood. Our travel book says Norwegian sailors intentionally switched the names of Iceland and Greenland in order to fool people into going to the wrong place, hence the expression: "Iceland is green and Greenland is icy," which should be changed to: "Iceland is icy and Greenland is even icier than that."

When we get back to the hotel, my fiancé and I decide it would be romantic to open a bottle of champagne and we have already begun to meet our hotel neighbors when the night security manager tells us there's a policy against going door-to-door and we should have asked the concierge for a corkscrew. As we wait for the restaurant to open for breakfast, we watch German TV and eat bags of peanuts from the mini bar.

Sunday, the 10th of February 11:00 a.m.
Greenwich Mean Time

The sun is not yet risen and my fiancé feels out of sorts due to 60 hours without sleep, but I don't care because overnight I realized that I was never in love.

We pay a visit to the famous nearby church, Hallgrímskirkja, where we see people asking the Lord for forgiveness for sins. I guess the worst He can say is "no" or "go to hell."

We leave the church just as a blizzard hits the city. Everyone walks unhurriedly, as if blizzards do not matter. Icelanders are a hardy people, loath to cry, as the wind and low temperatures freeze the tears in their very eyes. Blinking is painful for Icelanders: a people loath to blink. I realize their eyeball brinksmanship makes them ideal for membership in NATO because you can really spook most people by remaining unblinking.

Sunday, the 10th of February 4:00 p.m.
Greenwich Mean Time

The sun is at its most intense, though it does not shine so much as infuse the sky as if the heavens are no more than a massive old-fashioned glazed office window. My fiancé and I must be acclimating because the light is painful and bothersome.

We go to the National Museum of Iceland but it is closed for renovations until 2002 and we're not so sure it's full of treasures, anyhow, so we go back to the hotel to change for dinner.

I ask my fiancé to no longer speak to me. It turns out my fiancé was going to ask me the same thing.

The hotel concierge, whose name is "Thorra"—which is a real name in Iceland—suggests that we try the fresh seafood at the restaurant Kighósti Vonlaus on Stkdiavördustigur and we tell her to shut the fuck up.

We decide to abandon the quest for the perfect ice. There is ice to be had, but it is imperfect ice. Obviously, the Icelanders have ruined Reykjavik the way mummers have ruined the image of King Tut with their shop teacher's eyeglasses and string banjos.

We stop by a local bookstore to look for the latest edition of the *International Herald Tribune,* but the English language section has nothing but poetry by Sylvia Plath and a translation of André Gide.

On the way to the restaurant, we see a mother pushing a baby stroller down the street. We follow her to the lake in the center of town, where she and her clumsy toddler tear bread to feed the ducks and swans and this is how Icelanders teach children about socialism. It's hard to feel sorry for people like that. It becomes very obvious that Iceland and the United States are two very different nations. For instance, our guidebook tells us that Icelanders call gnomes and elves "the hidden people," whereas this is what we call sales help at Tower Records.

Monday, the 11th of February 5:00 p.m.
Greenwich Mean Time

The sun has set and there is nothing left to look forward to.

We spend the day packing and weeping quietly.

On the way to the airport bus we see plenty of ice—none of it perfect—so we throw the guidebook at somebody's car.

As we sit on the plane, I calculate that we have spent 81 hours in Iceland and seen 8 hours of sunlight.

The flight attendant says she can't serve drinks until we take off. I accuse her of picking a fight and of thinking she is better than everyone. She fools no one by acting beautiful and polite.

"Maybe I'm not an educated woman," I tell her. "Maybe I never went to your tall schools and fancy enterprises and the state didn't teach me my colors and flavors and smells, but I'm an American and I have American money and *you* are the perfect ice."

Coda

Icelandair reserves its right to deny its passengers Brennivin in-flight.

It may very well be that Iceland is for lovers, but you can find sturdy canvas tote bags there—the large-capacity ones with longer handles.

For JMS~ Zip! Goes another nickel

M. Sweeney Lawless

Ambitious Trip

Cathy Guisewite

Playing by the Numbers

HONESTLY, RICHARD, SOMETIMES I THINK OUR RELATIONSHIP IS NOTHING MORE THAN A GAME TO YOU!

Liebe Lamstein

The Race

Tuesday

I had a blind date tonight. He was really nice, but I'm afraid he may be too much of a noodle. I'd mow him down in a minute! His name is Sam.

Friday

Sam called today and left me this message: "Hi, Lily, it's Sam giving you a call. I haven't heard from you since our date on Tuesday and I just want to tell you I had a really great time with you that night and I'd love to see you again. As a matter of fact, I've been thinking of you ever since and I sure would love another look at those beautiful blue eyes. How about breakfast tomorrow? Or Thursday? Or any day over the weekend? Give me a call. I really think we may have something here. I know we just met but I just have a feeling. I look forward to talking to you. Bye."

I am standing over the answering machine with my mouth open down to my toes. "Gag!" is my first thought. "Who do you think you are? You don't even know me!" are my second and third thoughts. Then an enormous grin spreads not merely from ear to ear, but around my whole head, engulfing me briefly before the panic sets in.

The guy was showing a little moxie. I like that. That's what I was worried he didn't have any of, right? Why, then, do I feel like I used to feel in the eighth grade when a boy I liked turned out to like me? Ill. So very ill.

I am overcome with feelings of inadequacy. I should be ecstatic but all I want to know is: "What kind of a dope do you think I am, Sam? You think I just fell off the hay truck? I know your type. I've been around the block, buddy. I've already been married and divorced, remember? I'm not that easy. So if this is some kind of a lousy joke, I'm on to you, asshole, and you can find some other bimbo to stroke your ego!"

I guess I want him bad, huh? Does it show?

I've always wondered what it must be like to be pursued. Now that it's happening I feel completely out of control. And the critical voices in my head are euphorically beating my self-esteem to a pulp in ravenous anticipation of my self-loathing devouring the gooey mass that will be all that's left of me in another twenty-two seconds.

"Why on earth do you think he'd go for you?" the voices sneer. "He must be an idiot, not worth his weight in boogers! And you must be exorbitantly desperate to believe a line of gewgaw like: '. . . I sure would like another look at those beautiful blue eyes.' You know, as soon as he really gets to know you and finds out what a false alarm you are, he's going to dump you. (Actually, you won't have to worry about that because the relationship will never get that far.) 'What on earth was I thinking?' he'll wonder to himself by this evening and you'll never hear from him again."

I am now sufficiently tenderized and ready for consumption by that insatiable soul-snatcher known as "Self-loathing." Before she takes me down, however, I get one phone call.

"Hi, it's Lily calling for Sam, please . . . Thank you . . . Hello, Sam? It's Lily. How are you?"

"Fabulous! I'm so glad you called. I was really hoping you'd call." (Lily: One. Vicious Voices: Zip!)

"Well, I got your message; how could I not?"

"I don't know. I hung up and I thought, 'I hope I didn't scare her by coming on too strong.'"

"I don't scare that easily," I say laughing flirtatiously to cover up my utter terror of having been found out only four seconds into the conversation. (Maybe I spoke too soon.)

"Great," he says. I can hear the smile in his voice. "When can I see you again?"

"Um . . . well . . . " (The familiar feelings are lining up at the starting gate in rapacious anticipation of the capital race of the week that is about to begin. Terror, I Need An Out, No Self-Esteem, Just Keep Your Distance, I'm Worthless, Big Liar, and, oh yes, that scrawny little stiff, Contrition, are ready to go. A posse of allegorical horses prepared to stop at nothing for that evanescent moment of glory when they trample me like a grape; make off with my senses; and declare world domination!)

". . . I'm actually very busy this week with rehearsals for this play I'm doing. We're about to start tech week so I'll be at the theater 'til all hours." (And they're off! It's Terror in the lead; followed closely by No Self-Esteem, and Just Keep Your Distance along the rail.)

"You have to eat, don't you? Maybe I could meet you down at the theater during your dinner break?"

"Um . . . " (Oh my, ladies and gentleman, will you look at

that! This is going to be a very exciting race indeed. Coming
from behind, gaining from the far outside; she's an early foot
from wire to wire . . . It's Big Liar!)

" . . . We're not organized enough to know when our dinner break will be . . ." (Big Liar breezes past the stands; gaining
nimbly on No Self-Esteem and Terror . . .)

"How about Sunday? I'm having breakfast with my friend
Ellen at 10:30, before my rehearsal (Big Liar leads by a hair . . .),
but we could go for a walk before that at 9:00 . . ."

(Now it's I Need An Out dusting the railbirds and round-
ing it out along the back stretch. She's pressing the bet on Just
Keep Your Distance and getting the edge on No Self-Esteem.
I'm Worthless tries to give I Need An Out the hat trick, but the
latter pulls ahead. She's a cyclone. Neck and neck with that
speedball Big Liar. . .) "I just have to be on the road by ten so I
can make it to Ellen's on time." (. . . I Need An Out gets the bat.
She's puttin' on the ritz—she's nose to nose with Terror but
can't quite steal the lead.)

"Sure, that'd be great."

"I'm sorry it's so early. I'll have more time after tech week
is over . . ." (Holy moly! Coming from behind—as if out of
nowhere, ladies and gentlemen—it's Contrition—that glue pot
without a prayer. What a race this is turning out to be!)

"I'll look forward to seeing you bright and early Sunday
morning, then . . ." beams Sam.

(Contrition picks up speed . . .)

" . . . Get my day off to a wonderful start. Shall I come pick
you up?"

(Terror still leads by a nose with Just Keep Your Distance
now sneaking into second . . .) "Oh, no, you don't have to do
that . . . (Big Liar is jammed in the middle. She puts the chill on
Just Keep Your Distance and muscles her way back to number
two . . .) I'll bring my own car; that way I can go straight to
breakfast with Ellen."

(I'm Worthless and No Self-Esteem hang on to a tight
tie for third, giving Just Keep Your Distance a bad day at the
office . . .)

"Okay, I'll see you Sunday . . ."

(. . . And whatd'ya know? As they come thundering down the home stretch, that neverwuz—Contrition—is all but out of the race.)

". . . Have a great two days," offers Sam.

"Thanks. You, too."

"Thanks."

"Bye."

"Bye . . . Thanks for calling back."

"Oh . . . well . . . my pleasure, really." (It's going to be a close one . . .)

"'Kay, bye." Sam doesn't want to hang up, either, but I have no choice. My palms are so sweaty I'm in danger of being electrocuted any minute . . .

"Bye."

(And the winner is . . . Terror, by a breath! Big Liar glides into second. Just Keep Your Distance and I'm Worthless tie it up for show and No Self-Esteem and I Need An Out bring up the rear.

What a race, ladies and gentlemen! What a race!

The horses are walking it off now, already looking ahead to their next heat which could come at any moment. Tireless beasts, these ponies live to win—unmitigated cerebral domination or bust.)

Despite the infinite stamina of the "horses" in my head, I hang up the phone, still master of one or two of my senses and feeling relatively intact. World domination is not to be theirs just yet. I take a deep breath and notice that even "Self-loathing" has momentarily lost her appetite for my soul.

Boy, this dating thing is exhausting—and I haven't even left the house yet. If Sam and I ever have sex, I'll probably pass out before we've even popped the first button. I need some milk.

Yeardley Smith

Among Other Thoughts On Our Wedding Anniversary

Over the years,
When the sink overflowed
Or the car ran out of gas
Or the lady who comes every Friday to clean didn't
    come
Or I felt pudgy
Or misunderstood
Or inferior to Marilyn Kaufman who is not only a
    pediatric surgeon but also a very fine person as
    well as beautiful
Or I fell in the creek and got soaked on our first
    family camping trip
Or I bruised my entire left side on our first family
    camping trip
Or I walked through a patch of what later turned
    out to be plenty of poison ivy on what later
    turned out to be our last family camping trip.
Or my sweater shrank in the wash
Or I stepped on my glasses
Or the keys that I swear on my children's heads I
    put on top of the dresser weren't there
Or I felt depressed
Or unfulfilled
Or inferior to Ellen Jane Garver who not only
    teaches constitutional law but is also a wit plus
    sexually insatiable
Or they lost our luggage
Or our reservations
Or two of the engines
Or the rinse that was going to give my hair some
    subtle copper highlights turned it purple
Or my mother-in-law got insulted at something I
    said

Or my stomach got upset at something I ate
Or I backed into a truck that I swear when I looked
    in my rearview mirror wasn't parked there
Or I suffered from some other blow of fate.
It's always been so nice to have my husband by my
    side so I could
Blame him.

Judith Viorst

On Being Married

Paige Braddock

CHAPTER 2

Bears with Furniture

―――――

Some of the best comedians right now are women, and the best of the women comedians is named Rita Rudner. She does great bits on men, and in one of them she says: "Men don't live well by themselves. They don't even live like people. They live like bears with furniture."

I always wondered about that furniture part.

Since the observations of female comedians, women lawyers, my aunt Gloria, the entire membership of Hadassah, the League of Women Voters nationwide, and the woman who lives across the street from me don't count as empirical evidence, researchers at the University of California at San Francisco have done a study that shows that men need to be married or they starve to death. They studied 7,651 American adults to come to this conclusion.

This is why we think scientists are wasting their research money. This study says that men between the ages of forty-five and sixty-five who live alone or with somebody other than a wife are twice as likely to die within ten years as men of the same age who live with their wives. "The critical factor seems to be the spouse," said a professor of epidemiology and biostatistics who, incredibly enough, seems both to be surprised by these findings and to be female. She also noted that researchers were not sure why men without wives are in danger of an earlier death, but that preliminary analysis suggested they ate poorly.

Let me explain how you might do a study like this. Let's say you have a package of Stouffer's macaroni and cheese, a tomato, and a loaf of French bread. Let's say that it is seven o'clock. Pretend you are a researcher for the University of California and observe what the woman between the ages of forty-five and sixty-four will do with these materials:

1) Preheats oven according to package directions. Puts package in oven.

2) Slices tomato and sprinkles with oil, vinegar, and ground pepper.
3) Slices bread and removes butter from refrigerator.

In about an hour the woman will eat.

At the same time researchers can observe a man between the ages of forty-five and sixty-four living alone using the same materials:

1) Reads package, peers at stove, rereads package, reads financial section of paper.
2) Looks at tomato, says aloud, "Where the hell's the knife?"
3) Places tomato on top of frozen package, leaves both on kitchen counter, watches Monday Night Football or a National Geographic documentary on the great horned owl while eating a loaf of unsliced French bread.

This can be compared and contrasted with the man living with his wife. When the wife goes out, the result is exactly the same as in example 2, except that when the wife returns and says, "Why didn't you eat dinner?" the husband between the ages of forty-five and sixty-four will say "I wasn't hungry," in exactly the same tone of voice he would use if he were to say, "I have bubonic plague." (These results are occasionally skewed by observed occasions on which wife returns home and finds house full of smoke. Such incidents are particularly reliable indicators of longer life for men between the ages of forty-five and sixty-four, since they enhance the well-documented "I told you not to go out and leave me alone" effect, which promotes a generalized feeling of well-being and smugness.)

Every woman I know finds the California study notable only because the results seem so obvious. But I find it helpful to have anecdotal observations confirmed by scientific analysis, and besides, it gets me off the hook. I am frequently accused of feminist bias for suggesting that the ability to do a simple household task without talking about it for weeks is gender-based. If I were to suggest that a man without a wife is a man overwhelmed by dust balls, pizza cartons, and mortality, I would get an earful from the New Age men. The New Age men appear in many stories about lifestyle matters; there are five of them, and they are the guys who actually took those paternity leaves you've been hearing so much about. One of them makes a mean veal piccata, which is habitually featured in stories about men who cook.

If they're unhappy with this conclusion, they've got science to arm-wrestle with. $E = MC^2$, some guy once said, perhaps while eating a loaf of French bread and wondering why his wife had to visit her sister. And 1 man minus 1 wife = bad news, according to researchers at the University of California at San Francisco. Bears with furniture. Rita and I have biostatistics on our side.

Anna Quindlen

For the Woman Who Has Everything

Wendy Wasserstein

CHAPTER 3

Light Reading

Book Clubbing

I had a feeling I needed more mental stimulation when, in the middle of telling my husband about my day, I began to gaze off into the distance and drool.

So my friend Shirley suggested that I join her book club. It sounded perfect: intelligent discussions on literary themes, lively debates based around popular works—and lunch at a different restaurant each month.

The only problem was that I would have to read a book. And not just any book mind you, chances are it would be a long one with an intricate plot about casts of people set in far-away places.

Now don't get me wrong. I love reading, but the last book I finished had a sturdy cardboard cover, large colorful pictures, and a thinly disguised plot based loosely around a group of talking animals and the sounds of the alphabet.

But, since I was desperate to have a conversation with other human beings on any topic other than bodily functions, I decided to try it.

This month, the club was reading *Memoirs of a Geisha*. Luckily, it was a thick book so if I couldn't finish it, at least I could put it on the top of my stack of other unread books and make a nice drink table.

I whipped it open at the first sign my children were going to play quietly together. If I was quick, I might be able to get through a whole page before a fight broke out.

"Mommy, what are you reading?" my seven-year-old daughter asked.

"*Memoirs of a Geisha*," I said, hoping that would satisfy her enough to go away.

"What's a geisha?"

"A type of woman entertainer."

"Oh." I could tell by her face that I wasn't going to be let off the hook so easily.

"What does she do?"

"Mostly sing and dance," I said.

"Why is her face white?" she asked, looking closely at the cover.

"To make her look pretty."

She considered this for a moment. "Nuh-uh," she said. Then she ran over to her little brother to break this unbelievable news to him.

"Nuh-huh!" he cried.

I made it all the way to the end of the page before she kicked over his block castle.

Then my childless friend Lisa suggested I try books on tape. "That way," she said. "You can listen to it in the car when you're driving around."

So I bought *Memoirs* on tape, and naively slid it into the cassette player on my way to my son's soccer practice.

Now, in most cars, you have a choice between tape player or the radio. However in my car we receive KKID, a local station with an exceptionally persistent signal that broadcasts out of my backseat twenty-four hours a day.

"Mommy, how fast are we going?"

"I'm cold."

"Did you know there's a grape on the floor and it looks like a bug."

"Gross!"

"I'm hot."

"Did we bring snacks?"

"Are we almost there?"

"Why is that so loud?"

"Mom. Mommy? Mommeeeeeeee!"

I actually got through one whole chapter by the day of the meeting and, if I tried real hard, I could probably remember what it was about. But, I decided to go anyway and just focus on the beginning. After all, with enough wine, maybe no one would notice.

This month's meeting was held at an upscale Italian restaurant. When Shirley and I approached the table, she introduced me to the other members of the club: nine intelligent-looking women, all with *Memoirs of a Geisha* arranged neatly next to their plate. I smiled and tried to cast a knowing look that insinuated I was intimately familiar with the book.

The discussion started even before our wine order was taken. At this rate, they'd be through with chapter one before the salad arrived. I just hoped I'd get to finish the main course before they found out I was nothing more than a nonreading wannabe book club crasher out for a good time.

"Who would like to begin?" One of the women asked.

I raised my hand.

"I thought the first two paragraphs were riveting," I offered, trying to throw them off my track.

"Exactly," the other women agreed.

"And the setting was . . . was . . ." I stammered, "perfect."

"Exactly." The other women agreed.

A long silence followed and I began to get nervous. What if they were on to me and asked me something hard, like what happened in chapter two?

Then a very smart-looking woman raised her hand to speak. "Do you know that Wynonna Judd is getting a divorce?"

"No!" Gasps of disbelief.

"Yes, it's true. I read it while standing in line at the grocery store," she said. "By the way," she said pointing to me, "where did you get that leather bag? It's fabulous."

"Yes," everyone agreed. "It's great."

By the time desert arrived we had discussed the best way to take red wine stains out of a carpet, the debate on backpack versus over-the-shoulder purses, and all of the sexy scenes in the latest Harrison Ford movie.

When we were finished, we made plans on where to meet next month. Then we tucked our books smugly under our arms and walked to the car.

This book club was going to work out after all.

Debbie Farmer

Closet Commuter

Nurit Karlin

Why We Can't Stay Married

Many people are making lots of money writing books about why men and women can't stay married. They have titles like: *Men Who Love Women Who Love Too Much*, *Women Who Love Men Who Can't Find Their G-Spots*, *Couples Without Time To Love Because She's Always Driving the Car Pool.*

The thing that makes me angry about this is that I'm not one of the writers making money writing these books. And the reason that makes me angry is that I have the answer, which I'm going to give to you right here, for free.

The reason husbands and wives can't stay married is: large appliances.

Large appliances break up far more relationships than do sex, money, household chores, and relatives. My personal historical research proves it. Just watch *Wagon Train* some time (that's how I do most of my personal historical research). Those people had to put up with sex (under a wagon, yet), money, house- (or wagon-)hold chores, and relatives. Okay, I'll give you relatives, since most of them were moving away from their in-laws, which saved several marriages right there. But do you see people on *Wagon Train* getting divorced? I think not! And they didn't have large appliances, either. They beat their laundry with rocks in a creek.

If you check statistics you'll find that American marriages started falling apart in the 60s, just a decade after people acquired several types of large appliances.

"Imagine," my friend Lauren said to me, "finding out that there is only one correct way to load a dishwasher, and I am married to the only man in the world who knows it. And who is more than happy to share the technique with me."

My chin dropped, the way it does when I've found a soulmate (such as someone else whose car clock is an hour off for half the year because they don't know how to change it back from Daylight Savings Time).

"Oh, no!" I gasped. "There is one other person who knows the one correct way to load a dishwasher," referring to my own husband of a quarter century. "It must be a secret society."

Lauren and her husband are still married, but then they have a young son to consider.

But I estimate the dishwasher is a minor league marriage-buster compared to that mainstay of American kitchens, the hulking refrigerator.

"Where is the leftover pizza?" calls my husband from the kitchen. I shudder. I know that my answer, "On the right side, second shelf," will only add to his aggravation when he is unable to locate the mozzarella-covered prize. So I join him, feigning puzzlement, in front of the open fridge.

For a while we both stand there in silence, basking in the glow of the light and the chill of the frosty air pumping out at us. Of course, I see the pizza perfectly well because it's sitting right there on a red plate covered with clear plastic wrap; if it were any closer I would be in danger of inhaling the Saran and suffocating to death. But I let a reasonable amount of time pass before I say, "Oh, could that be it?" and my husband, mumbling about how anyone could find anything in "there" retrieves it and I return to the safety of the next room.

Faced with a similar situation, the uninitiated bride too often rolls her eyes, pulls out the pizza, and hands it to her chagrined mate, who attempts to save face by lashing out at her about some unrelated issue, such as the S&L crisis or call forwarding. She lashes back at him and their marriage becomes another victim of large appliances.

Even if her marriage survives the refrigerator challenge, the "what-were-you-doing-when-you-broke-it?" menace awaits.

"It just started beating itself against the basement wall like it was trying to commit suicide."

"What did you put in the washer?"

("Your underwear and a bag of cement," she mumbles under her breath, gritting her teeth.)

"The laundry," she replies slowly, as if speaking to a small child.

"What were you doing when it started ramming the wall?"

("Plowing into it with the Toyota.")

Did you spot the trend? One spouse, usually the male, forms a series of questions aimed at finding out whose fault it is. Large appliances provide the easiest available way for a husband to blame his wife for an expensive inconvenience for which she was in no way responsible. For reasons that no one has been able to discern, this makes him feel better. For reasons that are perfectly obvious, this makes her feel like keeping the washer and trading in the husband.

Large appliance manufacturers do not want you to know any of this, of course, and they will, no doubt, demand that I retract my statements. They'll probably argue that I, a woman who has been married to the same man for twenty-five years, have no right to abuse large appliances, several of which I own and use daily.

However, I stand firmly behind the facts I have presented here and, if you'll excuse me, I have some laundry to catch up on.

May I borrow some rocks?

Marcia Steil

Men Who Like Housework

Gail Machlis

CHAPTER 3

You Say Dumbo and I Say Rambo

The ultimate intimacy is an act so fraught and resonant that a couple probably shouldn't do it before they have a candid and detailed discussion, freely revealing personal histories and preferences. They certainly shouldn't do it before the third date. I mean, of course, renting a video together.

Video rental is one of those activities that makes or breaks a relationship, like canoeing. In fact, I (not my real name) have observed a problem on the cusp of becoming a trend and, Oprah willing, a national malaise: Video Incompatibility Syndrome.

When a couple enter a video store, basic issues come into play: Who's going to accommodate? By what route will you reach an accord? Does his fear of leaving Classics for a dip into Cult suggest other timidities? Is it significant that she's happy to rehash her romantic past but reluctant to disclose the fact that she has seen *Jason and the Argonauts* twenty-three times?

Divergent tastes don't always signal disaster; Dumbo and Rambo can find happiness. And yet.

Says my friend K (her real initial, but she's not really my friend): "My ex would only rent pretentious, boring things like *Dersu Uzala*, or *Ursu Derzala*, a Russian film about a Japanese guide or a Japanese film about a Russian guide standing silently in a field of snow for three hours. If I ever see a copy again, I'll crush it slowly."

He automatically vetoed her suggestions, she reports, especially ridiculing her passion for Schwarzenegger classics from his pre-smiling period.

"We took to renting separately," she says, "which I think is a real trouble sign in a marriage." It could also be the sign of a healthy independence. We'll let Oprah decide.

Phil Keller, the manager at Couch Potato Video on East Eighth Street in Manhattan, confirms the spread of Video Incompatibility Syndrome. "*Fried Green Tomatoes* was a big fight-producer," Keller says, "although movie choice generally doesn't fall along sex-stereotyped lines. But it's almost always a guy who gives in." (He has also seen some ugly battles over who's responsible for late fees, and has turned down parents offering cash incentives to say he's out of *Barney* tapes.)

Keller politely declines when sparring couples ask him to referee. "The only intervention I'll make is to say, 'You know, if you rent both of them, you get a third one free.' "

I wouldn't presume to point out a national malaise if I didn't have a suggestion for a solution. I propose that film makers take some responsibility and start splicing up genre-bridging hybrids expressly designed to solve the problems of the renting diad.

Ten Potentially Top-Grossing Films
for the Video-Incompatible Couple

1. "Terminators of Endearment."
2. "My Own Private Benjamin."
3. "Honey, I, Claudius, Blew Up the Kids."
4. "A Few Good Men in Tights."
5. "Henry V, Portrait of a Serial Killer."
6. "Scenes From a Mall and the Night Visitors."
7. "Pretty Woman Under the Influence."
8. "Jennifer 8-1/2."
9. "Shoahboat."
10. "A Guy Named Joe's Liver." (From Reader's Digest Pictures, the only documentary on the list: Spencer Tracy and Sharon Stone get an anatomy lesson they'll never forget.)

These carefully wrought composites will, of course, maintain the artistic integrity of the originals; I'm not advocating an intercut of *Howards End* and *Buns of Steel,* or an all-Smurf version of *The Piano.*

Certainly, the plan is not without risks. Already many a mise-en-scène is marred by prominent product placement; if video blending goes commercial, how long will it be before we're watching "When Amana Loves a Woman" or "The Return of the Monistat 7?" (Actually, I trust the industry to police itself; it's not as if there were three Amy Fisher movies.)

Whether or not Hollywood heeds my cry, full-frontal rental will remain a private matter between (or among; who am I to judge?) consenting adults—and a potential source of friction.

I hear that one Solomonic video incompatibility therapist is using a radical technique: couples who refuse to compromise are forced to choose between *Heaven's Gate* and a head-cleaning tape.

Judith Stone

Sex on the Silver Screen

Jan Eliot

The Silent Partner

Can we talk? I'm rarely at a loss for words. As far as I'm concerned, talking is a natural biological function, like breathing—I do it all the time. Yet, my husband can hold his breath for hours, even days at a time.

The silence seems deafening. "Is something bothering you?" I ask, even though I realize that trying to pull words from the mouth of a man in the midst of a mute spell is as pointless as trying to make a telephone call when the line is dead.

Duke shakes his head. "Uh-uh," he mutters.

Unfortunately, talking is like tennis. You need two people to play. "It's a big problem in a lot of marriages," says family therapist Marcia Lasswell, who adds that the quiet one is usually the man.

Why? "Men have an easier time being silent than women," she explains. "Silence is almost a macho characteristic. Clint Eastwood, Gary Cooper—they don't say many words, they're all action. The strong, silent type is a masculine myth. But women get very frustrated."

Yup. My friend Léon was once married to a man of few words. "Not only didn't he speak, but when I did, he said, 'Shh!' " she recalls. "He wouldn't answer things like, 'Let's buy a house' or 'What did you think of that movie?' I tried notes, I tried signal flags; he wouldn't answer. Once, after a prolonged period of his not talking, I went outside the house and rang the bell. He opened the door and asked, 'Where have you been?' "

"At first, I thought all that silence meant that he knew the secret of the universe and that in time he would impart it to me," Léon says. "But when it was not forthcoming, I began to think that if I killed him slowly, at least he'd say something like 'Ouch' or 'Stop it.' "

Nope. Threats won't make him talk. In such extreme cases, "it's like trying to force someone who isn't coordinated physically to dance," Lasswell says. "These really silent types are basically shy. Somewhere along the line, they learned that speaking up didn't get them anywhere."

Shutting up doesn't get them anywhere either. "I had a couple where the man was so nonverbal that he really had a terrible time," Lasswell recalls. "His wife yearned to hear the words 'I love you,' and he just couldn't get it out. So, we practiced and practiced. I told her to say it first so that he would feel safe. So she turned to him and said, 'I love you.' And he said, 'Ditto.' "

Recently, starved for conversation, I called my friend Claire. "I'm trapped in the Silent Zone," I said with a sigh.

"He must be angry," Claire concluded. "Fred always clams up when he's absolutely furious. I figure it's just as well, because if he said something, it would be something that I didn't want to hear."

"Duke's not mad," I assured her. (It's easy to tell when a quiet man is mad. He storms into the house, slams the door, and hits the wall, and when you ask what's wrong, he snaps, "Nothing.") "He's just not speaking."

"I'd go insane," Claire said. "I'd send myself into a busy little circle wondering why he isn't talking. Pretty soon, I would start tossing plates around."

We don't have that many dishes. Besides, "you shouldn't take the silence personally," Lasswell insists. "You've got to remember that he didn't just start being silent when he married you."

Don't I know it. After a year of dating, I still didn't know where Duke went to high school. It's not that he conceals anything. He just doesn't go out of his way to reveal it.

Some day, I expect to find a ticket to Stockholm lying on the dresser. "What's this?" I'll ask. After ten minutes of cross-examination, he'll reluctantly inform me that he's won the Nobel Prize.

Now, if I ever won, I'd tell everyone in the city in a matter of seconds. So would my friend Jane, another life of the party, who's been married to a taciturn man for thirty-seven years. She's still trying to adjust. "You can't out-silence them," Jane marvels. "Things come up in this world like 'Hello' or 'The house is on fire.' You've just got to teach them that it's important to say, 'I'm home' when they walk through the door so you don't have to worry it's a robber."

I suspect that it's easier to teach a dog to "speak." So does Monica. "Jack can go through an entire family outing without saying a thing," she laments. "But it makes me very nervous. So the last time we went to my parents' for dinner, I asked him to please try to act interested. He said, 'I can't. I don't relate.' I said, 'Just try to say something to do with something they're talking about,' and he replied, 'I've got to be me.' Finally, I asked, 'Could you at least lean forward when they're talking?'"

Sometimes I feel guilty for talking more than my mate. But someone has to shoulder the conversational burden. "I suppose the worst thing for a man who doesn't talk would be a woman who doesn't either," Jane says. "He'd go crazy."

Experts agree. "I enjoy someone who's pretty much of a brass band more than someone who's just a flute," declares Glen Esterly, coauthor of *The Talk Book: The Intimate Science of Communicating in Close Relationships.* Esterly, a self-described "silent man in a state of flux," admits: "An extrovert takes away the pressure to avoid what's referred to as awkward silence. If I'm going through quiet periods and I'm with a quiet woman, there's a lot of dead air time. I'm not uncomfortable with the silence, but most people are."

Yup. Duke is lying in bed, reading about irregular Spanish verbs. "Soon, he'll be able to be silent as fluently in Spanish as he is in English," I think. "Buenas noches," I say, giving him a kiss.

"*Mi charladorita,*" Duke says fondly. "My little chatterbox."

Margo Kaufman

Berflegump

My lover and I will be out for a ride. He'll be driving and say,
"I'm taking Route 295 to the bridge. What do you think?"
And I say, "Berflegump hipple dip."
He'll say, "I'm hungry. I'm stopping at that diner.
What do you think?"
And I answer, "Quiddy diddle quank blurp."
Why am I speaking gibberish?
Because I understand.
He's one of those new *sensitive* kind of guys,
who knows enough to ask me what I think—
But he hasn't quite evolved to the point
where he *cares* about the answer.

Flash Rosenberg

If Men Could Menstruate: A Political Fantasy

A white minority of the world has spent centuries conning us into thinking that a white skin makes people superior—even though the only thing it really does is make them more subject to ultraviolet rays and to wrinkles. Male human beings have built whole cultures around the idea that penis-envy is "natural" to women—though having such an unprotected organ might be said to make men vulnerable, and the power to give birth makes womb-envy at least as logical.

In short, the characteristics of the powerful, whatever they may be, are thought to be better than the characteristics of the powerless—and logic has nothing to do with it.

What would happen, for instance, if suddenly, magically, men could menstruate and women could not?

The answer is clear—menstruation would become an enviable, boast-worthy, masculine event.

Men would brag about how long and how much.

Boys would mark the onset of menses, that longed-for proof of manhood, with religious ritual and stag parties.

Congress would fund a National Institute of Dysmenorrhea to help stamp out monthly discomforts.

Sanitary supplies would be federally funded and free. (Of course, some men would still pay for the prestige of commercial brands such as John Wayne Tampons, Muhammad Ali's Rope-a-Dope Pads, Joe Namath Jock Shields—"For Those Light Bachelor Days,"—and Robert "Baretta" Blake Maxipads.)

Military men, right-wing politicians, and religious fundamentalists would cite menstruation ("men-struation") as proof that only men could serve in the Army ("You have to give blood to take blood."), occupy political office ("Can women be aggressive without that steadfast cycle governed by the planet

Mars?"), be priests and ministers ("How could a woman give her blood for our sins?"), or rabbis ("Without the monthly loss of impurities, women remain unclean.").

Male radicals, left-wing politicians, and mystics, however, would insist that women are equal, just different, and that any woman could enter their ranks if only she were willing to self-inflict a major wound every month ("You must give blood for the revolution."), recognize the preeminence of menstrual issues, or subordinate her selfness to all men in their Cycle of Enlightenment.

Street guys would brag ("I'm a three-pad man") or answer praise from a buddy ("Man, you lookin' good!") by giving fives and saying, "Yeah man, I'm on the rag!"

TV shows would treat the subject at length. (*Happy Days:* Richie and Potsie try to convince Fonzie that he is still "The Fonz," though he has missed two periods in a row.) So would newspapers. (SHARK SCARE THREATENS MENSTRUATING MEN. JUDGE CITES MONTHLY STRESS IN PARDONING RAPIST.) And movies. (Newman and Redford in *Blood Brothers!*)

Men would convince women that intercourse was more pleasurable at "that time of the month." Lesbians would be said to fear blood and therefore life itself—though probably only because they needed a good menstruating man.

Of course, male intellectuals would offer the most moral and logical arguments. How could a woman master any discipline that demanded a sense of time, space, mathematics, or measurement, for instance, without that built-in gift for measuring the cycles of the moon and planets—and thus for measuring anything at all? In the rarefied fields of philosophy and religion, could women compensate for missing the rhythm of the universe? Or for their lack of symbolic death-and-resurrection every month?

Liberal males in every field would try to be kind: the fact that "these people" have no gift for measuring life or connecting to the universe, the liberals would explain, should be punishment enough.

And how would women be trained to react? One can imagine traditional women agreeing to all these arguments with a staunch and smiling masochism. ("The ERA would force housewives to wound themselves every month": Phyllis Schlafly. "Your husband's blood is as sacred as that of Jesus— and so sexy, too!": Marabel Morgan.) Reformers and Queen Bees would try to imitate men, and pretend to have a monthly cycle. All feminists would explain endlessly that men, too, needed to be liberated from the false idea of Martian aggressiveness, just as women needed to escape the bonds of menses-envy. Radical feminists would add that the oppression of the nonmenstrual was the pattern for all other oppressions. ("Vampires were our first freedom fighters!") Cultural feminists would develop a bloodless imagery in art and literature. Socialist feminists would insist that only under capitalism would men be able to monopolize menstrual blood . . .

In fact, if men could menstruate, the power justification could probably go on forever.

If we let them.

Gloria Steinem

Light Reading

"I'VE DATED ELEVEN ENIGMAS—I
WANT AN OPEN BOOK."

Liza Donnelly

Henry

Retirement? No big deal. When the time came, I said good-bye to the bookkeeping field, picked up my pension and went. Pretty soon I was busier than ever. Yoga class, art tours, my Great Books group, my matinee ladies, and candy-striping at the hospital once a week. But Henry . . . .

The firm threw him a big party at Le Bernardin, and the next day he started his life as a vegetable. He was never the great communicator—with his clients, yes, but not with me. I thought maybe being thrown together now, we'd make up for lost time. But instead, he practically stopped verbalizing altogether. Just sat in front of TV, eating carrot sticks and salt-free pretzels, and mourning his lost kingdom. This went on for months. Gradually I began to notice a change in his appearance. Nothing specific. But he seemed softer, rounder, more . . . cushiony. I told him he should get some exercise.

One evening, he emerged from the bathroom with a towel around his middle. It was unmistakable: Henry had breasts! I didn't say anything. Why upset him? But during the next few weeks I observed him closely as, to my—what—horror?. . . astonishment? . . . delight . . . he slowly changed into a . . . woman. And I must tell you, it's made a tremendous difference. Henry is a new person. He's learning macramé, tap dancing, and Mandarin Chinese cooking at the Y; he's taken up the accordion again, which he hadn't touched since high school. And talk! We can't seem to find enough time for everything we have to say to each other. The world has opened up for both of us. I admit I miss the sex a little. But in every other way, Henry and I are much happier.

June Sigler Siegel

Road Signs

Jennifer Berman

The End

*He would like to close
his eyes and have
you just go away*

Men are good at a lot of things. Breaking up is not one of them.

When a woman wants to break up with a man, she invites him over for dinner, cooks his favorite dish, then tells him she's seeing his best friend. It's all very straightforward. But men have this weird aversion to endings. They prefer to take the passive mode, allowing the relationship to end itself. Men can't be bothered with dramatic farewells, the questioning of motives, discussions. They are bored. They want out. Good-bye.

I remember the first time a boy broke up with me. We were in the seventh grade. He invited me over after school, said he just wanted to be friends, then had his mother drive me home. It was all downhill from there. In more recent years, a doorman informed me that my date was not coming down. Ever.

A friend called her boyfriend and found out he had moved to a new city.

A coworker happened upon a personal ad placed by the man she was dating.

Every woman, with the possible exception of supermodel Cindy Crawford, has a story like this. You may have dated the man a few weeks or a few years. You may have shared a cab or an apartment. It doesn't matter. For some reason the man thinks that the decision to break up is none of your business. (Of course, some women do the same thing. But then again, some women mud wrestle.)

Often a woman senses a breakup brewing and tries to get the man to sit down and fess up. No deal. The average male gets this beam-me-up-Scotty look on his face as soon as you mention the word "discussion." He treats you as if you were trying to serve a subpoena. Then, when you finally work up the nerve to ask him what the heck is going on, he pretends you're imagining the whole thing. It's all part of the game, and evidently the winner is the one who can quit the game without ever talking about it.

Some men admit they avoid confrontation because they're afraid we'll cry. Of course we'll cry; we cry at Hallmark commercials. What they don't understand is that we're not crying because of them, we're crying because now we have to get naked in front of someone else.

It's a rare and brave man who breaks up in person. Most likely he has sisters and does volunteer work. He'll say things you've heard before: "I'm unable to make a commitment. I don't have time to be the kind of boyfriend you deserve." Then he'll add, "I hope we can eventually be friends. I'd really miss your company." It doesn't matter if he's lying, telling the truth, or quoting something he read in a woman's magazine. At least he's trying.

Most men, however, think that even making a phone call to end a relationship is excessive. "What's the point?" they want to know. The humane thing, they've decided, is not to call, but instead to disappear like the Lone Ranger.

These men believe in "Close your eyes and make it go away." They believe in the Fifth Amendment. They believe in absentee ballots. They may ski black diamonds, walk barefoot on hot asphalt, skydive for fun, but measured on their fear of confrontation, these guys are wimps.

They'll say they're going to the rest room and never return. Then they'll meet friends for drinks and say, "She just doesn't get it" or "What do I have to do, spell it out for her?"

It's not that we don't get it. After about three weeks of shampooing with the water off—just in case he calls—we get the picture. But we'd like to feel we're more than just a notch in somebody's bedpost. Stranded without an explanation, we sound like the neighbors of a murderer. "He seemed nice. Kind of kept to himself. This came as a complete surprise." Underneath, of course, we know.

You can spot a woman who knows her relationship is disintegrating, because her answering machine gives hourly updates of her whereabouts. "I'm at work now, but I'll be home by six." "I'm at aerobics." "I'm in the shower." Meanwhile, a man's machine has the same message as always: "I'm not home. Later."

So what happens is this: you refuse to bow out gracefully, and he refuses to confront. His only option is to make you so miserable that you break up with him. We're talking emotional terrorism.

During this period he won't laugh at your jokes. He'll ask you out, then act like you're imposing. He'll shred what's left of your confidence by saying "You're wearing that?" or "Didn't you have time to change after work?" He may even tell you he'd like to end the relationship but continue sleeping with you. Then he'll act surprised when you bash in his headlights, stuff his favorite tie down the disposal, and ignite his baseball-card collection.

So what's the right way for a man to break up? I suggest the following steps:

Advice to Men Who Want to Break Up

Step One.   Choose a reason. Inevitably your girlfriend will ask why you're leaving, and you should be prepared to explain. If you know that your reason is petty and immature, make up a nicer reason.

Step Two.   Select a date that doesn't conflict with birthdays or major holidays. "I didn't plan to break up with her on Valentine's Day," a male friend once explained. "It just happened to coincide."

Step Three.   Talk to her. You're both adults. It might go surprisingly smoothly.

Step Four.   Hide your baseball cards.

One final note: Since writing this piece I experienced one actual face-to-face, special-trip-to-my-apartment-to-end-it breakup and I am now convinced I may have been too quick to criticize the Lone Ranger method.

Cindy Chupack

Battle Lines

Jan Eliot

Better From Behind

So you're leavin'—forgive my starin'
But, I want to freeze this picture in my mind
Riding out into the sunset
Lookin' for that open sky
Been a fool for your pretty face
and the way your silver buckle shines
But now I know the simple truth, dear:
You always look better from behind.

Yes, you always looked better from behind
It's the view I always knew would linger in my mind
Well, you know I like your Stetson, and the twinkle in
    your eye
But honey, I can't help it—
You look best from behind.

Better pack for nasty weather
'Cause a cowboy never knows what he might
    find
Take your lasso and your leather
Take your heart, 'cause you're not takin' mine.
Turn and face me for a minute
So I can see you one more time
Flash that smile with nothin' in it
I confess, you look better from behind.

Yes, you always looked better from behind
It's the view I always knew would dazzle someone
    blind
Well, you look like you're in movies
And you sing like Patsy Cline
But honey, I can't help it—
You look best from behind.

Git along little dogie, get you gone
But walk a little slower, as you're movin on . . .
And if I see you next December
Waitin' on the check-out line
You'll turn around and I'll remember
How you always looked better from behind

Yes, you always looked better from behind
Pardon me if I must be a little less than kind
You were handsome as the devil, so I took it as a sign
No regrets when you left
Like the sun when it sets
Skip the rest—You look best from behind.

Michele Brourman and Robin Brourman Munson

Totally Useless Skills

When I told Barry I was going to write an essay about Totally Useless Skills he refused to understand what I was talking about. He said, "What do you mean?" I said, "What do you mean what do I mean? I mean what I said." Skills that are useless. Things you learned that have no use at all . . . like algebra. I'm 46 and I still have no idea what A plus B equals other than a headache. Barry is insisting the answer is X but I don't want to hurt his feelings by telling him that X is useful only if your mind has wandered and you can't remember how to sign your name. It is utterly useless as the answer to a math problem.

Uselessness is, of course, totally subjective. I know one guy who can eat Jell-O and then shoot it out his nose. Some people would say that that's a useless skill, but then they've never seen Brendan at a party.

The real trick to life is not the useless skills you know but the useful ones that you have been clever enough not to learn. If you know how to do things you invariably end up having to do them for those who don't. Things like typing, cooking, sewing, bookkeeping, beekeeping, and shark-cage cleaning. What were people thinking learning things like that? I try to stay as helpless as possible so that Barry has to do everything for me as I idly sit fixing my lipstick while working on an algebra problem.

To me, knowing how to wash dishes is a totally useless skill. What does that get you except clean dishes and you can buy those. Who ever got the Nobel Prize or the Pulitzer for squeaky-clean flatware? When was a dinner party ever more fun because after everybody left you got to scrub pots until even your elbows were pruney? When did a husband ever say about his wife, "She's beautiful AND she gets the water spots off glasses like nobody's business."

[NOTE: Make sure you train your man right from the beginning. Barry may suspect that I don't evaporate like the Wicked Witch of the West if I'm touched by water but there is no way he can prove it. I don't want the romance of our relationship marred by the image of me sweating over a steaming sink, which is why I always retire to the living room to read and finish my wine while he cleans up. Think ahead ladies. Your relationship is too important to mess with.]

I feel pretty much the same about all housekeeping skills. It would be useless for me to learn them because they wouldn't make me any happier. Take cooking for example. I don't know how to cook. I am great at eating. I don't have such a huge ego that I think I have to be great at everything. Barry, of course, knows how to cook but he's an overachiever and will have to live with the consequences. Thank you honey that looks delicious. Just a fork please and some salt. I'd get up but I'm very close to solving this equation.

Being a good cook is also, I believe, a socially irresponsible thing to do. What about all the poor chefs who have spent their lives learning their craft? If everybody else was a great cook no one would go out and these worthy people would be on the dole. By not learning I am relieving the taxpayers of what could be a substantial drain. Don't thank me. It's okay. Barry sweetie I have nothing to drink. You don't have to get me anything. I just thought it might be an interesting topic of conversa . . . oh thank you sweetie. I didn't expect this. Of course I'd rather have red wine but I'd never want to cause a problem. You just go ahead and . . . oh thank you. Lovely. You shouldn't have. [Obviously I thought ahead and never learned how to use a corkscrew.]

As I was saying, skills that don't make you happier are the ones that really should be defined as useless. Map reading for instance. What is the point of learning how to read a road map when I know Barry is going to ignore me no matter what I say? He's a man. He not only will never ask for directions, he's adamant that no woman could possibly be right when she says, "Exit 3 then take a left at the light." Fine. Suit yourself. I'm napping. Wake me when we get there (which will undoubtedly be a week from Tuesday, late in the day).

As for learning to change a tire, are you out of your mind? My sister does it herself. She thinks that's great. You should see her fingernails. How useful is a working tire when your finger is too greasy to point out your entree so the waiter doesn't snicker at your French? French, as you may or may not know, uses far more letters than are strictly necessary. It is, when you think about it, very similar to algebra.

It's very possible now that I think about it that algebra is the most useful skill I know. Sweetheart, I'm very close to discovering the meaning of X but I am simply parched again. Thank you baby.

Janette Barber

Sister City

Jan Eliot

Maxine's Friends

Marian Henley

The Coast Is Not Clear

I don't know. I really miss California, but my hair looks better in New York. It's the water. In NYC the water is soft and life is hard; in California it's the other way around. Out West, I'm a woman of simple needs and complex carbohydrates, serene and centered. Back East, I'm caffeinated, careening, and so crazed I worry I'll confuse control-top stuffing with stove-top panty hose and race into a meeting with giblets on my legs.

But I get so much more done in New York; I'm smarter and more interesting. Or am I mistaking histrionics for vitality? Maybe, but better melodrama than mellow.

My brain is a battlefield, Eve West and Eve East fighting for supremacy. In ten years on the right coast after a lifetime on the left, I fear I've become a hybrid, unfit for either. I move too fast for California, but I'm too cheerful for New York. (Although a couple more years here should take care of that.) Californians think I'm rude because I've picked up a New York practice that I call "participatory listening" and they call "interrupting." New Yorkers assume I suffered some sort of early-childhood citrus-induced neural damage that causes me to wait until they're nearly finished with a sentence before I respond.

Habits I've formed here get me into trouble there. Roach vigilance, for example, is part of even the toniest New Yorker's life. So finely tuned has my peripheral vision become that I reflexively swat at any small dark object on a countertop. On my last visit to my parents' house in California, I didn't even realize I'd struck without missing a conversational beat until mother asked gently, "Dear, why are you killing that raisin?"

I'm perpetually committing bicoastiality in my heart, measuring my two homes, my two selves, against each other. Though I miss it fiercely, I see now that leaving California's Edenic climate may not have been such a bad thing. Living in an eternal golden present makes folks think they're immune to mutability; decay and death come as shocking affronts, not natural events. Living through the four seasons forces Easterners to wake up and smell the cosmic coffee. California can be a fool's paradise. But on days when my feet are freezing and sleet is performing unauthorized acupuncture on my face, I sometimes think, "Better a fool's paradise than a fool's hell."

The coasts come out even in the "How-can-you-live-there-aren't-you-afraid-of _____" Olympics. I worry as much about psychopathic Manson-type killers as I do about psychopathic Son-of-Sam-type killers; I'm about as afraid of earthquakes as I am of muggers. Since I've breezed through a dozen tremors but never been mugged, I tilt toward the devil I know. But my greatest terror is not having an all-night photocopy place within walking distance, so New York may have a slight edge after all.

The West Coast is soothing, but deceptive. The ratio of good men to narcissistic, infantile louses is about the same as in the East—1.5 to 3—but it takes longer to find out who's who. Only in the West have I been wooed with the promise of a romantic Frisbee weekend. Only in the East have I spent a first date at the vet's with a man whose cat was on dialysis. What does this mean? You tell me.

More people live on my block than live in my parents' entire town. In one morning's pass through Grand Central Station, I see more souls, and the bodies encasing them, than my best friend in Oregon sees in a year. I don't think human beings were meant to lay eyes on so many of their species at once. You'd think the sight would be humbling and inspiring, like a night sky full of stars, making you feel small yet part of a grand plan. But gazing daily at a Milky Way of fellow citizens makes me feel like part of a large ant farm.

I've gotten kind of used to it, though. Now, when I'm out West I get lonesome. I just spent a couple of months in San Francisco looking out the window and thinking, "Where is everybody?"

A Quiz

1. On which coast did I see a sign on a grocery-store bulletin board inviting shoppers to gather and "raise a cone of energy to summon the goddess Astarte"?

2. On which coast did I see a very young Brooks Brother point excitedly at the horizon and cry to his companion, "There! That's the kind of jet I want!"?

Answers

1. right and **2.** left. See? You can't always tell. I've come to understand that the brusqueness of New Yorkers can mask a sweet sort of no-nonsense kindness. I've come to see that California "sharing" often turns out to be about as open as Donald Trump's ledgers. I believe the mix of nice people and human-waste products is equal on each coast.

But I keep having to fight with people who insist geography is destiny. Or density: Westerners think East Coast crowding creates a constant surge of stress hormones that eventually erode the brain's niceness centers, and I can't always offer solid evidence to the contrary. Easterners insist that the West's wide-open spaces are duplicated between the ears of its inhabitants, and that California's official nickname should be the Persistent Vegetative State. New York thinks if you're not there you're nowhere. California thinks it's more highly evolved than thou.

I can come up with ten stories supporting each stereo-type—and ten in rebuttal. I'm the Cassandra whose prediction is that soon the only thing the coasts will suffer from is irreconcilable similarities.

New Yorkers mock me because I can't remember what "regular" coffee is. To Westerners I'm a figure of fun because I ask for a bagel with a schmear. "Wouldn't you prefer a smudge?" they chuckle, poking each other knowingly in the tan. West Coast friends can't believe I still live in a form-fitting studio apartment; New York friends can't believe I'm dissatisfied with a rent-controlled anything, however tiny, even in a city where one in ten suicides is attributed to a lack of storage space.

I passionately defend both edges of the country against detractors and curse them both beneath my breath. I love them both. I hate them both. I work better in New York, but I sleep better in California. I say yes better in California, and no better in New York. Where does this leave me? On the continental shelf. In a holding pattern over some existential Omaha. I'll always be a misfit. The coast will never be clear.

Ah, well. Home is where the answering machine is, and that's New York at present. For good or ill, this town's given me something I never had before: attitude. As a Californian, if I felt wronged, I'd think to myself, "They'll be sorry when I'm dead." Now, after a decade as a New Yorker, I think, "They'll be sorry when I kill them."

Judith Stone

Moving—Hollywood Style

Catherine Siracusa

Good Morning Fort Worth! Glad to Be Here

Hidy, Fort Worth. Think of the fun we're going to have. The statehouse, the courthouse, the White House—mirth, glee, and hilarity to be found in abundance everywhere we look. It requires, of course, a strong stomach to laugh at politics in our time. But the only other options are crying or throwing up, and they're bad for you.

It is not my habit to write columns about writing columns, a subject about which damn few people give a rat's heinie. But since I'm new to y'all and y'all are new readers to me, I thought I'd start by telling you where I come from and a little about how I look at all this—then you can take my diamonds of wisdom with a grain of salt or a pound of salt, depending on your preferences.

I believe politics is the finest form of entertainment in the state of Texas: better than the zoo, better than the circus, rougher than football, and even more aesthetically satisfying than baseball. Becoming a fan of this arcane art form will yield a body endless joy—besides, they make you pay for it whether you pay attention or not.

It's all very well to dismiss the dismal sight of our Legislature in action by saying, "I'm just not interested in politics," but the qualifications of the people who prescribe your eyeglasses, how deep you will be buried, what books your kids read in school, whether your beautician knows how to give a perm, the size of the cells in Stripe City, and a thousand and one other matters that touch your lives daily are decided by the dweebs, dorks, geeks, crooks, and bozos we've put into public office. (You may believe yourself in no peril of ever landing in Stripe City, but should you happen to contravene a law made by the only politicians we've got, this too will become a matter of some moment to you. For example, if you happen to possess six or more phallic sex toys, you are a felon under Texas law. In their boundless wisdom, our Solons decided that five or fewer of the devices make you a mere hobbyist.)

While it is true that I believe all politicians are in a free-fire zone, and further that it is an important American tradition to make fun of people holding high office, I also believe there are heroes in American politics. They're just in damn short supply. I also believe Texas legislators are overworked and underpaid. But that doesn't excuse their performance.

Ronnie Reagan, who was not the brightest porch light on the block, used to go around proclaiming, "Government is not the solution; government is the problem." Me, I think government is a tool, like a hammer. You can use a hammer to build with or you can use a hammer to destroy with. Whether government is good or bad depends on what you use it for and how well you use it. On the whole, it's a poor idea to put people in charge of government who don't believe in using it.

I believe government should be used in order to form a more perfect Union, to establish justice, ensure domestic tranquility, provide for the common defense, promote the general welfare, and secure the blessings of liberty to ourselves and our posterity. God, as the architects say, is in the details.

I believe that all men and women are created equal. That they are endowed by their Creator with certain unalienable rights. That among these are life, liberty, and the pursuit of happiness. I believe that governments are instituted among men and women, deriving their just powers from the consent of the governed, to secure these rights. And that whenever any form of government becomes destructive of these ends, it is the right of the people to alter or abolish it.

I dearly love the state of Texas, but I consider that a harmless perversion on my part, and discuss it only with consenting adults. If Texas were a sane place, it wouldn't be nearly as much fun. Twenty-five years of reporting on Texas and I still can't account for that slightly lunatic quality of exaggeration, of being a little larger than life, in a pie-eyed way, that afflicts the entire state. I just know it's there and I'd be lying if I tried to pretend it isn't.

I am so tickled to have Fort Worth as a home base. I've loved the town for years—it seems to me characteristic of Fort Worth that it still thinks of itself as a town, not a city. Dallas is a city. My great-aunt Eula lives in Fort Worth. Once when I was visiting, I said to Aunt Eula, who's had that same black telephone for at least forty years, "Aunt Eula, have you ever considered getting a new phone? You know they make them now in a lot of different colors and fancy shapes."

Aunt Eula said, "Why would I want a new one? This one is perfectly good." I think "Perfectly Good" should be Fort Worth's municipal motto. Another time, when I was driving for Aunt Eula, she said, "Turn left where the green water tower used to be." I am contemplating writing a guide book to Fort Worth with "Turn Left Where the Green Water Tower Used to Be" as the title, it being the kind of town where everyone knows where the green water tower used to be.

When Jan Morris, the famous British travel writer, wrote a piece on Fort Worth several years back for the *Texas Monthly,* she of course flat fell in love with the place, as all right-thinking people do. For years I've feared that Fort Worth would be "discovered" and become chic and self-conscious. Horrors. I raced over after Morris's gushing article came out to see if any damage had been done. It was the talk of Juanita's, and I joined several prominent citizens, many of whom had been interviewed by Morris, in mid-discussion. They all thought the article was "real fine, real nice."

"So interesting about Jan Morris," I said. "You know she used to be a man." One of the fundamental Fort Worth expressions, benign puzzlement, set on every face. "Yep, she used to be John Morris and she was a don at Oxford and a famous mountain climber, but then she had this sex-change operation and now she's a woman, but she still lives with her ex-wife, 'cause they love each other." Silence ensued. Finally one of them said, "Well, she seems like real nice folks." The others all nodded and said, "Yep, real nice folks."

Fort Worth is a town where people know what's important.

Molly Ivins

Cafe Society

Jan Eliot

CHAPTER 4

My Momma Told Me

Pre-School Yuppies

Wendy Wasserstein

Nanny Tyrannica

I used to worry about losing my husband to another woman," the twins' mother confessed at my son's toddler program while stashing two color-coded pacifiers into a diaper bag. "Now," she sighed wearily, taking out two color-coded bottles of apple juice, "I'm more afraid of losing my *nanny* to another woman. She's terrific with Matthew and Molly. Because of her, they sing all of Gilbert and Sullivan's *Pirates of Penzance*. She's taught them Chinese stretching exercises. Anyone seeing her in the park would want to snatch her right up. They don't know she's a health-food fanatic. I can't bring a potato that wasn't organically grown into the house. She forbids us to eat chocolate. Did you ever binge on *carob?*"

The kids moved from story time to singing time. My son launched into monotonous rounds of "Row, Row, Row Your Boat." Without missing a syllable the twins, not yet two, piped, "When constabulary duties kill enjoyment, kill enjoyment . . . a policeman's lot is not a happy one."

Their mother looked at me and shrugged. "So tonight we're having free-range chicken and hydroponic yams."

Nobody can ever realistically anticipate the changes brought about by a new baby. Double those when the baby is followed by the arrival of a nanny. It's not easy having a stranger come into your house. Gone is the freedom to raid the refrigerator naked; you have to put on a trench coat just to get juice. Sex, of course, is now restricted to the bedroom.

And along with your privacy, you relinquish control of your baby. Each time you go into the nursery for a little kiss and nuzzle, you find yourself asking permission of the nanny.

At baby gyms, swim schools, and Suzuki lessons, mothers complain about their help, all of whom are in varying degrees intrusive. Even if they initially appear eager to please, soon they evolve into tyrants and bullies. Whether she's a British-trained nanny, a French au pair, or a Salvadoran housekeeper, she's the one who sets policy, determining her hours and responsibilities, dictating how your child will be fed and disciplined.

In the canyons of Wall Street, a junior partner this assertive would certainly be dismissed; but in tiny-tyke America, a nanny quickly gets tenure. Once she's established a warm relationship with her charge, the nanny has nothing to fear. The love of the child is her job security. She can beg, borrow, and belittle without risk of reprisals. Rather than change nannies and perhaps upset the child, parents will tolerate affront after abuse.

"I don't know what to do!" a mother at the ice-skating rink wailed. "After eighteen months, Jessica is very attached to our live-in. We were okay with her too until she got a boyfriend. Our arrangement was she could leave for her day off once Jessie was asleep. Last week her boyfriend showed up early and started honking. She tried to put Jessica to bed at five o'clock!" She shook her head, baffled. "Her last employer said she was a gem."

Former employers have been known to lie—maybe they want to dump this "gem" before any more sterling vanishes—and besides, each household has its own quirks. You can interview like Mike Wallace and study her chest X-rays to make sure she's not a smoker, but it's still impossible to predict how she'll fit in. Landing the right nanny is all luck, which is why some parents are brave enough to import from abroad someone they've never met.

Hiring a nanny sight unseen is an act of faith, today's version of an arranged marriage. How do you know you won't wind up with a subversive? A Madonna clone? A slob?

A mother at the park who'd flown over a French au pair smiled impishly when I asked if she'd been concerned about surprises. "I wanted a wallflower," she admitted. "That's why I had the girls send pictures. The last thing I needed was someone like Catherine Deneuve moving in when I didn't have my waist back yet. The homelier, the better! I wanted the *kids* to fall in love with her, not my *husband!*"

The mother at the next swing laughed. "We brought a young nanny over from England," she reported. "One morning, maybe eight months after she'd started with us, she looked up from feeding the baby and said, 'I'm quite fond of life here in America.' I didn't know what she was driving at. 'I think I'd like to become a permanent resident,' she continued. 'But there's a bit of a problem with my papers.'

"She was great with Alexandra," the woman went on. "Certainly we wanted her to stay. I offered to find a good immigration attorney for her. 'Oh, I've spoken to a solicitor,' she said. 'It would make things much simpler if I were married to a citizen.' I figured she was telling me she'd need a morning off to do this," the mother laughed. "Wrong! She then said, 'I thought maybe your brother would marry me. We wouldn't have to *consummate* the marriage . . .'"

She laughed again, an edge of hysteria creeping into her voice. "My brother won't even let me fix him up on a blind date! I should tell him to marry our nanny?"

Listening to mothers, one suspects there's a course in chutzpah at nanny school. A nanny, particularly a British-trained one, assumes the status of Chairman of the Board. If she's willing to do laundry at all, *she'll* pick the wash cycle. As far as childcare is concerned, she looks upon parents, pediatrician, and relatives as obstacles to the performance of her job.

This type of nanny takes pride in raising stoic male babies and sensible female ones. If you intended to feed the baby "on demand" (perhaps to stem relentless crying) and the nanny believes in "a schedule" (feeding every four hours), your offspring will learn the virtue of patience. As a first-time parent, afraid to trust yourself, you'll listen to anyone proclaiming herself a professional in the field. And even if you've had kids before, all of whom were successfully fed on demand, you'll give in. You're savvy enough to understand how inconsequential the timing of a baby bottle is compared to the bigger problems ahead—drugs in the fifth grade and teenage pregnancies. You learn to pick your fights, because you know ultimately the baby will quiet down; the nanny won't.

Having established herself as commander-in-chief of the nursery, the nanny puts out her scent in other parts of the house. "I made the mistake of saying, *'Mi casa, su casa'* to our Guatemalan housekeeper," a mother announced at infant CPR class. "She took me literally. I came home and found our gardener packing up his spades and trowels. Consuela didn't like the way he looked at her. An acre and a half to mow," she said, shaking her head, "and he's on his way back to Kyoto. My husband is fed up. He says with Consuela running things, he feels like a fraud checking Head of Household on our tax return."

With our son's first birthday approaching, my husband and I felt it was time for me to stop nursing and resume working. We started making inquiries about childcare. Friends asked their nannies if they knew anyone looking for work. Although five nations were represented among the neighborhood help, this effort was unproductive. "In all of NATO," said my husband, Martin, laughing, "there's no one to take care of Nicky."

"Scout the parks," we were advised. "If you see a nanny you like, make an offer." I couldn't follow through. Not because of ethics, but because it was winter and the parks were deserted except for a couple of three-card-monte hustlers.

An agency was our final option. The receptionist at International Domestics told us their fee was 75 percent of a month's salary.

"Hers or mine?" Martin joked. Hearing that graduates of nanny schools get upwards of $400 a week, we decided to go for a housekeeper, someone experienced in caring for children who would also do some cleaning. The first to emerge from the back room was Rosario. In her late 50s, she shuffled in slowly, as if her knees were tied together. I ruled her out; Nicky could swallow an entire bottle of Windex before she'd get to him.

"We can only pay $150 a week," I volunteered, hoping Rosario would turn *us* down. "Is that enough for you?"

"*Sí!*" Rosario mumbled, studying her lap.

"Talk to them," the receptionist instructed, "in English."

"Jes."

"We're vegetarian"—me, trying another tack. "There's no meat in our house. Do you eat tofu?"

"*Sí* . . . jes."

While I wouldn't expect a recent arrival from Central or South America to finish the *London Times* crossword puzzle, I wanted someone who could make herself understood to 911 and be able to read instructions on the bottle of Ipecac.

The parade of candidates continued. After we'd met all the possibilities, the receptionist, perhaps perceiving our indecisiveness, offered a suggestion. "If I were you, I'd hire Gloria. She's happily married. With a young baby, you don't want a girl who runs around with a lot of fellows. She'll catch something. Next thing you know, the baby's got it."

If she was trying to scare us into hiring Gloria, it worked. Immediately upon leaving the agency, we picked up a copy of Linda Wolf's *Tell A Maid Child Care, Spanish/English* so I could give instructions like, "*siempre mantenga cerrada la puerta de la piscina*" (always keep the pool gate closed).

We lucked out. Gloria was a good choice for us. The hours she selected approximated those we would have picked ourselves. She's gentle and loving with Nicky. After two years, she's an essential part of our household. Her assertiveness is useful: Gloria's the only one who can persuade Nicky to take a bath, wear shoes, and chew his vitamins. She alone knows where the parts of Mr. Potato Head are buried.

Gloria may not have the panache of a British nanny, and Nicky doesn't sing operettas, but he leaves the twins in the dust when it comes to "*Quando Caliente El Sol.*"

Sybil Adelman

Nanny Dearest

Anne Gibbons

Welcome to Kindergarten, Mrs. Johnson

(Lights up on simple schoolroom set. Ms. THOMAS is at her desk, stage L. She is wearing a bright smock. As MRS. JOHNSON enters, MS. THOMAS crosses to her.)

MS. THOMAS: Welcome to kindergarten, Mrs. Johnson.

MRS. JOHNSON: How do you do? It's a pleasure meeting you. Janie has told me so much about you.

MS. THOMAS: It's a shame you couldn't make it last week with the other mothers.

MRS. JOHNSON: I'm sorry. I was speaking at a conference in Zurich.

MS. THOMAS: Well, come along. *(crosses back to her desk)* I've been observing Janie very closely. Have a seat. *(MRS. JOHNSON starts to sit in a miniature kiddy chair and nearly falls off onto the floor. MS. THOMAS is oblivious to her difficulty)* Sit straight. *(singing)*

She's a very bright girl, Mrs. Johnson.
She works beyond potential—
A model for her peers,
Exploring at a level
That's way beyond her years.
And I'm sorry
But it's getting on my nerves.

MRS. JOHNSON: *(speaking)* I'm sorry . . .

MS. THOMAS: *(speaking)* Don't fidget, Mrs. Johnson. *(crosses to Mrs. Johnson, singing)*

She's a difficult girl, Mrs. Johnson.
She helps the other children—Lord knows where it will lead,

And I've learned that when my back is turned
She's teaching them to read.
I'm to say the least dismayed—
What does she think this is, third grade?
She's independent.
She's assertive.
She's always self-assured.
Now I don't know where she's getting that,
But it's not to be ignored—
And it generally starts at the home.

(Ms. Thomas sits back at her desk. Speaking)

Did you know that Janie's the only child in class with an even reasonable self-image? Now who's responsible for that?

MRS. JOHNSON: *(a bit thrown)* I am.

Ms. THOMAS: I'm sorry?

MRS. JOHNSON: *(louder)* I am.

Ms. THOMAS: I am what?

MRS. JOHNSON: I am, Ms. Thomas.

Ms. THOMAS: Good. Well, how do you expect her to be intimidated by simple authority?

MRS. JOHNSON: Well, I . . . *(starts to sit on her hands)*

Ms. THOMAS: Keep your hands where I can see them. *(MRS. JOHNSON jerks her hands up. Ms. THOMAS sings)*

Now, I'm not saying you're a bad mother,
Even though you missed our pageant
And the Halloween parade.
No, no one's saying you're a *(produces Bad Mother flash card)*
Bad mother,
But your cookies at the bake sale,
Well, they clearly weren't homemade.

MRS. JOHNSON: *(abashed; speaking)* They were Pepperidge Farm Mint Milanos.

MS. THOMAS: The other mothers baked.

MRS. JOHNSON: I know, but . . . but I hate baking.

MS. THOMAS: Janie was humiliated!

MRS. JOHNSON: She never said a thing to me!

MS. THOMAS: Well . . . *(singing)*

> You're a busy little bee, Mrs. Johnson,
> Zipping off to Zurich.
> I hear next week it's Rome.
> Is there really any wonder
> Things are suffering at home?

(MRS. JOHNSON starts to protest.)

> Oh, there's no need to object.
> It's all here in Janie's artwork—
> You can see that I'm correct.

(She produces a large pig made out of a Clorox bottle and decorated with hearts. She shows it to MRS. JOHNSON.)

MRS. JOHNSON: *(speaking)* It's a pig! Made out of a Clorox bottle!

MS. THOMAS: Oh, come on, Mrs. Johnson. There are domestic problems written all over this pig. I know what I'm talking about. I've taken psychology courses.

MRS. JOHNSON: *(starting to stand)* But . . .

MS. THOMAS: *(raising pig over MRS. JOHNSON's head)* If you have something to say you raise your hand! *(MRS. JOHNSON sits abruptly, MS. THOMAS sings)* Now, no one wants to be a—

(MS. THOMAS flashes card at MRS. JOHNSON.)

MRS. JOHNSON: BAD MOTHER.

Ms. Thomas: And I think we can do better
If we just make up our minds,
'cause we all know what happens to a—

(She flashes card again at MRS. JOHNSON.)

Mrs. Johnson: BAD MOTHER!

Ms. Thomas: And there's every indication
That this suits your situation
Here is my evaluation—
Take it home and have it signed!

(She picks up an evaluation with "Bad Mother" marked on it and pins it on Mrs. Johnson, who is crushed.

Now, wasn't it nice meeting and getting a chance to chat like this?

Mrs. Johnson: *(fighting back tears)* Uh-huh.

Ms. Thomas: Did you know we have these parent-teacher conferences every Monday at four o'clock?

Mrs. Johnson: *(shaking head)* Uh-uh.

Ms. Thomas: Well, I hope I'll be seeing you again very soon.

(She replaces the pig.)

Mrs. Johnson: Ye-yes, Ms. Thomas.

Ms. Thomas: That'll be all. *(MRS. JOHNSON tears out of the classroom.)* No running in the halls.

(She sees the next mother waiting.)

Welcome to kindergarten, Mrs. Feldman. Have a seat.

(blackout)

Marta Kauffman

Billie's Parents

"You must be Billie's parents. I'd recognize you anywhere!"

Brenda Burbank

How to Talk to Your Stepmother

Your stepmother answers the telephone.
"Hi, is my dad there?"

Your stepmother has just announced that it is time for dinner.
"I'm not hungry."

Your stepmother has just put a bottle of salad dressing on the table.
"This isn't the kind we have at Mom's."

Your stepmother has just put the chicken on the table.
"I don't like chicken in funny sauce."

Your dad, your stepmother, and you are going to the movies. You don't want to see the movie she wants to see.
"My mom says that movie is too violent for me."
Alternatives
1. "My mom says that movie is too scary."
2. "My mom says that movie is too sad."

You want to watch television. Your stepmother says no.
"I'll ask my dad."

You ask your dad if you can watch television. Your stepmother informs him that she already told you you can't.
"I'm not talking to you. I'm talking to my dad!"

Your dad is out in the afternoon and you turn on the television. Your stepmother says to turn it off.
"You're not the boss of me."

You want your stepmother to take you to a movie that she thinks your dad doesn't want you to see.
"Look, you're my stepmother. You're in charge. You don't have to ask him."

Your stepmother picks up you and your friend after the movies.
"Hi, where's Dad? Why didn't he come?"

Your dad says you are not allowed to sleep over at your friend's. Absolutely not. It's out of the question. Tomorrow's a school day. Your stepmother says nothing.
"That was your idea, wasn't it?"

Delia Ephron

PTA

SIGNE
PHILADELPHIA DAILY NEWS
Philadelphia
USA

Signe Wilkinson

Hedge(hog)ing Our Bets

Your son has fallen in love, my friend calls to report. They have just come from the pet store.

Alden gets on the phone, breathless. "Please, Mom. Please. I saw this pet and I have to have it."

I thought our pet issues were over. I'd heard about the lizards. The hamsters had come and (mercifully) gone. We had succumbed to the cat. The beagle has topped the wish list for months, though temporarily displaced by the pig from Vietnam. Even Alden knew that the pig wouldn't fly.

"It's a hedgehog. It comes from Madagascar."

Half an hour later, Alden is home. A child possessed.

"Mom, it's so cute. I have to have it. Mom, I'll do everything for it. I'll clean its cage. I'll wash it. I'll feed it. I'll do everything for it. It eats cat food."

It eats cat food? To the cat, I'm sure, it *is* cat food.

"No, Mom, I asked. The man said it would get along with the cat. He said they wouldn't mess with each other."

No problem. We'll just tell the cat not to mess with it.

Alden, these are wild animals. They belong in the wild.

"They're very friendly. The man said so. He said they only bite if you mess with them."

From his vocabulary it is obvious the helpful gentleman in the pet store is a native of Madagascar and thus an expert in hedgehog behavior.

These animals are not meant to be kept in cages, I tell him. It's not natural: a hog in chips.

"I don't have to keep it in the cage. I figured it out. I can buy a used playpen and it can be in the playpen all day."

When it's not out of the playpen. Or in the cat's stomach.

"And it's very inexpensive to keep, Mom. It only eats cat food. And not that much of it. Just cat food. And worms."

What could be simpler?

How big is it, Alden. (Knowing that asking will be regarded as the first step in a process of capitulation.)

"Not big. Two inches. Or two feet. Or something. Mom, I just have to have it. I'll do everything for it. I'll find out all about it. I'll read everything about it. I'll do *research*."

The kid knows how to push our buttons.

"Mom, did you ever feel that you just had to have something? You just had to or you didn't know what would happen."

Yes, Alden. That's how people feel about their romances.

"But those are just people, Mom. You can always get another one. But I don't think there will be that many hedgehogs after they sell this one. This might be the only one."

How much is it, Alden?

"Well, it's sort of expensive. But Mom, I'll give up my allowance forever. Or at least until next year. I'll make my bed. I'll take a job."

How much, Alden?

"Three hundred dollars."

Three hundred dollars? Don't worry, Alden, I don't think they'll sell it so fast.

"Mom, I've figured it out. I can take money out of the bank for it."

No, Alden, you cannot raid your bank account to buy a hedgehog.

"I'll never ask for anything again."

He promises to give up his allowance. He promises to work for it. He promises to give up all claims to his parents' estates if he can have the hedgehog.

We don't need a hedgehog.

"You never listen to me. You don't care how I feel."

I do. And I do.

"Then please, just think about it."

I'll think about it. (I've thought about it.)

"Mom, I've looked it up. It's not really a hedgehog. It's a kind of hedgehog but it's an insectivore like a hedgehog. It's actually called a tenrac. There are two kinds, the long-tailed kind and this one. Mom, it's so cute. And in winter they hibernate."

They hibernate all winter?

"Yes, Mom. It's hibernating now."

Three hundred dollars for a hibernating animal?

Alden, I just had another thought. How do you know it's alive? Come June, it's time to wake it up, maybe it won't wake up. As a matter of fact, I'd like to get into this deal. Direct line to Madagascar. Hello, I'd like another few dozen of the "hibernating" hedgehogs. Yeah, regular air is fine. The cargo hold will keep the bodies—oh, pardon me, the hedgehogs—cool.

Sunday morning. Long face. Distracted air. Announces he can't even watch the cartoons and has no appetite. Has been raving about the hedgehog almost nonstop for the past thirty-six hours.

"Mom, Dad. I can't get it out of my mind. It's just so cute. And I would do everything for it. I just love it."

Father feigns snoring.

"DA-ad. You're not being nice. You're not listening to me." Tears. Storms out of room.

Alden, don't you see? Your father is just pretending to be a hibernating hedgehog. He's trying to amuse you.

"Can I have it. Please?"

Alden . . .

"Please. Just consider it?"

Alden.

"Please."

Okay, I'm considering it.

"When will you know?"

Bring up old theme: I don't approve of keeping animals in a cage.

"But Mom, look at it this way. It's already in the cage. No one is going to send it back to Madagascar. And we'll be so nice to it."

Oh, Alden.

"Just consider it. Just think about it."

I'm thinking about it.

Monday morning, though I know this is probably one of the dumbest moves I've ever made, right up there with starting those tap dancing lessons, I go to the pet store to see a Madagascar hedgehog. Sure enough: a sign for $299—not $2.99, as would seem reasonable—on the cage. It looks like a miniaturized anteater. It's hibernating but it does seem to be alive. Moves very sleepily. Sort of like Alden and his father in the mornings.

Afternoon. Phone rings at office.

"Mom, you went to see it?" Excitement in the voice.

Who told you?

"Dad did. And I told him that we would give it such a loving home. And he said that these were noble feelings, so we could reopen the issue and talk about it tonight."

I don't want to be home tonight. As a distraction, offer to take child to dumb, violent movie. Hedgehog matter put to rest. Momentarily.

7:30 a.m.

I go to Alden's room to wake him up. For the first time in memory, the bed is made. And made neatly. Alden is feeding the cat, another rare event. He is completely dressed.

8:00 a.m. leave for school.

"I made my bed and got dressed so I could get the hedge-hog."

Naturally, this information stuns me. I thought that Alden's behavior was simply the result of a decision he'd made to lead an exemplary life.

"Do I have any after-school plans?"

Not that I know of.

"Then we could go get the hedgehog today."

H Day plus fifty-six hours. Still hedging.

Dale Burg

Wild Things

LIVING LEGENDS

THEY'RE FREE RANGE CHILDREN.

Yvette Jean Silver

CHAPTER 4

St. Bernadette

O ne of my favorite films of all time is *The Song of Bernadette* with Jennifer Jones. It's a real classic, usually shown around the Easter season. I first saw it when I was a little girl; I loved it then, as well as now. Basically, Bernadette was a peasant girl who was visited by the Blessed Virgin Mary in a grotto in Lourdes, France. There, she performed the apparent miracle of creating a spring of water from a grotto rock. Now, as you know, Lourdes is where people go to get healed from various maladies. I suppose Evian owns it now, but still, people visit. Bernadette, being an innocent, just knew that she saw a beautiful lady who gave her cryptic messages and promised a better life.

I was riveted. *I* loved the Lady too. I was surprised that the blessed Virgin wore so much face makeup and red lipstick. But hey—she was making an appearance.

I felt that if I could just suffer enough, I, too, could become a saint and know the beatific serenity of Jennifer Jones. But being from Commack, Long Island, wasn't enough suffering. I prayed that if I could maybe develop boils and go mad, I, too, could become a saint.

I set out on my destined course.

I enlisted my younger sister Mary.

"Mary, I'm gonna be a saint—and you're gonna help! I need a robe. Saints wear robes."

So we went into my mother's closet where she kept the beautiful orange-gold kimono that my father brought home from Japan when he was there during WWII.

Next, I needed a halo to show my divinity.

We took a wire hanger, bent it into a circle and stuck it on my head.

We didn't have gold paint, so we took Mom's can of Streak and Tip and spray-painted the hanger while it was on my head.

So now I'm a nine-year-old with frosted hair. And a kimono. I looked like Mrs. Luftig down the block.

Next, I had to suffer. All saints suffer—it connotes humility. We were to say the Rosary three times a day on our knees, but not in the plush comfort of our carpeted room. Oh, no. In the gravel. In the driveway.

"Hail Mary, full of Grace, the Lord is with thee . . . . Our father who art in Heaven, hallowed be thy name . . . . Glory Be to the Father and to the Son and to the Holy Ghost . . . ."

Mary left after a minute to go play kickball.

Mary had no will.

"Hail Mary full of Grace the Lord is with thee . . . . Our Father who art in Heaven, hallowed be thy name, thy Kingdom come thy will be done . . . . Glory Be to the Father and to the Son . . . ."

I felt a presence.

I looked up.

The Lady was wearing a kerchief, a green parka and smoking a Lark.

"Julie Lynn, what the *hell* are you doing? Take my Kimono off! And what happened to your hair? Rinse that out and get in the car—we're going to Modell's."

Modell's—where we bought all our groceries, and sometimes our winter coats! I walked around trying to spot the Lady. Maybe I just hadn't suffered enough.

"Ding . . . Ding . . . Ding . . . Shoppers, aisle nine, mops on sale. Aisle nine, mops on sale."

I looked everywhere for the Lady. I searched produce.

Nothing.

"What the hell are you doing, Julie Lynn? Why can't you keep up?"

"She's looking for the Blessed Virgin Mary," my sister Mary said.

They both started laughing. Mary was holding her stomach she was laughing so hard.

Out of nowhere, a beautiful woman with a blond pageboy and a white deli coat spoke from behind a counter.

"I'll watch her. She's not doing any harm."

We were startled. She had appeared out of nowhere.

Finally, my mother said, "All right, stay here—but don't stray from the area." And she gave the Lady a look.

The Lady was *so* nice. She gave me free slices of bologna, she told me what a quarter pound was and she told me the macaroni salad wasn't fresh. She knew everything about everything. She told other people the macaroni salad wasn't fresh.

I wanted to ask her if *Song of Bernadette* was her favorite film, but I didn't.

And then she gave me the largest sprinkle cookie I had ever seen.

Suddenly my relatives were back. Mary wanted a sprinkle cookie too. She started to sputter and whimper and mew. She was *mewing*.

"Sprinkle cookie, I want a sprinkle cookie!!"

We turned to find the Lady. She had vanished—I mean, vanished! I searched the deli counter, the back room, everywhere. Gone.

Mary cried all the way home.

I just ate my sprinkle cookie. Slowly.

Sometimes there's God so quickly.

Julie Halston

Honoring Genius

" ISAAC NEWTON WENT TO A LOT OF
TROUBLE TO DISCOVER GRAVITY THE
LEAST WE CAN DO IS USE IT."

Martha Campbell

Babes in Toyland

The news that Barbie had been caught shoplifting sent shock waves through the world of little girls.

"Why did she do it?" said one. "Barbie had everything. She had jumpsuits, business suits, and an astronaut uniform with a lavender helmet. She had a Corvette, a beach cottage, and Ken."

Quickly I riffled through the newspaper, where there was a sidebar to the main arrest story by a child psychologist: "Barbie's Booboo—What to Tell Your Children." It said that petty theft often masked deeper problems and was a cry for help.

"It was a cry for help," I said. "A manifestation of some need, perhaps unmet in childhood, for affection and a feeling of belonging."

I thought of Barbie, with her impassive feline face and one-and-a-quarter-inch waist. I wasn't buying it. I explained that it might have been a mistake, that Barbie might have slipped those pantyhose into her Sun-n-Fun tote bag intending to pay for them, and then had just forgotten. It occurred to me that Barbie might have been set up by foreign toy manufacturers who wanted to flood the market with cheap imitations, dolls named Ashley or Melissa with lounge-singer wardrobes and boyfriends named Rick.

Like so many parents, I had learned my lesson from the Pee Wee Herman scandal in 1991. Over the years, the people in children's television have usually fallen into one of three categories: father (Captain Kangaroo, Jim Henson), puppet (Big Bird, Lamb Chop), or animated (Daffy Duck, *et al.*). Despite the suggestion by the Reverend Donald Wildmon some years back that Mighty Mouse appeared to be snorting cocaine in a cartoon, these characters rarely get in trouble with the law.

But Pee Wee Herman was none of these. Suddenly that summer there were stories everywhere telling parents how to explain to children that the weird little guy in a bow tie and lipstick who appeared on Saturday-morning TV with a talking chair and a pet pterodactyl had wound up in the clink, charged with exposing himself in a triple-X movie theater.

At seven one morning, looking at the tabloids, I knew that before my first cup of coffee I was going to have to face two small boys and explain the difference between cartoon characters and real life, a difference I was a little fuzzy on myself, having lived through the Reagan years. So I did what anyone would do under the circumstances: I hid the papers.

"If they don't get their questions answered by their parents, where will they?" one child psychologist said to a wire-service reporter.

Simple: They'll get their questions answered on street corners and in the back of the bus to day camp.

After archery, I did explain the difference between characters and the actors who play them, the difference between being arrested and being convicted, the difference between private and public behavior, as well as the rules for keeping your pants on, which I can assure you we've been over a hundred times.

I explained that even grown-ups make mistakes, and that despite published reports, what the actor who played Pee Wee was accused of doing was in no way comparable to mass murder, although in his mug shot he did look like a member of the Manson family. This made it easier for the kids to separate television and reality, although for a long time afterward they kept asking who played Peter Jennings on the evening news.

Pee Wee, of course, was history. This is a very unforgiving country, particularly after you've been famous enough to be made into a doll and sold at Toys 'R' Us.

So when the Barbie story broke big, it occurred to me that I might be witnessing the twilight of a career. I was not sorry. I had never wanted American girls to have a role model whose feet were perpetually frozen in the high-heel position.

Well, as you know, that's not the way it turned out. The next day Barbie's agent started spin control, and before you could say "dream house" there was a Sad-n-Sorry Community Service Barbie, with the navy blue shift and the open letter about how even dolls make mistakes. Little girls read it in the toy aisles and their eyes filled. "It wasn't a cry for help," I said. "It was a public relations stunt." But by that time the little girls I knew had gotten Community Service Barbie from their grandmothers, and they didn't care.

Anna Quindlen

CHAPTER 4

Intimacy

The main thing I know about intimacy is that I am not very good at it. Yes, I'm happily married, I have friends, and I appear extremely accessible. But closeness makes me uneasy. I don't really want to hear about your problems, not when there's something good on television. If I don't remember the names of your family from conversation to conversation, it's because, frankly, I don't care that much. But please don't be offended if my eyes glaze over when we discuss your ongoing problem of finding someone to love, being paid what you are worth, or your inability to accessorize. It's just that I find what goes on in my head so much more fascinating than anything you could tell me.

There, my dirty little secret is out in the open. I suck at intimacy, communication, nurturing, caregiving, all those squashy pink fuzzy "girl" words. But, you ask, isn't intimacy a woman's *job?* Traditional wisdom has it that we females are hard-wired to care more about other people (husbands, children, coworkers) than ourselves. Some think if women ruled the world we'd have no more war and violence, just lots of quilting parties and sharing and eating of chocolate. Look at the racks of self-help books, all designed to bully women into cultivating the intimacy garden. John Gray has built an empire on the ridiculously simplistic concepts in *Men Are From Mars, Women Are From Venus*. There are so many of Gray's books that soon we'll have *Chicken Soup For Men From Mars Made By Women From Venus*. It is our task, we're told, to buy and read these books, figure out the dynamics of relationships, open the discussion. When it comes to the relationship business, women do the heavy lifting.

Many men, on the other hand, are told to resist women's encroachment into their psyches. To men like these, women are the intimacy police, enforcing the draconian law of open communication with the Miranda warning: "We need to talk."

Where does all that leave me? Yes, I'm biologically female, I love makeup, I cry at old movies, but I'm also as self-centered a "me first" alpha dog as anybody this side of Stone Cold Steve Austin. I might as well admit it, I've never worried about lying on my deathbed and thinking, "I spent too much time at the office!"

Male or female, nobody in my family is good at intimacy, either. We all love each other, but we never say it. We don't hug, other than a ritual peck on the cheek at greeting. The main way we communicate, in my family, is through humor. The nastier the joke, the deeper the concern. But please, don't ask us to be direct, and please don't tell us what's going on inside of you. Because we don't want to know.

I found release for my own need for intimacy as a performer of autobiographical solo material. It is perfect: I'm alone, on stage, the center of attention, talking in spectacular detail about my life and my emotions. Members of my audiences are amazed by my honesty. But I'm not honest with them about the essential component of the equation: they're listening to me, but I don't have to listen to *them!* If there's one thing I hate, it's when, after my show, members of my audience tell me their secrets. Shut up and tell your shrink, not me. Yes, it's unfair, but this is my playground and it's my rules.

My husband is a nurturing, caring man. He's conversant with his emotions, and annoyed that other men's emotional vocabulary begins and ends with "Let's pound beers and break stuff." When first we met, I was amazed and happy that I had found someone who loved me so much and was so open. I like to think that's had a good effect on me, overall.

But if I'm not careful, I slip back into old patterns. Bury my head in a magazine rather than talk, become distracted by the television during intense marital discussions, mutter, "I dunno" when asked, "What's the matter?"

But that doesn't mean I'm ready to care about everyone who flies into my radar screen. Intimacy's a dirty job, but somebody's gotta do it. Just not me, okay?

Elisa DeCarlo

CHAPTER 4

Taxes, Freedom and Gefilte Fish:
A Passover Story

Last week, I was startled to realize that Passover and tax time occur around the same time of year. Now, you might not see the incredible coincidence in this. After all, Passover is a celebration of freedom and rebirth, while tax time is a season of frustration, dread, and remorse over shoddy filing habits. And yet, as I began preparing my return, a childhood Passover ritual came to mind and suddenly the relationship between these two sacred events became clear.

It all started with memories of the search for leavened bread or *chametz* (which is pronounced by making a brief gargling sound, then saying "mates." Guess you'll just have to wait for the audio edition). You see, according to tradition, during Passover no foods containing flour are allowed in the home. So what are Jewish families supposed to do with their loaves of rye bread, Entemeyer pastries, and boxes of rigatoni? Well, back in the old country (or so the story goes), the Jews gathered up such food and gave it away. Of course, in 1970s suburban New Jersey where I grew up, this was a little trickier. I can't quite picture my family driving over to the local mall and passing out half-full boxes of Ritz crackers and loaves of Wonder Bread. I think my mom stashed much of it in the freezer.

But back to tradition. The night before Passover begins (all Jewish holidays start in the evening—it's a lunar thing) there's a ceremonial search for any last crusts. (It's kind of like an Easter egg hunt, except it will never take place on the White House lawn.) When I was growing up, my dad would hide pieces of a bagel and we kids would hunt them down with a dustpan and broom.

But whether it was my great-great-etc.-grandmother in Russia cleaning between the floorboards (if she had floorboards) or my mother scrubbing with Top Job, the result was the same: Passover cleansing becomes spring cleaning.

So what does this have to do with taxes? you wonder, enthralled though you are with this small piece of Jewish culture. Well, while Jewish families around the globe were searching for bread, I was searching for business receipts. And while most were in my accordion folder, I was fully aware that a slew of errant receipts lay hidden elsewhere, just waiting to be discovered. And discover them I did, neatly folded in my wallet, stuffed in the recesses of my checkbook, serving as bookmarks in unfinished novels. In my search for tax write-offs, I searched through Visa, phone, and insurance bills; duplicate check stubs, lots of drawers (including silverware and sock drawers), not to mention several jammed manila envelopes still lying around from my last move.

Amid this paper hurricane, I felt a sudden desire to recycle the small edifice of newspapers growing under my desk, to arrange and label my computer diskettes, to even, yes, clear out and reorganize my filing cabinet! Momentarily, I considered that this is just an avoidance technique for ignoring my taxes, but then revelation struck! Just as Passover is the impetus for kitchen cleaning, tax time is the stimulus for office rebirth!

The Passover Seder itself is a long, formal, ritual-packed meal containing as many courses as it does prayers. In fact, "seder" is Hebrew for "order." So, as I began filling out tax forms, I was again stunned by similarities: the word "order" kept leaping into my brain.

Consider this. During the Seder, prayers over the wine, the matzo, and the green vegetable must all be said at very specific times. So too is there a specific time for the asking of the four questions, the reciting of the ten plagues, the eating of the gefilte fish. And, it's exactly the same with taxes! I started filling out the popular 1040, but right around line 12 where it asked for Business Income, I had to beat a hasty retreat to Schedule C. This is the place where I put to use those 783 receipts I've located, classified, and totaled. My efforts paid off until about line 13, where I had to fill in my depreciation figures, so I headed over to Form 4562, then back to 1040 until I got to line 25, which sent me scampering to Schedule SE. The whole thing reminded me of *"Had Gadya,"* a song about a goat that we sing at the end of the Seder: "Then came the fire that burned the stick that beat the dog that bit the cat that ate the goat my father bought for two *zuzim*."

My version? "Then came the Schedule SE that satisfied Line 25 that completed Schedule C that contained line 13 that needed Form 4562 that will bring us back to "doe"! Doe, a deer, a female . . ." Oops. Wrong song.

I could go on drawing comparisons, but it wouldn't be fair. Figuring one's taxes isn't really like wandering in the desert for 40 years; it just seems that way. And various IRS evils (self-employment tax, limits on home/office use) don't really measure up to the magnitude of vermin, locusts, or any of the other ten plagues. (Then again, considering what the military does with our money . . .)

But finally, there comes that moment when the final calculator key is pressed, the final box filled in. Suddenly, the Red Sea parts and a completed tax form emerges! Next Year in Jerusalem! Next year . . . it all goes to an accountant.

Ellen Orleans

Mom Is Always Right

Gail Machlis

Bullwinkle

I learned about sex watching *Love American Style*. Remember that show? Every punch line had something to do with a big brass bed. I was maybe six years old, but I was conditioned to laugh whenever I saw a bed.

Then one day, it occurred to me, "What could a man and a woman do in bed together that could be funny, every single time?" I thought about it, and thought about it, until it finally came to me. Oooo, that must be sex.

So I asked my mom. She liked being scientific. Without confirming or denying my suspicions, she took the chalkboard down from the kitchen wall, the one used for shopping lists. She wiped it clean with a fresh wet Bounty paper towel. She propped it up on the breakfast bar and made a diagram.

She drew this:

I said "Oh, is it a bullwinkle?" And she said, "No, it's your uterus, and those aren't antlers, those are your Fallopian tubes. That's where your eggs come from." Then she walked away.

My eggs? My eggs? What eggs? I walked around in a stupor for three days. I couldn't eat omelets for a month.

But whenever I was sad or confused when I was growing up, my mom would get out the board. She relied heavily on her extensive knowledge, her warm authority and her ability to draw with chalk. For the tough stuff, she'd give me a bowl of Mallomars or Entenmanns so I could wash these concepts down with cookies. (You know Entenmanns, thirty-six varieties of cookies and they all taste the same.) And, piece by piece, cookie by cookie, it all made sense.

I know it seems like the next thing I should write is "And thus began my eating disorder." But, really, it wasn't like that. Halfway through Entenmanns . . . Pimples, Boys, Not Getting Picked. Getting Picked On, Divorce, Republicans . . . made sense. (Well everything but Republicans.) And I'd feel better.

So now I'm grown. I'm an actor, writer, and comedian, living in New York. My mom passed away last year. I miss her

terribly. In her final days she'd come to rely on me to sometimes map things out for her. I don't mind. I would bring the
cookies.

Not long ago I was standing on a subway platform. I
looked up at one of the subway maps, and it made me think of
my mom. The subway map looked like this:

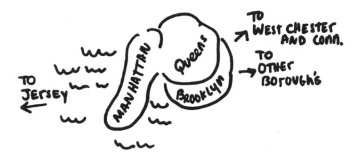

Well what do you know? That's exactly what mom drew
when I asked, "What do men looked like naked?" It seems fit-
ting if you think about it. The shaft is Manhattan, the boroughs
are balls. It was like mom was just checking in, saying "hi." I
had to laugh.

Thanks mom.

Susan B. Murray

Coupon

When I first moved to New York City I was broke.
Mom was worried that I didn't have enough money to eat.
So she sent a small check for food
accompanied by the sweetest note:
*"Your father and I really believe in you,
and we hope things will turn around soon, dear."*
But in that envelope, along with note and the check,
was a coupon for
"$1.00 OFF WASH•AWAY•THE•GRAY"
. . . with a Post-it note attached:
"Thought you might be able to use this!"
A message of loving practicality,
without a trace of sarcasm.
Mom is always trying to be helpful.
But it made me cringe.
Because you know you've been taking money
from your parents too long when
there's a *WASH•AWAY•THE•GRAY* coupon
in with the food check.

Flash Rosenberg

Mommy Dearest

Wendy Wasserstein

A Parental Proposal

The "help wanted" pages are filled with job descriptions that defy comprehension. This probably explains why so many parents can't quite figure out what it is their children do for a living. And it can lead to parental queries like this one from my mother-in-law to my husband Mark:

"Tell me exactly what your job is. Go slowly. I have to write it down."

Mark hadn't switched employers or secured a promotion; he's been doing essentially the same work for ten years. So why the sudden curiosity? Because his parents recently attended a wedding packed with inquisitive relatives. Relatives who appeared to be more interested in Mark's career than they were in the bride and groom.

"Jeff/Harry/Beth is doing great. He/she's a CPA/GYN/PHD," they reportedly said. "So how's Mark? What did you say he does?"

"Something with computers," my mother-in-law answered at first. "And banking, I think."

"That's sounds nice," they responded, "but what exactly does he do?"

"Well I'm not sure, but I know it's very important. So doesn't Sheila make a lovely bride?"

"How could you not know what your own son does for a living?" they prodded, refusing to be distracted by something as inconsequential as the bride's appearance. "What is he—some kind of spy?"

"Everyone thinks you're with the CIA," Mark's mother complained the moment she came home. "They kept me so busy with their questions, I almost missed dessert. The only way I got to the ruggelah was to promise to write and explain precisely what you do. So what do you do?"

For the next hour I listened as Mark tried to describe his job, and his mother grew more and more confused. Do other people have this problem, I wondered. So I decided to ask some friends.

"I just tell my folks I work with numbers," an economet-rics expert told me. "It doesn't really satisfy them, but it's the best I can do."

"All my parents know is I work with lab rats," said a sci-entist friend whose job I can't begin to describe.

"I do junk bond work," replied a securities attorney. "How would you like to explain that to your parents?"

The solution to this job generation gap came to me as I lis-tened to the tenth description of an indescribable job. From now on, at least once a year, we should take our parents to work with us. After all, there's already an annual Take Our Daughters To Work Day and a strong move afoot to include sons. But, shockingly, nobody has protested the exclusion of parents. Such blatant discrimination goes to the very essence of parenting — parents' inalienable right to brag about their kids.

Imagine the educational benefit of parents sitting with their children at the conference table/laboratory/computer room. Witnessing their daughters' demos and their sons' presentations. Watching their offspring interact with bosses, clients, co-workers (both enemies and friends). Gazing as their progeny dodge phone calls, pound keyboards, glare at computer screens, and curse the invention of the fax machine.

There are risks, of course. Dad may cross-examine the boss about health insurance and the company's retirement plan. Mom may whip out a tape measure and compare office footage on her hands and knees. Both will conclude you're smarter than your boss and make sure to let him know it.

And you can be sure that one of them will demand to know when you're getting a promotion.

But despite the risks, we owe it to our parents to expose them to our work environments. Besides, a discreetly whis-pered warning is usually all it takes to get parents to behave. The warning? "If you get me fired, I'll move back home."

Mark is very excited by my idea and plans to try it at his firm next month. What does Mark do? Something with com-puters. And banking, I think.

Madeleine Begun Kane

Happily Ever After

Carol Lay

Make Me A Grandmother

All anyone talked about were biological clocks. The whiners on TV's *Thirtysomething* chewed it over like a piece of tough meat every week.

They talked openly of artificial insemination, surrogate mothers, and frozen sperm. (Giving new meaning to designer genes.)

I didn't care about any of this. I wanted to be a grandmother and I was teetering between senility and death. My interest span was becoming limited, patience was in short supply, and I was beginning to forget all the cute games and nursery rhymes. I was out of touch with new toys and TV shows for children. In a few years, I'd throw the baby up into the air and forget to catch him.

All my friends had grandchildren. Me? I was as out-of-sync with my contemporaries as I had been in the '50s when they were dropping babies like lottery balls and I was burning candles to Our Lady of Impossible Conception.

I didn't want to labor it or put pressure on my kids. I just called them every day and left a message on their answering machines, "Why are you punishing your mother?"

It wasn't like I was asking for major sacrifices. All I wanted was for them to get married, live in borderline poverty, drag around for nine months with a little nausea and eight pounds of stomach to stuff under a steering wheel, and surrender two weeks of pay to present me with a small bundle I could play patty-cake with and buy cute presents for when we traveled.

I fancied myself as Auntie Mame. There was so much to teach them about life and *so little time*. I wanted to show my grandson how to bluff his way out of an inside straight. I wanted to take my granddaughter to the mall and dress up like dance hall girls in a saloon and have our pictures taken together in a little booth.

I wanted people to stop me in a supermarket and say, "Your baby is beautiful!" and I would fan myself with a pound of bacon and protest, "Oh puleeese, I'm the grandmother."

I probably wanted revenge.

It is a fact of life that your children never appreciate all you've gone through until they've been quarantined with three kids with measles . . . during Christmas . . . when the washer isn't working . . . and neither is your husband.

They have to experience the exhilaration of kids spitting out their gum in their hands . . . or washing three small faces with one small handkerchief full of spit . . . or having their offspring take their checkbook to school for Show and Tell to have the proper respect for the profession.

Actually, I did lust for the smooth little bodies with breaths that smelled like milk and little heads with the faint aroma of baby powder. I wanted little fingers to grab onto mine like they needed me and little eyes that followed me around the room when I came into it.

I was beyond the point of just talking about it; I was beginning to have dreams of what life would be like with Grandma Bombeck.

The dream always started out the same. My son would kick open the door and drag in a hobby horse (taking a large chunk of wood out of the wall) and yell, "Mom! You home? We'd have called first, but we were running late and couldn't get the real sitter. We knew you wouldn't mind watching Christopher for a night."

"You didn't have to bring the rocking horse, dear," I smiled. "You already left the corral and we eat off the space ship stored in the kitchen."

"He wants the hobby horse, Mom. Reach in my pocket. See that list? He has a small cold. Give him a spoonful of the red stuff three times a day and a little white pill just before he goes to bed. The vaporizer is in the bag and all the doctors' numbers. He *has to take* the pills on a full stomach and he'll spit the syrup in your face, but keep throwing it in until he swallows it."

As he leaves, his brother is coming up the walk with his two children in tow, Velcro Fingers and Terminator II. Within thirty seconds, they have taken the bathroom door off the hinges, clogged up the toilet with a shoe, put mealworm in the refrigerator for their hamster, which is in the middle of the coffee table, crayoned on the fireplace, flooded the patio, and sold me two chances on a pony.

My teenage granddaughter stops by to tell me she wants to move in with us where she'll have more freedom. Besides, my car isn't run often enough and she'll take care of that. It's okay with her mom if it's all right with me. She introduces me to her boyfriend who wears an earring and has a four-letter word on the bumper of his pickup truck.

The baby falls off the hobby horse. Velcro Fingers wants to know if he can keep the wax apple he has already taken a bite out of and Terminator II has drawn a picture of his hand on the wall behind the sofa.

They move on to the piano where they play ''Chopsticks'' over and over. I threaten to destroy their puppy. The baby wipes its nose on the new slipcovers.

I promise to read them all a story, but they want to sit in the middle of the floor and play poker. They all cheat.

As the teenage grandchild makes a long-distance call that lasts sixty-five minutes before she splits, I try to get up from the floor when one of them comments, "Grandma, you oughta lose those thighs."

I tell everyone it's nap time. They tuck me in and crank up the TV set.

I always awake from these dreams in a cold sweat. What am I thinking! This isn't the way grandparenting is. It's a high-level consultant's job. Grandparents criticize when things aren't being done right, exchange wet bottoms for dry ones and crises for fun times. Grandmothers have three major objectives: keep billfold pictures current, buy whatever their grandchildren are selling, and give kids impractical gifts that parents have forbidden them to have.

The reality is the first child to place a baby in my arms that grabs my finger, stuffs its foot in my mouth, and smiles at me when I say, "This is your grandma"—gets it all.

Erma Bombeck

CHAPTER 4

In the "Family" Way

Once upon a time, when a woman declared her homosexuality, she could be assured of at least one thing: escaping society's (and her parents') expectation of children. Not anymore. During a visit home a few years ago, my father stunned me by following up his obligatory question, "Think you'll move back to New Jersey?" with a new one: "Are you and Lori considering children?"

His inquiry left me speechless, while at the same time informing me that lesbianism was no excuse for not adding to the pool of grandchildren.

Of course, dykes and their kids aren't really news: there have always been lesbians who have children within heterosexual relationships. After coming out, these women simply raised their children on their own or with a lesbian partner.

And, way back when (before AIDS and trendy lesbian parenting), if a dyke wanted a baby, she merely went to a bar, selected a man with pleasing physical attributes and a reasonable I.Q., engaged in a 3-minute heterosexual act, and—hopefully—found herself pregnant the following month. As detached and clinical as this image might be, it *was* an efficient conception method. The hardest part was dealing with the lesbians who considered motherhood a "manipulative patriarchal construct."

Alas, things are not so simple anymore. Now, there are so many choices! We have doctors providing in-office inseminations with medical-student frozen sperm. Then there are elaborate and complicated sperm banks, where one chooses a donor based not only on physical appearance, musical ability. and favorite hobbies, but also on his answers to required essays such as "Why I Am Donating My Sperm" and "Message to My Future Child."

If all this seems too futuristic, you can bypass the anonymous donor approach and go with someone you know. You can select a donor based on whether he will be a supportive co-parent, won't sue for custody rights, or stay out of your life—depending on your personal preference.

There is also the semi-anonymous donor, in which case you find a trusted friend to run interference. Only this person knows both the donor's and the mother's identity. Additionally, there is the double security method: one middle-person knows only who donated the sperm, and a second middle-person knows only who received it. I'm sure there's a purpose to this kind of arrangement, but I've yet to figure out what it is.

My favorite arrangement is when a brother of the partner not carrying the baby donates the sperm. The neat part here is that one partner becomes the mother and the other becomes the aunt, giving her a legal relationship to the child. Also, both women's parents become grandparents, which can be helpful or problematic depending on their opinion of lesbian motherhood.

Now, you may be wondering why I'm writing about babies. Am I pregnant? No. Is Lori pregnant? No. Are we working on it? No. Am I considering it? Only in the most abstract, eight-years-from-now, if-I-have-a-steady-income-and-stable-emotional-state-kind of way.

Babies? Heck, I still haven't managed to get in touch with my lover's inner child, much less any flesh and blood versions we might create. Right now, feline children are the only babies for which I'm willing to take responsibility.

Still, I like human kids. Just last spring, I signed on for a 3-hour child patrol shift—that is, I told my friend Annie I'd watch her daughter while she went to an appointment.

At the time, Stella was nearly two and immensely fascinated with every aspect of the world. Normally, I would have been content to examine pencils, rubber bands, and shoelaces right along with her; that day, however, I was in "accomplish mode."

Feeling restless, I proposed a stroll to the grocery store, a mere five blocks away. Stella agreed. I asked her if she wanted to ride in the stroller. No, she wanted to walk. So off we went. A half block from the house, I realized I hadn't counted on something: toddlers walk very slowly. Unlike walking an overeager dog, I was not dragged ahead, but instead had to take a step, wait, take a step, wait some more. It wasn't so much that Stella had shorter legs than I; it was simply that just as every pencil, rubber band, and shoelace had been marvelous and mysterious, so now was every stick, pebble, and blade of grass. After two interminable blocks, I had a brainstorm: I decided to carry Stella on my shoulders.

I soon realized there was something else I hadn't counted on: since I'd seen her last, Stella had gotten bigger. And heavier. Nonetheless, through an alternating pattern of carrying and toddling, we eventually reached our destination.

The walk home was even slower, since I couldn't carry both the groceries and Stella, who paused to examine cracks in the sidewalk, large rocks, and a variety of bugs.

Fortunately, Annie met us half way, and with a mother's muscles, hoisted Stella up for the remainder of the walk. As we journeyed on home, she asked, "Why didn't you take the stroller?"

"Stella said she didn't need it," I replied.

Annie laughed. "The point of a stroller is not that Stella needs it. It's that you need it. Unless, of course, you want every walk to proceed at ten inches per hour."

Clearly, I have a lot to learn about being a mother. Guess I'll go practice on the cat.

Ellen Orleans

Meet Your Family

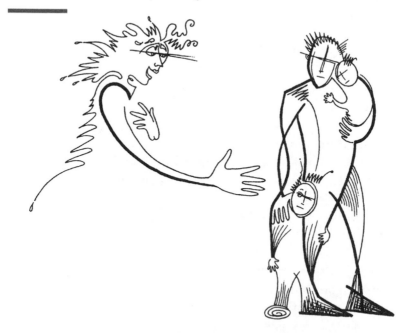

I was spending a miserable Thanksgiving in Penn Station.
Trains weren't departing but people kept arriving until the place
was packed with squalling kids and weary parents . . .
and me, strangely envious:
Where's MY husband? Where're MY kids? How does that happen?
And then I discovered the secret:
*Will Doris Johnson please come and meet her husband and children
at the Information Booth?*
Aah Haa! So I waited there all day listening for:
*Will Flash Rosenberg please come and meet her husband and children
at the Information Booth?*
So I could rush over and introduce myself.
I always knew I had a family here somewhere.
We just haven't been paged to meet yet.

Flash Rosenberg

Exit Laughing

A Lighthearted Tale About a Family Plot

My mother calls to tell me she doesn't want the plots. At first I thing she's saying *plotz*.

"We live in Florida now," she says. "It doesn't make sense to be buried in Westchester."

The family plot. My grandmother loved it. "The view!" Nana would say, visiting it Sundays. "Have you ever in your life seen such a view?"

"Anyway, I've decided," Mom says. "I'm signing them over to you."

"I have to be buried by myself?"

"There are four plots," she says firmly. "You have two. Your cousin Joan has two."

"*Joanie?* I only see her Thanksgiving!"

We laugh. A week later, the deed to Plot 034, Section 24, comes in the mail.

Down in Florida over Christmas, my mother takes me shopping. She's discovered it's easier to drop bombs in the car when she's looking straight ahead. "You got my letter?" she says, tooling down Palmetto.

"If this is about the plots again, Ma, I don't want the plots. I've decided. I'm getting cremated."

"*What!*"

I remind her of the last time Dad took me to see his father's grave in Brooklyn. Jacob Volk's stone was listing. The plot was overgrown. Swastikas were sprayed all over the place, and every piece of glass that protected the photographs on the headstones was smashed. I remind her how somebody had Granny Ethel exhumed and moved next to Great-Aunt Ettie, who was buried with two decks of cards so they could play in the afterlife.

"I'm going to be cremated, Ma. No one's going to vandalize my grave."

"Still," she says "the thought of it . . . "

I tell her about my friend Madeline, who keeps her parents in matching urns in the basement. She waves to them every time she does the wash.

My mother cracks up. What I really want to say is: *You can't die until I can't make you smile.*

"I checked out the local crematorium down here," she says a few weeks later. "I asked the fellow if I could see how it's done. He said no one had ever asked him that before. I had to explain I didn't want to actually watch, I just wanted to make sure the place was nice. You know me—I like people to be comfortable." We howl.

Saul Bellow calls death "the dark side of the mirror that allows it to reflect life." This is no surprise coming from the man who wrote *Mr. Sammler's Planet.* But that's Saul Bellow, and these are my parents. I've always had my parents. I can't imagine not being able to pick up the phone and talk to them. Should I be trying to? Why is my mother thinking about death so much? Just because she's in her 70s? She just got her master's and has a nice practice, so what's with all this death talk?

I check out the books on my night stand. There's Ellen Currie's *Moses Supposes,* which opens with a story about a man who suspects his father is suicidal. There's the insomniac's companion, the *1989 Guinness Book of World Records,* which lists ten categories under Death. (Tonga has the lowest death rate.) There's *A Doctor's Visit,* by Chekhov, whose death in Baden-weiler, Germany, at age 44, is fictionalized in the last book, *Where I'm Calling From,* by Raymond Carver. What's going on? All these books about death? Everything I'm reading now is about death?

I go into the living room and look at the shelf where I keep the books that churn my heart. There's Nathanael West, Dostoyevsky, Virginia Woolf, William Kennedy, Louise Erdrich, Don DeLillo, Joyce Cary, Toni Morrison, and Bruce Chatwin. So I look at my Paris-in-the-30s shelf, and there's Hemingway, Joyce, Fitzgerald, Jean Rhys, Ford Maddox Ford, and Gertrude Stein. So I look at my Southern shelf, and there's O'Connor, Welty, McCullers, all of Walker Percy and Faulkner. Is it possible that death informs everything? Are we born, as Beckett wrote "astride the grave"? I decide to find one book, any book, that doesn't have to do with death. There are two: *Basic Italian* and *The Films of Mae West.*

Studying the slim, chestnut-haired 20-year-old in the photo Mom has always kept on her dresser, I ask if Dad still looks like that to her.

"He seems just like the day I met him," she says.

Sitting on his patio, overlooking a lake, my father says: "This isn't a bad last view, is it? This isn't a bad way to go."

"Where'ya going?" I say.

Knock wood, ward off the evil eye, I can't picture anything happening to them. They both love their work. They both play killer tennis. They've both had run-ins with scary things, but what does that mean? Most people I know would be dead if it wasn't for modern medicine.

"We're not afraid to die," they've told me. "There comes a time when you're ready. We couldn't have imagined that at your age either."

Sometimes I see myself at my father's funeral. Gripping both sides of the lectern, I pause the way Dad would. I develop eye contact. Then I launch into the one about the man who tells his wife he wants his ashes scattered in Bloomingdale's so he can be sure she'll come visit. The idea that something could happen to them won't seem real until it has to. Why should it? What good does it do to taint the present with the inevitable?

The elevator door slams. I get the mail. There's a letter from the university I went to asking to be remembered in my will. There's a bulletin from the Authors Guild; they'd like something too. There are bills, magazines—and what's this from Florida?

RE: Florida Statute 765.05—Living Wills

I, Audrey Volk, willfully and voluntarily make known my desire that my dying not be artificially prolonged under the circumatances set forth below . . . .

I consider the misspelling. Is this document valid? I'm supposed to let my mother go?

I punch her number. "Ma? I got your present today."

Silence.

"I wanted to get you a Hallmark card. Something appropriate like:

> Your living will means lots to me.
> A gift that suits me to a T.
> Or maybe:
> You gave me life?
> I help you die!
> You're as sweet as
> Apple pie!

We laugh. Hurtling toward the apocalypse, we gasp for air. After we hang up, I start flipping through the magazines. Right there, in a column called "What's Hot," is an item about a man in the town my parents moved to. He's bringing mummification back. Prices go from $7,700 for your basic linen wrap to $150,000 for a jeweled sarcophagus. I send it off. Mom will get a kick out of it. I can hear her laughing now. Meanwhile, know anyone interested in prime Westchester real estate, one six-hundredth of an acre, nicely landscaped, riv vu?

Patricia Volk

The Clock Is Ticking.
Can We Tock?

Something's Happening Here

My jeans are shrinking.
The president of the United States is young enough
to be my husband.
I need reading glasses.
My thighs are falling.
Trolls are back.

I never expected to live past thirty, and now I've shot past thirty-something right into the great unknown middlesomething.

How can this be happening to me? And, please, I need to know:

Am I Ever Going to Be As Dorky As My Parents Were When They Were Middle-Aged?

No? You really mean it? Thanks. That's the way I feel about you, too. None of us can be that dorky, ever, because we're part of the hippest generation that ever lived. Time is on our side. We were born during an incredible wrinkle in history, when anything was possible, and it still is. Sure, we're getting a little older. But that doesn't mean we've turned into June and Ward Cleaver. We're still cool. We're still the biggest generation of rebels that this world has ever seen.

We invented sex.
We invented drugs.
We invented rock and roll.
The next step for us boomers?

We Will Invent a New Middle Age

Sure, why not? There are 76 million of us, and if we say HELL, NO, WE WON'T GO, we won't. Who says we have to plunge into the midlife doldrums like our folks did? We're much better prepared. We've got stair-climbing machines, Retin-A, and spandex. Most importantly, we've got ATTITUDE. (Sure, our parents and the Generation X people behind us might prefer to call it "denial," but that's just sour grapes.)

So let's begin deconstructing this traditional middle-age myth right now. If you're special, like we are, you never have to be really middle-aged, driving big cars and buying the Mrs. a mink and cooking tuna casseroles and actually liking Lawrence Welk and talking about the weather and falling asleep in a Barca-Lounger with your mouth open and wearing ugly eyeglasses on a string around your neck.

Of course, we do drive minivans and buy our beloveds shearling coats and cook pasta and listen to Harry Connick Jr. and occasionally watch the Weather Channel. But hardly any of us fall asleep in front of Letterman since he moved up an hour. And some of us do wear glasses around our necks, but they're designer glasses with neon strings or handwoven attachments made by natives, and part of the money goes to save the rain forest.

So, it's clear: we're different. These years ahead of us are going to be a truly unique experience, much cooler than anything our parents ever went through. This is not your father's Oldsmobile. This is a vibrant, fulfilling, hip time of life for us. Call it New Middle Age. Or, if you cringe at the mention of middle and age together in one sentence, call this time ahead of us the Relaxed-Fit Years. Whatever you dub them, these are the crowning years of our mature young adulthood. The attitude? I'm stuck in the middle with you, and I plan to have a hell of a lot of fun while I'm here.

Checklist: Signs That You Might Be Halfway Up That Stairway to Heaven

- ✔ You've started musing about the shallow value system of people in their twenties.
- ✔ You tune in more often to the local news than to MTV.

✔ You wince when the scanner hits a rap station.

✔ You find yourself telling your babysitter about your first boyfriend/girlfriend.

✔ Many of the doctors in hospitals look like Doogie Howser to you.

✔ You suddenly desperately need your first reading glasses, crown, arthroscopic surgery, extramarital affair, Armani suit, elastic waistband, fiber-laden cereal, sports car, baby, inheritance, root canal, dye job, hotel getaway . . .

✔ You truly enjoy the Disney Channel specials featuring ancient rock stars of the past who look "hey!—pretty good."

✔ There are house repairs you've been meaning to do for over a decade.

✔ You know the difference between Sinead O'Connor and Sandra Day O'Connor.

✔ All of the professional athletes you admire are at least ten years younger than you.

✔ You no longer care as much if you don't go out on Sunday night.

✔ You yearn more wistfully for former repairmen than for certain ex-lovers.

✔ You've begun to go toward the lite-lite beer, lite rock, lite butter, lite literature . . .

✔ You are too old for Doc Martens, but too young for Doc Kevorkian.

Cathy Crimmins

More Brain Lint

Brain Lint by Amy Krouse Rosenthal

I was checking in at the gate at the airport and the woman asked, "Have your bags been with you at all times? Has anyone asked you to take a package for them?"

I just love the conspiracy it implies! The international drama! My inadvertent foray into a world of traveling incognito! What kind of wig would I wear?... But then she hands me the boarding pass and I go buy some gum.

amy@suba.com

Brain Lint by Amy Krouse Rosenthal

Confession:

I never write down the order # when ordering from a catalog even though I pretend to do so when the sales person says "Do you have a pen handy? I'm going to give you your order # now."

Sponging kitchen counter

Yeah... OK. 642-311-9. Got it.

amy@suba.com

Brain Lint by Amy Krouse Rosenthal

I saw this sign in a public restroom:

> PLEASE DO NOT FLUSH EXCESSIVE AMOUNTS OF TOILET PAPER, OR SHOES, DOWN THE TOILET.
> Thank you —

I so want to meet the person who flushed a shoe down the toilet and made a sign like this necessary.

This is so exciting! Tell me everything!

OK. I had this shoe and...

amy@suba.com

Brain Lint by Amy K.R.

When a waiter says "Good choice!" after I order, I feel good, proud even. But when he says it to someone else and not me, I feel like I've failed some sort of restaurant pop quiz.

The risotto? Excellent choice!

I knew I shoulda ordered that...

amy@suba.com

Amy Krouse Rosenthal

CHAPTER 5

Somewhere a Time for Us

Roz Chast

Daylight Savings

"I HATE CHANGING TO DAY LIGHT SAVINGS TIME."

Theresa McCracken

Can We Tock?

I'm sick of hearing about my biological clock. I can't pick up a magazine or eavesdrop on a luncheon conversation without detecting its inexorable tick. No one, however, is telling me what I really want to know about this internal, infernal, time-keeper. Does it come with a snooze alarm? What if it turns out to be a biological clock-radio: Is there any chance that my ovaries could suddenly begin blaring out traffic reports or "Born in the USA" while I'm at an important business meeting or arguing with my landlord?

Sure, I understand that basically we're all on Genetic Standard Time: the body's DNA programs precisely how long we remain fertile and indeed, barring accident, sets the hour of our bucket kicking. Science has recently found the masterclock of our daily rhythms, a section of the hypothalamus called the suprachiasmatic nucleus, not much bigger than a pinhead. It seems to govern the hundreds of bodily functions that ebb and flow in a regular pattern throughout the twenty-four-hour cycle of our waking and sleeping. These include body temperature (it peaks at 4 P.M.), levels of various hormones (high tide for testosterone is A.M.), and tolerance of pain (greatest in the afternoon).

But how come we never hear anything about the other interior chronometers that are just a important as the Big Ben of babymaking and the Rolex of rhythms? What about, for example:

The Botanical Clock: Perhaps regulated by the pituitary, the Botanical Clock fixes the precise point in a relationship at which a man stops sending flowers. It is closely related to the **Astrophysical Clock,** which controls the length of time a loving couple will have stars in their eyes.

The Tautological Clock influences redundancy, repetition, and redundancy. It is also responsible for making an otherwise pleasant friend or mate say things like, "Well, listen, you'll either get the job or you won't."

The Ontological Clock: By maintaining a delicate balance of brain chemicals, this clock determines how long you remember the definitions of really rather simple words that won't stick in your head, like *nonplussed* and *ontology* (the one that does *not* recapitulate Phil Donahue; that is onto*geny*. Ontology is, of course, the branch of philosophy dealing with being, something I can tell you with great confidence, having just looked it up for the third time this year.) Nutritional deficiencies can cause some genetically vulnerable individuals to forget the difference between *oligarchy* and *plutocracy.*

Not all body clocks are governed internally. We all own a **Cultural Clock,** which has to do not with how soon we get fidgety at the ballet, but with how our culture views time. Never mind the globally acknowledged oscillations of the atomic clock, the transit of the sun, or even the vaunted suprachiasmatic nucleus: we pick up the tick tocked by our parents and grandparents. Thus, while in remote parts of Brazil it is acceptable to appear at a dinner party several decades late and feign surprise that the host and hostess have passed away, in some Swiss cantons it is considered rude for a guest to enter a room in such a way that his hat arrives before his shoes.

Intimately related to the Cultural Clock is the one that controls differences in the way the sexes perceive time. I call it the **Genderological Clock,** and who are you to stop me?

I must thank the late Lorne Greene for leading me to the discovery of this clock and, ultimately, to the Alpo theory of rapprochement between the sexes. One night I was watching his classic dog food commercial, idly wondering whether those mutts get their residual checks figured in dog-years or people-years, when all of a sudden I thought, "Hey! I wonder if there are man-years and woman-years!" That could explain a lot. For example: A certain man tells a certain woman he will call "in a couple of days." Two weeks pass. He dials her number—and is shocked by her cold response. She's wrong to think he's been toying with her. He said two days—*and for him, that's all it's been!* Applying a formula very similar to the one Lorne Greene uses to figure out the age of a golden retriever, you can convert man-time into woman-time. (Roughly seven woman-days = one man-day, when you're dealing with relationships. Different for-mulae apply to work situations and personal growth issues.)

Looking back, I can see unheeded hints of these divergent perceptions of time in my own true life. When I was sixteen, for instance, my boyfriend and I stayed late at a riotous New Year's Eve party in a town about an hour from home. Rather than risk the roads that night, we stayed, quite chastely, with friends. I called my parents to tell them where I was and that I'd be back in the morning.

When we pulled up at 11 A.M the next day, my father was raking so furiously in one spot that the lawn was bald. "Where the hell have you been?" he barked. "I said I'd be home in the morning," I whimpered. My father's reply, now famous in our family: "Eleven o'clock isn't morning where I come from!" Since I know for a fact that my father comes from Boston, I should have realized right then that man-time and woman-time are out of sync.

Maybe it's because so many little boys first learn about time from games like football, in which an announcement that there are ten minutes left in the final quarter means you have the leisure to catch several trout, finally finish *Sister Carrie*, jog a mile, shower, and reestablish yourself on the couch just as the two-minute warning sounds. Whatever the reason, it is a sci-entific fact that just because a man and a woman share a Zip code, that doesn't necessarily mean they live in the same time zone.

Judith Stone

Seasonal Disorder

Lynn Johnston

Egg Cups

Why do they make bathing suits with those stupid egg cups on them anyway? Is there a woman on earth they're designed to fit?

I consider myself to be average, okay? Average, average, average. By the time one's age-o-meter has clicked past forty, "average" is considered to be a plus. There are millions of us out there—and whenever we're not juggling careers, chaos, and the challenges of raising teenage children, what are we doing? We are trying to track down a garment manufacturer who sews for the body that is ***@?!!average**!!!

What's with the mastiff shoulders, gorilla-length arms, six-inch waists, and skirts designed to gird the loins of an undernourished twelve-year-old boy?!! And . . . what's with the bathing suits?

Summer fashions appear at the exact time we are trying to find clothing for spring. March is when the bathing suits arrive. March is when the average female begins the fruitless foray into the land of Lycra, hoping to find a bathing tog that will (A) cover, (B) flatter, and (C) allow for some participation in water sports.

Hoping for two out of three, we search once more for a suit that's suitable. Hah! This is a project for the Discovery Channel!! Two years ago, I accidentally found a three-out-of three!! Shocked and grateful, I ordered four of them (all the same) so I am set now for multiple seasons to come!! Alas . . . this doesn't mean that I don't still (on a "thin day") try on those high-thigh, egg-cupped disasters with the hope that maybe I can look like the siliconed sylph in the window.

Why do we do it? Every year, we allow our self-esteem to be reduced to the size of bacteria. Every year we struggle in Port-a-John-sized cubicles, trying to get into and out of a garment that's guaranteed to disgust. And, every year we do this (heaven forbid) at the risk of exposure!

It's that old nightmare, isn't it? The average person's worst fear (aside from public speaking) is to be seen naked, or nearly naked, by someone other than one's spouse!

The fear of being seen in one of these egg-cupped creations was the catalyst for this Sunday strip. As a form of therapy, I guess, I had a hapless heroine streak through a shopping mall in "the bathing suit from hell."

After all, isn't it nice to see the things we fear most . . . happening to someone else?

Lynn Johnston

The Swimming Suit

There are moments in every woman's life
When she faces the humiliating fact
That time is no longer on her side,
As she performs the simple, yearly,
Humiliating, death-defying act of . . .

Buying a swimming suit.
I can't believe I'm here
Buying a swimming suit.
I do this every year.
Putting myself through
Eight kinds of hell
Searching through spandex
And nylon fortrel for a

Flattering swimming suit . . .
Oxymoron . . .
A flattering swimming suit.
I feel like a moron.
Take a deep breath . . .
A Prozac . . . a pause . . .
And try to remember
The swimming suit laws.

Rule number one . . .
No stripes horizontal
Unless you weigh thirty-five pounds.
Rule number two . . .
Accentuate the good parts.
Make them look up . . .
Never look down.

Buying a swimming suit.
There are questions when
Buying a swimming suit.

Here's one suggestion.
When thinking of ways
To improve the bra size,
Remember that foam
Is the last thing
That dries.

Rule number three . . .
Keep them distracted
With ruffles and sequins and belts.
Rule number four . . .
Don't squeeze the flab.
If you pull it in here
It comes out somewhere else.

And the lady who helps you is seventy-five
With glasses and rolled-down hose.
She says, "Dahling, this one is so good for the thighs."
I look better naked than I do in those.

Still . . . I'm buying a swimming suit.
How I hate this!
I'm buying a swimming suit.
I can't . . . wait!
Here's a nice little speedo.
Maybe I'll take this one after all.
Or maybe . . .
I'll just stay inside . . . till fall!

Could I see something in a wet suit, please?

Amanda McBroom

Healthy Appetites

Anne Gibbons

Dieter's Prayer

Lord, won't you help me?
It's that time of year.
Winter has come and gone.
Springtime is here.
In this season of flesh,
Won't you show that you care?
Lord, won't you heed
This dieter's prayer?

Teach me tonight
To love cottage cheese,
Grapefruit, and celery,
Lord, if you please.
Make me believe
That tofu's a food,
And not something you made up
When you were in a bad mood.

Lord, won't you help me?
Show that you care.
Lord, won't you heed
This dieter's prayer?

Make me believe
That ice cream's just awful.
That the devil is hiding
Inside every waffle.
That mayonnaise is nothing
But a communist plot.
That broccoli is good for you
And chocolate is not.

Keep me away
From the refrigerator door

When life is a trial
And love is a bore.
Save me from nachos,
And tacos, and chips.
For what goes in my mouth
Always lands on my hips.

Oh, pizza, oh pasta,
Oh popcorn, oh pork!
Get thee behind me,
Oh knife and oh fork.
And chicken fried steak
From the deepest of south . . .
Oh, lord, if you love me,
Won't you please shut my mouth?

Oh, lord, do you hear me?
Honk if you're there.
Lord, won't you heed . . .
You know my need . . .
Oh, lord, won't you heed
This dieter's prayer?

Amanda McBroom

A Perfect Model Keeps Her Full Mouth Shut

I normally don't buy fashion magazines, pretty much for the same reason I don't subscribe to *Nuclear Fission Monthly*. Unless I'm going to suddenly grow about seven inches and lose about four pounds per inch, or if it's discovered that plutonium can safely rid your shower of nasty soap scum, why should I read these publications?

Last week, however, as I was trying to calculate the unit price of my pork-rind value pack while waiting in the grocery store checkout line, an issue of *Vogue* caught my eye. One of the headlines on the cover read: "Nobody's Perfect: Five Supermodels Face Up To Their Flaws."

Feeling fat, ugly, unintelligent, unsophisticated, inarticulate, short, nearsighted, old, and out of shape (and this is my post-PMS state of mind), I thought this article might lift my spirits. Maybe Christy Turlington, Naomi Campbell, Linda Evangelista, Cindy Crawford, and Nadja Auermann would admit that they, too, are convinced that a hideous, beer-bellied, troll-like creature resides in their bathroom mirror.

Okay. Maybe that's just my own problem. But at least they might own up to a pimple, a split end, or the hint of a wrinkle.

So I read the article. And while I'm still thoroughly disgusted with myself, I've let go of my hope-your-miniskirt-splits hostility toward Christy, Linda, Cindy, and Nadja. These four supermodels had the good sense not only to point out their flaws, but to wisely emphasize that they exercise like maniacs and diet constantly.

Naomi Campbell, on the other hand, apparently has an intense desire to be hated by every woman in America. As the article's author diplomatically points out, "There's virtually nothing about Campbell that she isn't, shall we say, extremely fond of."

That's an understatement. I know it's healthy to have a good self-image, but this woman is head-over-stiletto-heels in L-O-V-E with herself.

For starters, she just *loves* her backside: "My butt is high. I also like the point where my legs meet my butt. In certain pictures you can see it. It's quite defined."

Is anyone thinking about now that Naomi really needs a hobby?

Butt there's more.

"I can wear almost anything, and it can look good. People always say, "We'll give you the worst outfit, Naomi, because we know you can make it look good."

Well, Naomi, that's your take. It's equally possible, though, that while you're strutting down the runway in a gunny sack and combat boots, members of the Paris practical joke society are having a major hoot.

At this point in the interview, I'm guessing the reporter is thinking that four supermodels would have been plenty. But Naomi's on a roll: "I have a little button nose. My lips are quite full, but they're not huge . . . like my shoulders . . . My face is very animated. My smile is very genuine. My waist is 22. My hips are 33 or 34 . . . my body's in proportion."

Okay. If Naomi would have stopped there, I could have cut her some slack. After all, several studies have shown that repeated exposure to flash bulbs, pancake makeup, and push-up bras can result in a condition known as BIMBOS (Boring Inane Mindless Body Obsession Syndrome). In fact, from Milan to Manhattan, BIMBOS benefit concerts are being held in conjunction with the new fall fashion season.

But Naomi crossed the line. Without a hint of apology, she matter-of-factly noted that she neither exercises nor diets.

It's time someone has a little chat with her.

Maybe she's not aware that if she ever wants to have a woman friend, this is the type of information you take to your grave. Since only 0.005% of the female population stands over 5 feet 9 inches and weighs under 97 pounds, I think I speak for many women when I request that, in the future, Ms. Campbell, do us a big favor.

Wearing one of your genuine smiles and using your quite full, but not huge, lips . . . lie.

Carrie St. Michel

Less Than Perky

Yvette Jean Silver 2001

Yvette Jean Silver

(It Must Be) Fun
To Be Perfect

Where'd you get those cheekbones honey?
How'd you grow that hair?
People
Who don't even know you stop and stare.
God must have had a happy day when he painted on
    your face.
Setting you as the example for the human race.

      It must be fun to be perfect.
            Fun to be perfect.
            Fun
                To be
                    Perfect.

Where'd you get those eyebrows honey,
You don't have to pluck?
Was it
In your gene pool,
Or just luck?
You probably gaze into your mirror
Just imagining the potential attributes of your future
    offspring.

      It must be fun to be perfect,
            Fun to be perfect.
            Fun to be perfect.
            Fun to be
            Perfect.

    I believe that living would be easy.
    If only I could be perfect, too.
    I'd sail right through my life so free and breezy,
    Reacting like
    Perfect people do. . . .

Where'd you got that body baby
Always tan and tight?
You don't even exercise,
Let alone eat right.
Down here, on the planet Earth I'm working up a sweat.
I don't know, but something tells me
That I'm not there yet.

> It must be fun to be perfect,
>   Fun to be perfect.
>   Fun to be perfect.
>   To
>   Be
>   Perfect.

Julie Gold

Personal Olympics

Jennifer Berman

The Vegetable Lament

The Lament was written when my husband was a vegetarian and I was not. One night he made a reckless reference to my "consumption of dead flesh."

Well! One can't let these things go, and I didn't.

Do radishes scream when they're pulled from the
    ground?
If you listen closely, can you hear the sound
Of vegetables wailing while their roots are flailing?
Do cabbages cringe when you reach for a leaf?
Does all the wheat tremble when you cut a sheaf?
The eyes of potatoes weep for lost tomatoes . . .

    Does chopping up celery
    Remind you of Ellery
    Queen?
    Might stalking asparagus
    Be truly analogous
    To a murder scene?

Do cucumbers care when they're plucked from the
    vine?
Do grapes leave the stem quite content to be wine?
Might all garden salads deserve tragic ballads?

    Each vegetarian
    Is an agrarian
    Beast.
    Heartlessly harvesting,
    Ripping up everything
    For a selfish feast.

So—darling—remember, your favorite part
Of eating an artichoke is cutting out its heart . . .
And a meal without peeling an onion is hardly
    complete.
Thanks, but no thanks, you ghoul—
I'd rather eat meat.

Martha Trachtenberg

Goldilocks

Liebe Lamstein

Sometimes More Is More

Oh, I appreciate the plain black dress,
The uncluttered room.
The bare wood floor.
The Rothko painting, yes,
But sometimes lately, I'll confess,
It seems to me that less is less
And more is simply more.

Would a palace be a palace if it were small?
Would the Great Wall still be great, or just another wall?
How about the Taj Mahal—would it still impress?
I think not.
Sometimes less is less.

Would a quarter pounder be as filling as a half?
Would a little titter be as thrilling as a laugh?
Wouldn't you trade one perfect rose for twenty-four?
I'd say yes.
Sometimes less is less.
Sometimes more is more.

Oh, I adore a simple meal—
Half a sandwich—cafe au lait
But once in a while I might
Have a larger appetite
Then, baby, gimme the grand buffet!
A small Niagara Falls would simply be a drip.
Shrink the great Titanic, you've got one more sinking
    ship.
A miniature Grand Canyon would be just a crack
Face the facts!
Sometimes more is more—
Sometimes max is max.

And if you want a chic affair
Keep it sweet and simple and mature
But why try to be smart
Cause in matters of the heart
Less—is not—*l'amour.*

Oh, why does Schwarzenegger pump it up before a shot?
Why do we bring the trumpets in when the music's
    getting hot?
Why would a gal add silicone to what she's got?
What for?
Honey, can't you guess?
Sometimes less is less.
Sometimes more is more.

Michele Brourman

Paradise Lost

Gail Machlis

Mono

The following is an excerpt from the book by mononucleosis survivor Mary Jo Pehl entitled *Mono! My Courageous Battle With The Kissing Disease*. Pehl is the bestselling author of *What Do You Think This Is? A Guide To Making People Touch Bumps on Your Person And Tell You What They Think It Might Be*.

Chapter 592: I Am Diagnosed

After weeks of feeling achy and lethargic, I realize the random polling of my friends and acquaintances to determine what's wrong with me is proving frustrating and worrisome. Friends, neighbors and complete strangers with whom I've chosen to discuss my condition proffer conflicting diagnoses, like tuberculosis, cholera, pregnancy, diphtheria, leprosy, smallpox, bigpox and impotence. Is this what HMOs have wrought? I could no longer trust the health-care services my lay-friends were offering? After a long night, restless and steeped in my illness I decided to go to the doctor.

After pawing at my glands and mulling over the symptoms, Dr. Kathy thought perhaps I had a viral infection but she couldn't be certain until the blood tests came back. Then she leaned back in her chair, her hands folded.

"Mary Jo," she said, "I think you should be prepared for the worst . . . " She hesitated. "What I'm saying is—it's not uncommon for people in situations such as yours to have to . . . "

My stomach lurched. What was she trying to tell me? She continued, "To have to modify their lifestyles, sometimes even make drastic alterations in the way they live . . . "

My eyes brimmed with tears. "You don't mean . . . " I couldn't continue.

"Yes," she said. "I think it might be best if you lived in a plastic bubble." She handed me some pamphlets about bubbles and I took them with a trembling hand. In a torrent of tears, I ran out of her office as fast as I could, barely managing to grab the current *People* magazine from the waiting room and stuff it in my purse.

I went back to the telemarketing office and tried to act normal. Please, I prayed, don't let any of my coworkers mention plastic bubbles. I feared I'd betray my emotions and I only had so much fake nonchalance in me. I tentatively paged through the brochures the doctor had given me. I was feeling so sickly, maybe living in a bubble was my only option.

I began to brighten as I considered all the possibilities of a plastic bubble. I could furnish it with items from Sears or Ikea! I could put up miniblinds—I do so love miniblinds! I could have a puppy in my bubble! I was feeling better already. After all, I would still be *me*—I would just be in a plastic bubble! I picked up the phone and began calling every plastic bubble dealership in the metro area.

I was on pins and needles and other cliches as I awaited the results of my blood tests. At last the call came from Dr. Kathy.

"I'm afraid I've got some bad news," she said. I pressed the phone close to my ear so hard it hurt. Then I shifted it a bit so it wouldn't hurt so much.

"You have . . . mononucleosis," Dr. Kathy said gravely.

I was certain I had heard wrong. Me?! *Mononucleosis?!* How could my friends have missed this?

Dr. Kathy continued, "It's sometimes called the 'kissing disease.'"

I slumped over my desk—oh, how I wanted to scream and curse the fates but I had already gotten a written warning from my boss Debbie about personal calls. "Am I . . . ?"

"Contagious? Not through casual contact. Make sure you don't share eating or drinking utensils. And of course avoid kissing."

How much worse could it get? I would have to cease my rampant kissing sprees. My days of accosting perfect strangers and making out with them for extended periods were over.

Dr. Kathy took a deep breath. "Mary Jo, it might be a good idea to get your affairs in order."

"You mean . . . ?" Now I could not stop the tears and I crumpled to the floor, whereby I spotted an errant Whoppers Malted Milk Ball that had gotten away from me a few months earlier. I cradled it and wondered if this would be my last Whoppers as I popped it into my mouth.

"There's no treatment except plenty of rest—let it run its course. Listen to your body," Dr. Kathy urged.

But my body and I hadn't been on speaking terms for years. We had had a falling out when it insisted on continuing my menses, even after I had demanded it stop. After a very ugly confrontation, my body stalked out of the room, and though I ran into it here and there, we barely exchanged civilities.

"Oh, and stay off your spleen," Dr. Kathy admonished. I hung up and I stared at the phone. I had never felt so frightened and alone. Just then, Sherri from the next cubicle poked her head over and said, "A huge package from Plastic-Place just came for you."

Chapter 593: I Go Whining and Bitching into that Good Night and Begin the Painful Process of Suing Friends and Acquaintances for their Misdiagnoses.

Mary Jo Pehl

CHAPTER 5

Spiro Agnew and I

Monday. My birthday is coming up and not having had a midlife crisis at 40, I'm planning to have one now. I will be over 40 now! I can't focus. I have no energy. I think about Spiro Agnew more than other people do. Whatever happened to Spiro Agnew? Has he opened a restaurant, the way retired baseball players do? Spiro Agnew's Ribs. Or a used-car dealership? I can see his face so clearly, his hair combed straight back. It is the face of my youth.

Tuesday. Did you know that an anagram of Spiro Agnew is "Grow a penis"? Did you know the lead singer of the Red Hot Chili Peppers was convicted of sexual battery because he waved his penis at a fan after a concert? I heard this on MTV. I think it would be dangerous to wave it at a fan. I was always told to keep my fingers away from fans. And I always have.

Wednesday. How old was Spiro Agnew when he fell from power? Not much older than I am now. In the 60s, even the old people were young. But now! My birthday is *next week:* I don't have much time to determine exactly what form my midlife crisis will take. This is urgent. I could join a cult. But which one? And it seems a little strenuous for someone my age. Daydreaming about Spiro Agnew—I remember his tie clips best of all—I turn on the TV. *Mystery Science Theater 3000,* my favorite. That's it! I could become a *Mystery Science Theater 3000* groupie! Groupies are so youthful. You can do it from home in your spare time. No investment necessary. No special equipment. And I already watch the show twice a day, every weekday. A man and two robots sit in front of a big screen and we watch the backs of their heads as they watch bad movies and make wisecracks. Once, some devils in red leotards were writhing around plotting the demise of Santa Claus and one of the robots said: "Oh! Hell got an NEA grant."

Thursday A.M. Maraschino is an anagram for Harmonicas, Roast Mules becomes Somersault. Someone told me those, I didn't figure them out myself, I hate anagrams. *Mystery Science Theater 3000* is also on for an hour at 8. What am I doing? Anagrams? Four hours of bad movies a day? I must take up a more constructive hobby, a life-affirming hobby for my midlife crisis. Got a Smith & Hawken catalogue today, as I do every day. I will order English gloves and French watering cans and Japanese pruners. I will make things grow.

Thursday P.M. Yorba Linda, C-Span 2. Richard Nixon is standing in front of the Presidential Library and Birthplace. It's the 25th anniversary of his inauguration. My heart pounds with excitement, rejuvenated by the sound of his voice. He poses in front of a fountain with Gerald and Betty Ford. Does former President Ford really count as a vice president? Where is Agnew? Oh, it's all wrong. Nixon doesn't even look like his face masks anymore.

Friday. *US* magazine says the "deck is stacked against today's younger actors." Sounds promising. Perhaps I can take up acting. Although I'm sure I read somewhere else that actresses over 40 can't get any parts. So back to gardening. I already have several oddly shaped aloe plants the kids brought home from school as cuttings. I never water them. Maybe that simulates the harsh life of the desert. I wonder if Spiro Agnew gardens? If he doesn't already, he should. Gardening is what every celebrity does when he sinks into obscurity. Or do they raise horses? It seems so unfair that Agnew gets so little exposure, and he's not even a younger actor.

Saturday. I don't have to have a midlife crisis after all! I have discovered true immortality. I read in *Audubon* that ecologists in northern England are planning a "forest of the dead." People will be buried beneath trees to help enrich the soil, instead of wasting all those nutrients in crematories or cemeteries. You can choose your tree and the species of wildflowers you want to have planted above you. Pushing up the daisies, the Indian paint brushes; though blue bells and bunchberries might be more appropriate, more discreet. I've never had much luck with wildflowers, myself. I once bought one of those cans of seeds from the Smith & Hawken catalogue and sprinkled it on my mother's lawn near the septic tank, which had just been dug up, but the seeds washed away with the first rain or were eaten by birds, and she planted grass again instead. I wonder if the gardeners in Echoing Green, as the corpse forest will be called, will order their seeds from Smith & Hawken.

Sunday.   A birthday present has arrived! A pot of narcissus from Smith & Hawken, the first of a series of plants to come. Now I don't have to garden at all, just open cardboard boxes once a month. Well, it's 10 A.M. *Mystery Science Theater 3000* is on. But so is *The McLaughlin Report.* What will I do? Which will I choose? Life is so full, so ripe with possibility. And I am only in the middle of it! The scent of narcissus drifts through the room. I hate the smell of narcissus. But the name is so historically and psychologically suggestive, so rich with meaning. And they're awfully pretty in the windowsill by the twisted aloes. I am content. I have made up my mind. Someday, as I lie decomposing in Echoing Green, it is this species I will feed. For now, I could just sit here and gaze at narcissus forever.

Cathleen Schine

Totally Bitchin' Babes

Purgatory Café

Last Saturday night, I up and died
Don't ask me what happened, baby—Don't ask why
All I know is I awakened on the other side
It was some kind of weird, baby—some kind of ride.
I was greeted by a guy in an angel suit.
He said, Tell me your story girl—Now, what did you do?
So I told him 'bout the good and the bad times too
He said, Step aside, Hon—I gotta think about you.

A little while later, he calls my name,
He says, I got a few things I kinda got to explain.
See, I can't send you straight to Heaven on account of
  what you did,
But you can't go to Hell—Shoot, you're just a kid!
See, we got a little place kind of in-between
Where you'll spend a little time till your slate is clean,
So hey, here's wishing you a pleasant stay
And may I recommend—The Purgatory Café!

CHORUS: Purgatory Café
         Where the neon buzz and the jukebox play
         It's a heck of a place to pass your time away.
         Purgatory Café . . .

Now be sure that you ask for the special of the day
When you're sitting at the counter, Purgatory Café.
They got deviled ham sandwiches, angel food cake
And hot black coffee—But make no mistake
This might take a little while—You might have a little
  wait,
But the company is friendly and the food is great.
So leave your hat at the door—your sins at the gate
Sit anywhere you like—Purgatory Café

CHORUS: Purgatory Café . . .

Week after week, and wouldn't you know
The longer I stay, the more I don't want to go.
You see, Heaven is sounding just a little low-key
And that New Age music don't do nothing for me.
So I go to the guy in the angel suit,
I say, I ain't looking for trouble, man—I don't mean to be
    rude
But don't send me off to Heaven, 'cause I really want to
    stay
At the Purgatory Café.

Now, Angel Man, he looks at me a little annoyed
He says, You only get to stay if you are gainfully
    employed
We need a short order cook on the graveyard shift
You do all your own dishes, and you get no tips.
So here I am, baby—day after day
Flipping deviled ham sandwiches, angel food cake
Happy as a clam cause I get to stay at the Café.

CHORUS: Purgatory Café . . .

They tell you all about Heaven, tell you all about hell
Sometimes you know right where you're headed
Sometimes you can't tell
They tell you fire and brimstone, halos and lace
A little short on the details about that in-between place.
So listen to my story like you know that you should
And don't be too bad, but don't be too good
'Cause it's a heck of a place to visit—a cool place to stay
Eternity is really happening—Purgatory Café

Lisa McCormick

CHAPTER 6

The Montana Nine: A True Story

I don't remember exactly what year it was that this happened, but I do know it was in the wintertime. I had been on the road in the Pacific Northwest—Eugene, Oregon, Corvallis, Portland, Seattle, Vancouver, Spokane, Edmonton—and on this particular day I flew into Winnipeg. I took a taxi to the hotel—I don't remember the hotel's name, but it was small, maybe four stories tall, near the business district. My room was on the fourth floor. It's funny how some details stay with you while others don't.

As I unlocked my door to enter I noticed that directly across the hall from me was a room where it looked like there was a party going on—except it was not your typical "hotel party" type group. It was all women, all older women, in fact, all older women in flowered dresses with whitish-bluish hair. I waved a friendly "hello" and they waved back. I carried my guitar and suitcases into my room and started unpacking, when I heard a light tap on my door.

I opened it to find two of the old ladies standing there, looking a bit on the anxious side. "Excuse me," one of them said, "but we stayed in this room last night and now we can't seem to find our train tickets. Could we look around to see if they are still here?"

"Of course," I said, stepping aside to let them in.

For the next few minutes we all opened and closed every drawer, looked under the bed, on the desk—everywhere—but no tickets. I asked them what time the train was scheduled to leave and they said 10 o'clock. So, since it was around 2:00, I knew they'd find their tickets. I sometimes absentmindedly stick tickets in some pouch or bag while traveling, then spend what seems like hours searching for them, but they always turn up. I asked them where they were traveling to, and I could hear a note of excitement in their voices when they answered.

"We're taking a four-hour train ride north, then we take a plane up close to the Arctic Circle where the sun never rises!"

they answered. I asked them if they were scientists and they laughed. "No, we're friends. Every year we pick a destination, then for one week we leave our families behind—husbands, children, grandkids—and the nine of us have an adventure. Last year we went to Phoenix and that was okay, but this year we wanted to try something a little different, and the Arctic Circle seemed like a good idea, so here we are!" I asked them where they were from and she said they all lived in and around Billings, Montana. I wanted to talk some more, but they were worried about finding their train tickets, so they left.

I went back to my unpacking, and with three hours to go before my sound check, I decided now would be a good time to organize my purse. I have the kind of purse that turns into a black hole during long trips—things get tossed into it in one city, only to disappear, then reemerge two thousand miles later. So I emptied it out onto the bed and attempted to sort through a wrinkled pile of credit card slips, cash receipts, boarding passes, checks, American cash, Canadian cash, tissues, candy wrappers, phone messages—a boring task that suddenly made me feel very sleepy. I stretched out on the bed next to the contents of my purse and promptly fell asleep.

I awoke at 4:30—and only had a few minutes to get my gear together for the concerts that night. I splashed water on my face, packed a small bag with my performing clothes, guitar strings, batteries, and headed out the door. Right across the hall were all those old ladies, still crowded into that one room, and although I was running a little late, I was concerned that they might not have found their train tickets. So I went in and asked.

Yes, the tickets had been found, having slipped between suitcases in their room. I looked around and could see how that could happen—all nine of them were crowded into one rather small hotel room. I suddenly had an idea.

"Look," I said, "I've got two shows tonight—I won't be back until very late." I took my room key out of my pocket and held it out to them. "At least you can spread out a bit. Here, use my room."

They looked a bit doubtful, but one of them quickly grabbed my key. "Thank you," she said, "We will."

I had two performances scheduled that night—one at 7 P.M. and one at 10 P.M. The first concert ended at about 9:15 and immediately afterward I planned to get my Sharpie pen and autograph CDs in the lobby.

I always keep my Sharpie pen in the same section of my purse where I keep my money, so it came as a shock when I reached into that section for the pen and saw that there was no cash in there. I had been on the road for quite a while and re-membered having a substantial amount of money. My mind raced for a moment—could I have been robbed while onstage? Then I remembered—I had been cleaning out my purse at the hotel. What did I do with the money? I tried to reconstruct my moves . . . then I realized I had left the contents of my purse on the dresser in my room . . . *and then gave my room key to a bunch of strangers!!!* What was I thinking?

I immediately told the stage manager what I had done, and he offered to drive me over to the hotel between shows. But there wasn't much time, the old women were probably al-ready on their way to the train station, but more than that, in my heart I knew everything would be all right. The stage man-ager said perhaps I should have the front desk manager be made aware of the situation, but I declined. I had a feeling there was no need to worry.

I performed my second show that night, and got back to the hotel around 1 A.M. I retrieved my room key from the front desk, went to my room, slowly turned the key, and turned on the light. What would I find?

There, on the dresser, neatly folded, were my clothes. Next to that, in short stacks, was my money—separated neatly by denomination and country (U.S., Canadian). Next to that was a pile of receipts, again separated—U.S. and Cana-dian. Next to that were checks. Next to that was a sheet tally-ing up the amount of cash, checks, and receipts. (There was over $700 in U.S. money, over $600 in Canadian. Plus some coins.)

Next to all of that was a handwritten note on a small piece of blue-lined notebook paper. In beautiful script it said:

Dear Christine:

(We know your name because it's on your airline ticket.)
Thank you for your kind hospitality. You are a very
trusting soul.

> *Sincerely,*
> *Elsie of The Montana Nine*

    The Montana Nine, I thought to myself. The name conjures up images of a gang of outlaws, roaming the hills, stirring up trouble. But in reality The Montana Nine is a gang of old ladies, on their yearly adventure, and I had an encounter with them. They folded my clothes, added up my receipts, counted my money, then stole off into the night in pursuit of the Arctic Circle.

    Someday, if you're lucky, you, too, might see them. In their flowered dresses, with their blue hair. *The Montana Nine.*

> **Christine Lavin**

Domestic Delinquent

CHORUS: I'm a domestic delinquent
There are dishes in the sink
Dustballs on the floor
And the garbage really stinks
The wash is piled high
Oh what's a girl to do . . .
Just revel in the wonder and sit down . . .
And write a song or two.

My mama always told me
Not to worry 'bout such things,
You marry yourself a rich man
He'll take care of everything.
The Merry Maids will come
And they will do all your chores,

Just don't invite him in till you've got that diamond . . .
And the invitations are mailed . . .
And the honeymoon's bought and paid for . . .
Or he may walk out that door.

I went into therapy
A long time ago
To find the deeper meaning
Of why I let my housework grow.
That therapist, he called me
Immature and unaware (Imagine that),
So I left him a token of my thanks—
There's bubblegum stuck under his chair.

CHORUS: I'm a domestic . . .

I open up the fridge
The mold is climbing in the back
But it don't bother me.
They look like vines from Africa
A modern work of art.
Andy Warhol would agree
It's a source of inspiration
To the artist in me.

CHORUS: I'm a domestic . . .

Jackie Tice

Dishwater Rhyme

Sherrie Shepherd

True Story

This guy calls me up, asks me out on a blind date, then says, "Okay, so how will I know you? What do you look like?"

I said, "I don't know. Uh—I have brown hair. I'm five-four . . ."

He said, "Oh. Five-four. So you should weigh about a hundred-twenty pounds."

I said, "Yeah. I probably should."

True story.

Mindy Schneider

Butter

Butter, I remember butter
We were once like lovers
We were quite a team

Sugar, I remember sugar
Not much of a looker
Oh, but what a dream

I remember coffee-flavored Häagen-Dazs
Sweetening my lips.
Now it's just a memory
Right here on my hips . . .

Pasta, I remember pasta
Now, I'm not anti-pasta . . .
It always did the trick

Chocolate, I remember chocolate
But it became a habit
That was hard to lick

Oh, yes, and I remember Fannie May
But from where I'm standing now . . .
Looking at my fanny may
Remind one of a cow

Ohhh, butter, I remember butter
We were once like lovers
We were quite a team
I'll take some butter-smothered pasta please . . .
In a vat of . . . chocolate . . . cheese! . . .
Butter.

Megon McDonough

My Porch, and Welcome to It

I am a homeowner, a smart, dedicated and competent home-owner. Being smart, dedicated, and competent isn't all it's cracked up to be. I'm tired of having to know everything to keep my house up and running. Every time anything goes wrong with my house, I have to learn the language and the inner workings of the hardware involved. Then, I weigh and balance the repair technique, the cost of hiring out, or possibly, taking the risk to do it myself. Then, I always make sure that as a woman, I'm not taken advantage of.

I bust my tail to have the perfect lawn and the perfect flower bed. One can only imagine how fantastic my garage is on the inside. Rather than frustrate the men on my block, I keep the garage door open for long stretches on weekends just so these guys can covet my shelving units. They think it's about

Tupperware and casseroles? Think again, Harvey. Wait till you get a peek at those gigantic hooks I drilled into the crossbeam. Wanna watch me hoist my kid's bike upside down to hang for the winter? Check out how my weed whacker hangs in tandem from the pegboard with my rake and garden tools. My lawnmower goes in for sharpening at the end of each season. Every homeowner knows it's about the tools. After that, it's about storage and how pretty it all looks on the shelf.

Yep, I can take a little personality character trait like being anal compulsive and stretch it out over my homestead like weed and feed, where it can run free. But I wasn't always like this.

For the 18 years that I was married, I was the wife my mother thought I should be. I made dinner. I made beds. I made a baby. Then, role definitions became murky as the 1980s rolled into the 1990s. I always had my little jobs and worked outside the home. I also took out the trash and changed the light bulbs. I hired the people to do the jobs my husband couldn't or wouldn't do. I ran the show. And I was good.

My interest in running things might have started with my incredible flair for loading the dishwasher. I could stack like nobody's business; As many as five meals of dishes were loaded to save water with not one dish at risk. It was a thing of beauty. Then, I moved into organizing drawers, closets, and the entire garage and basement area. I know that typically these latter two arenas are reserved for the man of the house to mess up and reign over. My then-husband didn't care and so I marked my territory and was off and running. He was a smart man, my then-husband. On car trips, he knew enough to politcly step aside, allowing a master to pack the trunk. And I was good.

My spatial and mechanical curiosity bloomed and took me into the realm of power tools. I'll never forget my first experience with the electric hedge trimmer. I stood firm, feet apart shoulder width. I aimed, fired, and carved, creating the loveliest straight line our front bushes had ever known. Our house went from looking like Dickens's Miss Havisham's place to the Cleaver family dwelling with one stroke of my power trimmer. The buzzing force I wielded from my hands gave me a sense of control I felt all too comfortable with. I was unstoppable. I was Rambo on my Rancho. And I was good.

It was the staple gun that threw me over the edge and into my mechanical nirvana. I learned to use the gun while re-covering my kitchen chairs. Stretching fabric around the butt cushion had been so easy, I wanted to keep going. What else could I staple? The pull of that trigger, and the sound and vibration as it fired a staple deep into the wood turned me on. From my solar plexus, through my shoulders, down my arm and out my hand, I once again felt that power and control. I loved it, and I wanted more. I was good.

I had it in my mind that I could maybe rescreen the back porch. I was told it would be simple. All I'd need was shoe molding, a roll of screen, a miter box, and, of course, my new best friend, my beloved staple gun. I could do this. I couldn't spell miter box, but I could learn to use one.

My buddies at the hardware store loved me. When they saw me coming they knew I'd be packing cookies in exchange for a quick hands-on lesson. When there was something I needed, I knew I could count on them to teach me, show me, or walk me through the use of something they're about to sell me. Usually, if I'm packing Danish, they just do the task for me right then and there in the store. But I love that they want me to feel the empowerment that comes with ownership of a great craftsman tool. And so, with a few kinds words of encouragement, a stern warning to be exact with my measurements, they send me home. I'd be ready to fly solo.

At home, with my kid's boom box blaring, I pulled off the old shoe molding that held the screens onto the frame of the back porch. I cut new screens and attached them with my new best friend, my beloved staple gun. Around and around the screens I went. Eight large panels of screen with as many as 50 staples per panel. I was loud. I went fast. It was aerobic. I switched arms for an equal workout. I knew the porch was looking good. Hell, I knew I was looking good. The screens were up and I moved onto the next step. The shoe molding took a considerable amount of time due to this miter box. The miter box deal is not my best friend; nor would I call it beloved.

To miter means making angled cuts in the wood to make them match a similar but opposite angled edge. Aren't you just so impressed? I had to use wood nails to hammer the molding onto the porch frame. And I thought using lip liner was a bitch! I'm using a hammer and having way too much fun. The molding's up and all that was left was to paint, take a bow, pour a beer. And like that beer, I was good.

With the porch completed, I was motivated to wash down the furniture and scrape off the grill. Then, I was done. I lit a candle, poured a drink, and sat on my antique glider, marveling at my spectacular back porch. I thought about my home. The interior, the exterior and now, with this porch, I felt like a land baroness. I amazed myself for not only caring about my surroundings, but actually doing something about them. Rather than nag, beg, or hire, I took care of it myself. Then, suddenly, my serenity was interrupted by the high-pitched screech of my glider rocking. Oh sure, I knew that I could get up, grab the naval jelly and remove the rust and eliminate the screeching. A little WD40 would bring the quiet grace back to this inherited relic that came with my 70-year-old house. Then, unexpectedly, I felt a surge of testosterone. The husband variety. "Hell," I thought. "Tomorrow is another day." I continued to sit—and enjoy my glorious estate.

I sat, reflected, smiled and drank my cold one. I gave myself an emotional pat on the back. I allowed myself an indulgent moment of overinflated self-satisfaction. And I was good.

Sally Fingerett

L.A.F.F. (Ladies Against Fanny Floss)

When our stretch marks look like the New Jersey
   Turnpike
mapped from navel to knees,
when the bottom's best feature is its interesting texture
(the sign of a fine cottage cheese),
when we search for the perfect bathing suit
that will cover our asses (and still look cute)
is this an impossible, hopeless pursuit?
Or are we just hard to please?

When will we finally find the designer we need
who will heed our demand?
Or a style at the shore (where less is not more)
to guard the parts that are best left untanned?
We need more protection than spandex rags;
something cut larger than luggage tags
tied with dental floss onto our saddle bags.
Don't hide your heads in the sand!

CHORUS: We're talking to you, Fashion Avenue
              We're not going to take any more.
              We're your mothers and mistresses, wives and
                  sisters
              united from shore to shore.
              We are standing erect with our hands on our
                  chests
              four inches above the floor
              And we're asking you, Fashion Avenue,
              for a little more support.

Swimsuits abound for the 98-pounder
whose legs alone measure five feet.
Here's a fine idea: try a line this year
for women who actually eat.

Not for half-naked nymphs found posing between
the pages—of course!—of a sports magazine,
but swimsuits for those of us more likely seen
between pages of *Bon Appetit.*

Our legs do not end where our armpits begin;
we want a realistic design,
a little more coverage, a little less skin
(some vertical stripes would be simply divine.)
Swimwear that won't self-destruct with a wave,
fashion to flatter the not-so-brave,
at least let us know where to stop when we shave.
Where do we draw the line?

CHORUS: We're talking to you, Fashion Avenue
We're not going to take any more.
We're your mothers and mistresses, wives and
    sisters
united from shore to shore.
We are standing erect with our hands on our
    chests
two inches above the floor
(just like real life, this song is affected by
    gravity)
And we're asking you, Fashion Avenue,
for a little more support.

One day we may see our feminist family
rise from the underground,
despite Father Time and weird Uncle Gravity
constantly pulling us down.
This dysfunctional system will finally heal,
even our sisters with abs of steel
will all too suddenly know how we feel
ten years and two babies from now.

And when we connect and command your respect,
effectively paying our dues,
your very language shall be more correct.

Fat is a word you will no longer use.
Those negative terms only grate on our nerves.
Give adipose tissue the name it deserves.
Call it . . . "personal strategic energy reserves"
and call stretch marks "organic tattoos."

CHORUS: We're talking to you, Fashion Avenue
We're not going to take any more.
We're your mothers and mistresses, wives and
  sisters
united from shore to shore.
We are standing erect with our hands on our
  chests
upon the floor . . .
And we're asking you, Fashion Avenue,
for a little more support.

Camille West

The Story of Z

I've figured out the dirty little secret of women's fantasy lives. And it's got nothing to do with thumbing through *Herotica* or fondling Brad Pitt's backside or soaking in a penthouse Jacuzzi with Richard Gere. Sleep has become the sex of the 21st century. Sleep is replacing sex as that obscure object of desire that inhabits our daydreams—if we still have time for daydreams. When I indulge in an out-of-body experience during a particularly dull meeting, my richest, deepest, most rewarding fantasies aren't erotic. They're about checking out for hours and hours of glorious uninterrupted sack time. I'm not mentally undressing my dishy seatmate on the commuter train; I'm wondering whether he'd take offense if I catnap on his shoulder until we get to Hartsdale. My idea of a phone sex line is 1-800-M-A-T-T-R-E-S.

Arlie Hochschild interviewed dozens of working mothers for her book *The Second Shift: Working Parents and the Revolution at Home*. Time and again, they talked about sleep the way starving people talk about food. But this problem is not reserved to working mothers. Far from it. I read a column a few months back about the chronic sleep deficit that's sweeping the country. Something like 80 percent of Americans are seriously sleep-deprived. (Or maybe it was that 80 percent have lower back pain, or 80 percent think Heather Locklear needs to touch up those roots. I nodded off somewhere in there.) Experts estimate that chronic sleeplessness costs the nation as much as $70 billion annually in lost productivity, accidents, and medical bills. There was some maxim that if you fall asleep within five minutes of lights out, you can count yourself among the seriously sleep-deficient. (Wait, there are people who can stay awake for five minutes?)

I don't need Faith Popcorn or Gallup for confirmation. I know a trend when I'm living it. My friends and colleagues concur. Sarah says she would rather lay her head on a pillow than anywhere else. Maria says none of her friends want to fool around on the weekend; they just want to recover from the week (oh God, not another recovery movement). Barb claims that no one she knows is having sex—unless they're on some procreational full-court press to get those babies in before the buzzer sounds.

In fact, the only person to whom I expounded my sleep-as-sex theory who just didn't get it was a single, unencumbered, 20-something guy I work with. As I rambled on during one of my brief moments of clarity (the decaffeinated life is definitely not worth living), he rolled his eyes and said, "Sounds like all you need is a good nap." Which sounded suspiciously like a guy saying that all I needed was a good roll in the hay. Which proves my point exactly.

Obviously, for working parents, small children are the big problem. I guess I should have had an inkling of the trouble ahead when I read a *Parents* magazine survey a few months after our first child was born. In response to the question, "How do you feel about sex after the baby?" one new mom answered, "Fine, just don't wake me."

I just edited this wonderful new book by a physician whose sex therapy clinic has successfully treated thousands of couples. The doctor confirms that fatigue is a big problem in people's sex lives. But when I pressed her for some solutions, I couldn't help but feel a tad disappointed. She explained that we go through these R.E.M. cycles several times a night, one every ninety minutes or so, at which time we become aroused—only we're not aware of it because we're out like a light. She recommends you set your alarm to go off ninety minutes after you fall asleep. The idea is, when you wake up you'll be in one of your R.E.M. cycles, so you'll be in the mood. Yeah, you'll get me up after those precious ninety minutes when you pry my cold, dead fingers from around the pillow.

The women's magazines are certainly no help. *Cosmo* has yet to publish articles for the Exhausted Generation. How about "Douse His Candle: 15 Ways to Rev Up Your Zs" or "I Was the Office Narcomaniac"? And how long before the Surgeon General realizes that sleep is the ultimate safe sex?

I do see hope on the horizon. Two months ago my husband and I took our first real vacation—three days and two nights—away from our two small children. On our last pre-child vacation, we embarked on an exotic trip abroad with complicated transportation nexuses and an intricate itinerary. This time around, we didn't even bother picking a destination. Our only goal was so modest it was almost pathetic: to go to sleep at night and wake up whenever we happened to wake up—not when a tiny voice shouted "Uppies! Uppies!" in one of our ears.

The first morning we made it to 7:13. The second morning we lasted until almost 8:00. And I was a new woman. For the first time in memory, whenever I closed my eyes, they didn't pine to stay closed. I felt energized, alive . . . sexy! We were, in all modesty, animals. Two days after we returned, however, the inevitable exhaustion crept back in. We're looking forward to re-creating that connubial bliss soon—perhaps when the kids are in their surly, narcotized teenage years. In the meantime, my husband and I comfort ourselves that this too shall pass; we know that one day our lust for sleep will recede and truly smutty thoughts will regain their rightful pride of place in our fantasy lives.

Who knows? Perhaps that day will come sooner than you think, darling. There I'll be, draped in that low-cut black nightgown you bought me on our honeymoon in Florence, my hair back-lit by flickering candles, my limbs still moist from a fragrant tub, awaiting the caress of the massage oil that warms at your touch.

But for now, wake me and you're a dead man.

Elizabeth Rapoport

Sleep

You rock the baby, you feed the cat,
You walk the dog, babe, you're good at that
It may be reckless, it may be a sin,
But screw the alarm, I'm going to sleep in

CHORUS: Sleep, sleep, sleep is my good friend
        Late in the morning or at the day's end
        Pull down the shade, and turn out the light
        The only date I have is with the sandman
          tonight

Don't talk to me about how you need
Only two hours and you're on your feet
Saying where's the fiesta; well you can find me
At the siesta catching some Z's

BRIDGE: Gonna bed down, drop off, got sand in my
          eyes,
        Slumber, repose, get some shut eye,
        Get forty winks, nap, hit the land of nod,
        Catnap, knock off, go saw some logs

Give me eight hours, give me some REMs
Dreams like diamonds, ten carat gems,
Give me some respite, leave me alone:
It's a nice party, but I'm going home

Debi Smith

TechnoBabe

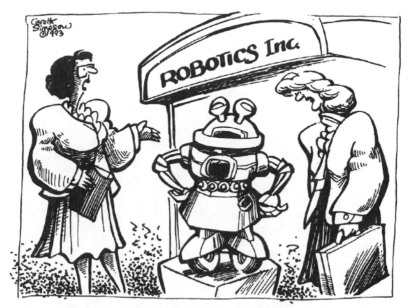

"Our old model did the work of ten men.
Our new improved version does the work of one woman."

Carol*Simpson

Tonight's Menu

I'm sittin' in my kitchen, oooh, I'm wishin' they'd love
   my cooking
Or they'd quit their bitchin'
Gonna put my foot down, make him take me uptown,
Dress like a debutante, go to a restaurant.
Baby take me out, . . . baby take me out to eat.

I want white cloth linen, and a cool pressed napkin.
A Zinfandel from an organic vineyard
Where they've got Evian on every table,
They let you sit and linger, long as your butt is able.
Baby take me out, baby take me out to eat.

> Don't wanna hit the hut! Don't wanna slam no
>   mac!
> Don't wanna run for the border!
> Don't you give me no Kentucky Fried yech!
> I ain't no seafood lover!
> Don't want no chili dog! No pizza burger!
> Baby, your baby ain't drivin' through
> Unless they've got a 5-star review!

I wanna leave my lipstick on fine bone china.
Give me decaf espresso, don't want no insomnia.
I'll drink my water from sparkling crystal,
Get a monkey in a tux running to my signal.
Baby take me out, . . . baby take me out to eat.

> They've got squid and leeks! I see those grouper
>   cheeks!
> How 'bout that garlic veal!
> Can't we put aside our politics for just one meal?

They got free-range potatoes, braised with a mango
Garnished with a twenty-dollar tomato.
I don't care if it's tasty, don't care if it's good,
I want you spending money.
I think you should.
Baby take me out, . . . baby take me out to eat.

Sally Fingerett

An Open Letter to the Firefighters of Engine Company 54, Ladder 4, Battalion 9 in the Glass Booth on the Corner of 8th Avenue and 48th Street

[*The author's long-standing devotion to firefighters predates the tragedy of September 11. This work dates from an earlier, happier time.*]

Dear Firefighters of Engine 54, Ladder 4, Battalion 9:

No matter what time, day or night, I pass by that little glass booth at the firehouse on the corner of 8th Avenue and 48th Street, you are all dressing and undressing like some firefighter version of Porky's, like it does not count officially as porn if sometimes you are saving lives. Maybe the Chippendale dancer guys are one big women's-bachelor-party cliché, but at least they are honest about what they do.

I have not seen much porno at all, but why do I think of you when I imagine some kind of porno ideal? Because you do so many porn things, such as:

1. standing in calendar poses
2. blowing on your coffee for a very long time
3. tossing back your head and laughing throaty firefighter laughter
4. twirling around in that big command chair wearing those form-fitting bright white T-shirts and is it me or do suspenders do things for a man? Sure, investment bankers try to wear them, but firefighters are bombshells in them. Speaking of which, how could anyone ever think that "bombshell" should be a term for women? Especially women who are not firemen who lift weights until their pecs and their biceps are just perfect little scoops of man flesh.

My friend Jennifer says, "Why don't you turn your head when you walk past—cross the street and ignore them."

Oh yeah? Okay, maybe I could see how if somebody was gay maybe they could avert their gaze. But I am hard-wired for firemen. It is just a physiological fact. Blame the victim, why don't you? It is not me making you firemen; it is not me telling you to flaunt your fireman lifestyle.

My friend Jennifer says, "Just because they take off their coats and shirts and strut around doesn't mean they're on display."

Oh, yeah? They're under glass. Like pheasants. Like in a jewelry store. Like a boy diorama in the Museum of Natural History.

My friend Jennifer says, "Not every half-dressed man in rubber boots wants you."

Oh yeah? Well, why not?

I am not saying that just because I happen to be interested; you are supposed to be after me like a cartoon skunk. I am just saying that I think everyone involved could have a very enjoyable time, is all. But you guys have given me low self-esteem. You made me hate myself until I felt like Shemp.

My analyst said to try aversion therapy. My analyst has told me time and again of the dark, Freudian significance of polishing and polishing trucks that already are shiny-clean. He says winding and unwinding those big, big hoses is obsessive-compulsive behavior. He told me to summon up images of those kookie barber shop quartet moustaches. This works for a little while, but the next time I look through the window, there is one of you humming and penciling in a report, leaning to one side to shift himself ever so slightly and again you inhabit my dreams.

What is the worst thing anyone can say about firemen? That they don't rescue kittens from trees anymore? And listen to this: the African American firefighters' organization named themselves "The Vulcans." How cool is that? Very.

Even firefighter boring day-at-the-office small talk must be full of sexy words like: hook and ladder, fireman's carry, jaws of life, cherry-picker. Hhhhhhhhhhhhh. I imagine you silently mouthing these words to yourselves over and over as you curl up in your cots all in a row, faces ever so slightly smudged with soot and your hair boyishly tousled. You are men who slide down poles as if it is nothing whereas I would find something fascinating about that.

I didn't want to bring this up, but I pay your salary. I never was in a fire. Also, I never turned in a false alarm, so no—no, I do not feel as if I have gotten my money's worth.

Writing this letter makes me as sad as when I heard that one time Janet Jackson and Michael Jackson had not seen each other for over two years.

Here are my demands:

1. A written apology displayed in plain view in your window for all to see. It does not have to say "Dear Meg" or even "To Meg" even if I deserve it more than most other people although I would appreciate that very much.

2. Someone in your fire station must get tired of all that four-alarm chili or whatever it is you are always eating when the guy up front says he does not have time to talk because he is covering because everyone is eating. It wouldn't kill one of you to call me up and maybe take me to dinner as a very personal apology that I would appreciate. My number is 555-2209.

3. Common courtesy is only polite. I nod—you nod back at me. I wave—you wave back to me. I say jump—you buy me some jewelry. It does not have to be that expensive and I would mention to everyone I talk to that it is jewelry from firefighters and you can't buy that kind of positive publicity. I guarantee that I would be as happy as the people on commercials if it was a real diamond and maybe we could spin round and round happily together in a kind of light-hearted dance if you gave it to me on the beach.

In conclusion, can't we just meet and talk this whole thing through? I'm sure it is just one big misunderstanding, and that when we look back on it together, all of us will laugh. It can work out for everybody. It is as simple as a nod, a wave, maybe some Speedos in the summertime. It will be so worth it for you to call me at 555-2209. Then I will tell all my friends to stop tapping at the glass.

M. Sweeney Lawless

Viagra® in the Waters

Just outside of Johnson City
On a dark and twisting road
In a Kenworth 18-wheeler
With a heavy, shifting load
He was pushing through to Binghamton
Though the hour was getting late
Pfizer's finest on a mission
To the pharmacies upstate
He was on a holy mission
There were men who couldn't wait
(for his twenty thousand pounds of Viagra®).

He'd clocked seven hundred miles
Since he climbed into the rig
Just another twenty-five or so
Would finish up that gig
But the trailer hit an oil slick
And down the hill did fly (oh my!)
'til it landed at the bottom
in the town's water supply
It was instant rigor mortis
What a hard way to die!

CHORUS: Save your sons
             Shield your daughters!
             There's Viagra®
             In the waters

All over Johnson City
People rising with the dawn
They drank their morning coffee,
Took their showers, watered lawns
And who could have predicted
All the changes up ahead?

Men were getting up for work,
And heading back to bed
So many called in sick,
You would have thought a virus spread.

Down at the courthouse coffee shop
Some stared in disbelief
As a pack of thirsty lawyers
Started filling out their briefs
But at the local college
Young men appeared much smarter
No chromosomal mystery
They simply studied harder
Now water on the rocks
Is the latest party starter.

CHORUS: Save . . .

The Johnson City firemen
Cursed their wretched luck
They could not get their fire hoses
Wound back on the truck.
Sprinkling holy water at a funeral,
Father Ryan said,
"I know I've saved their souls,
but I've never raised the dead.
Would a couple strong men help me now
To close the casket lid?"

Old man Weisberg
Took the shower of his life
Then he marched into the kitchen
And he called out to his wife
She knew something was up
As he stood naked at the table
Holding two cups of coffee
And half a dozen bagels
It had been at least a decade
Since the last time he was able.

CHORUS: Save . . .

Believers seeking miracles
The pilgrims came in hordes
The waters of Viagra®
Grew more popular than Lourdes.
The clergy quoted scripture
But they found it hard to sell
That those who chose to be anointed
Were pointed straight to hell
Despite the dire warnings
The crowds began to swell.

Some hardened politicians
Came into town one day
With their permits and their pipelines
Pumped the waters all away.
From the heart of Johnson City
Rose the mournful cry of men
But the women knew another truck
Was coming through again
Don't worry—there's a truck next week
We'll spread the oil again.

CHORUS: Save . . .

Camille West

Maxine's Viagra® Supplements

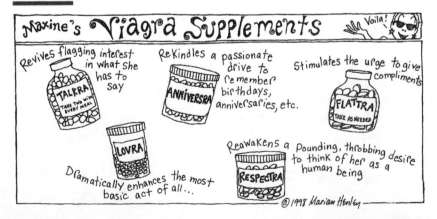

Marian Henley

What Was I Thinking?

It was a last minute invitation
I did not have a thing to wear
I ran into the store I said I need something black
something formal
other than that . . . I don't care.
I made it to the theater as the lights dimmed
the first act was brilliantly fun
but when I caught my reflection during intermission
I thought [pause] . . . what have I done?

CHORUS: What was I thinking?
what was I, blind?
When I bought this outfit
was I temporarily out of my mind?
What was I thinking?
just look at this dress!
I'm taking up drinking
my life is a mess

* My good friend said
I think you're gonna hit it off
I've known him for a long long time
and if I wasn't happily married myself
in a heartbeat I would try to make him mine.
So I figure OK I'll take my chances
what harm could it do?
Makes you wonder 'bout the motives of your married
   friends
when something like this happens to you

CHORUS: What was she thinking?
Who is this guy?
Maybe I'll just choke on this porkchop
and conveniently die.

What was she thinking?
Quick, sharpen this knife
my endorphins are sinking
I'm taking my life

BRIDGE: Oooh, oooh oooh
Ach! du lieber!
Ooohooohoooh
Ah! Wat da tien na!
Oooh oooh oooh
¡Oh, muy boja!
Oooh oooh oooh
¡Qué lástima, La Vie, au revoir!

(That's an international segment, so people will think this is world music, which I think is going to be the next big thing to sweep the nation and I want to ride that wave right into the beach . . . .)

It was late
I had insomnia
that TV stair-stepper started to look good.
I thought to myself should I buy it?
I heard Bruce Jenner say
"Yes, you should."
And that Snackmaster, that BeDazzler, that Thighmaster
    and
that Victoria Jackson makeup kit
now I can barely get around my apartment
it's so filled with all this stupid stuff.

CHORUS: What was I thinking?
Look at this junk!
I can't blame it on drinking
I've never, uh, hardly ever, uh,
right now I'm not drunk.
What was I thinking?
When will this end?
what was I thinking?

when will this end?
what was I thinking?
this song has no end
what was I thinking?
this song has no end!!!
what was I thinking?
this song has no end . . . etc.

(*Alternate second verse follows:)

My hairdresser said it's time for a new 'do
you've had that look for way too long.
So he showed me a perm in a magazine
and I thought sure, what could go wrong?
I should have known by the sounds he was making (ho
    boy)
something was going awry.
After two hours I put on my glasses
I could not believe my eyes

CHORUS: What was he thinking?
         I can't believe what I see.
         I look in the mirror
         Art Garfunkel's looking back at me!
         What was he thinking?
         Quick, steal me a hat.
         I should look on the bright side,
         unlike Art, it will grow back

Christine Lavin

CHAPTER 6

A Far Too Frequent Flyer

Dear Airline CEO,

I am a traveling musician, a singer/songwriter. On pretty much any given day there are scores of traveling musicians out there, flying all over the country (getting as far away as possible from the towns we played the night before). When we musicians get together, like at Folk Festivals and such, air travel is one of the most common subjects of discussion. So, on behalf of my many musician friends I would like to ask you a few questions and relate a few observations.

Who designed the seats on airplanes, Calista Flockhart? Some of us need more room than that. Also, all of us have shoulders. Don't the seating designers know this? We try though; we squirm into those seats, balancing stuff in our laps, moving stuff around on the floor with our feet. We buckle up and then try not to move much (since any movement at all affects the entire row). Of course what we really need, once we've squeezed into our seats and settled down, is Cokes and bags of peanuts.

Speaking of peanuts, here are the two most common complaints I've heard regarding air travel: it's too expensive and the food sucks. I have to wonder why food is served on airplanes at all. In our real lives, most of us can get through two, four, even six hours without eating. In airplanes we seem to need to eat constantly and the need is so great we will eat stuff that no one would even consider eating in any other circumstance.

It's not the *food* we want, is it? It's the distraction. We welcome the opportunity for any activity. And the challenge of opening lots of tiny little containers, deciding how to distribute our seven grains of pepper and eating a meal without moving our arms, is at least time-consuming.

We need to be distracted from the offensive, claustrophobic proximity of total strangers. Though we may have been sane when we arrived at the airport, by the time we get off the plane we have become people pushed to the very edge by someone's puffy coat sleeve extending way beyond their half-inch of the armrest, into our territory. Since providing a comfortable environment for your passengers is apparently out of the question, you instead create the appearance of room by allowing passengers to "recline their seats" . . . right into the lap of a now-homicidal maniac.

Speaking of creating appearances, airline ads portray their cabins as serene, spacious, welcoming. Smiling flight attendants are helping stow baggage in nearly empty overhead bins. While some passengers are engaged in pleasant, informative conversation with attractive men and women, others are stretched out in deep, peaceful sleep. Everyone is happy. And throughout, these kindly flight attendants bend lovingly to our every need.

I've never been on that flight. On the flights I've taken some of the passengers are wearing what must be whole bottles of perfume. The flight attendants are wearing buttons that say "Eat and get off." Fat men are snoring louder than the jet engines and no one (with the possible exception of a nine-year-old, or some huddled family fleeing a hideous regime) is at all pleased to be there.

Apparently "truth in advertising" is *very* broadly defined. Can you imagine if it weren't? An ad for one of your middle seats might read: "For sale: Terribly situated, insanely close-quartered, tiny, uncomfortable seat on airplane. We guarantee this seat will be surrounded by huffy people who will resent you for being there! That's right, this is the seat nobody wants! Not only do you not want to buy it, no one else wants you to buy it either! And when we sell it, it will probably be more expensive than the other seats because if you've waited this long to book and all of the other seats are taken then we've really got you, so we can sell this turn-you-into-a-psychopath seat for an astronomical sum. Call today . . . or tomorrow."

I think we musicians harbor an especially sincere resentment of your industry. Traveling with guitars on airplanes is such an atrocious experience that I imagine that's why God made Quaaludes. It's not just that we pay thousands of dollars for each of these guitars, and hundreds of dollars for each guitar's flight case and then another hundred or so for the padded ballistic nylon case that prevents the gentle baggage handling systems from shearing the metal latches right off the cases. No, we actually love these instruments, care about them, and know that each of them is one of a kind, irreplaceable.

When, because we must, we turn our guitars over to an airline, we are often required to sign a small piece of paper, which, the ticket agent will explain, "relieves the airline of any responsibility for loss or damage." It is still a shock to hear this. No one has ever answered the obvious question: "If I'm handing this to you and you're not responsible for it, who is?" The ticket agent hates this question and ignores it. I watch my guitars being tossed, upside down, onto the conveyor belt.

Still, here we stand, cursing and muttering under a constant barrage of loud-speakered instruction in long, long lines that wind like lower intestines because who else can offer us the possibility of breakfast on the East Coast and lunch on the West Coast on the same day?

I'll bet the airlines must have been ecstatic when they realized how greatly we value our time. Talk about "Eureka!"—who knew? Who knew we'd be willing to endure nursery school seating, sardinelike proximity, shrieking babies, foodlike substances, stupefying boredom, seething resentment toward some reclining idiot, a seatmate with a cold, a Gameboy and flatulence, the very real possibility that we and our bags might never meet again and that we might arrive at our destinations hours or even days late?

If I knew how to do it, I would try to organize people into a sort of strike against things like middle seats. I'd say to every prospective passenger "if a middle seat is the best they can do, tell 'em you'll find someone who can do better." I do not imagine, Mr. Airline CEO, that you are shaking in your boots.

A far too frequent flyer,
Cheryl Wheeler

Here's a song I wrote for your industry:

On the Plane

You will need to arrive at a quarter to five
if your plane is departing at ten.
When you called for a seat, we advised you
    to meet
at the gate and we'd let you know then.

The seats are so teeny you'll sit like Houdini.
Be quiet and listen to this,
If we should fall in a fiery ball,
kiss your own ass good-bye, then your kids.

On the plane, on the plane,
you will do exactly as we say.
You'll remain in your seat
with your bags at your feet
till the speech is complete on the plane.

If we sit on the runway from now until
    Monday
well all we can say is "too bad."
Up front there's free liquor and they get there
    quicker,
so those folks are not quite as mad.

You've paid your dinero, this movie's just fair
oh but here comes the part that's so good.
Then the pilot will cut in: "We can't see Cleveland,
but if it weren't cloudy, we could."

On the plane all is well,
just think of it as practicing for hell.
I'm in five, you're in four,
you lean back anymore,
you'll be shoved out the door of the plane.

We are not responsible for . . . anything.
And everything can go wrong.
We really don't know where we'll go or when.
And you may never see your bags again.
Such a shame, on the plane.

Your carry on stuff has to fit in this box.
If it doesn't and you make us wait,
you'll be pulled from the line with a hook from behind
and then beaten and shot at the gate.

The air that you're breathing's been recirculating
since Orville and Wilbur were boys.
If you should choke, here's a thimble of coke.
You do realize that coughing annoys?

On the plane, on the plane
People are we perfectly insane?
The skies are not so friendly.
Delta isn't ready.
I prefer the bus.
USAIR begins with US.
It's truly torturous
on the plane . . . on the plane.

Cheryl Wheeler

Santa Fe Chic

"I LOVE THE SOUTHWEST, PARTICULARLY
HERE IN THE DEN."

Mary Lawton

Who's Calling?

It's six in the evening and I'm thinking to myself:
"Should I take spaghetti or some beans down from the
    shelf?
Time to cook some dinner, kick back, watch TV—
But what is this I hear—who could be calling me?"

Now, my married name's "Jaworek," which I know's
    hard to pronounce—
And I don't mind announcers stumbling on it, when
    announced—
But when I pick up the telephone and hear someone say,
    "Ms. Jork?"
There's no doubt in my mind on the other end's a dork

CHORUS: "May I sell you something?
            Siding? Windows? Doors?
            How 'bout beachfront property at
            'Washaway Shores?' "

I say, "So you're going to try and sell something to me?"
He says with pride and confidence—"Absolutely!"
While I'm listening, a little song is running through my
    mind:
There must be fifty ways to leave this phone salesman
    behind.

Give the phone to your two-year-old who's learning how
    to talk,
Set it by the parrot who is practicing his squawk
Tell him you're in labor, would he please call 911,
And when you hear a pregnant pause, then you know
    you've won.

Tell him the house is burning and the fire truck's on the
    way,
Set the phone down on the counter and then just walk
    away,
Tell him you are in your car and a thief is breaking in,
Put the phone up to the car alarm and let the fun begin.

Tell him you've been at the dentist for a major overhaul,
(slurred speech) And you are really sorry but you just can't
    take his call,
Pass the phone to your teenage brother who's refining
    his techniques
Of playing "Feelings" on his armpits and slapping on his
    cheeks.

BRIDGE: Let your kid practice blowing his whistle
        "In the phone, son, have a ball."
        Let your dog obey the command, "speak,
          speak"
        and take over the call.

When he's finished with his spiel, say, *"Je ne parle pas
    Anglais"*
Or "My sumo-wrestler husband's in the biz, and you're
    just in his way"
Or tell him you're so glad he called, you were just going
    to call him
You're running a deal on cemetery plots . . . would he
    like to get in?

Debi Smith

CHAPTER 6

The Queen

Tonight, here in my house, I am the Queen. It's Saturday night and I will not be putting on makeup. I will not be worrying about what to wear. I will not be holding in my stomach for three hours while I stand holding a drink I don't even want.

Tonight I will stay home, watch movies and make brownies. I will have a Queenly blast.

My 15-year-old daughter EJ is in the basement with her gal pals. They are dancing obscenely to music, they are watching videos while dipping double-stuffed Oreos into questionable milk. They are leaving me alone with my TV and my brownies. They know better than to disturb the Queen.

Oh, sure, they come up to ask if they can use the phone. I nod. They curtsy and back away out of my regal living room. One of EJ's little friends nervously enters my space, holding an empty roll of toilet paper. She is too petrified to speak. I glance over. She waves what appears to be a white flag. It was the end of the roll, void (pardon the pun) of paper, just a small white flowing remnant. My daughter's guest shyly asks for assistance. I look down my nose, "Ask EJ, honey. She'll get it for you." Am I cruel to my subjects? I think not.

During the week I slave over raising EJ (Princess Dirty-Room), but come Saturday night, I take to the couch with an entire pan of brownies and Lipton's Gentle Orange Tea. Saturday nights I am Queen Couldn't-Care-Less. I give lazy a whole new meaning. I take selfish to new heights. All week, I'm Earth Mother Fantastic. I'm kind and loving, patient and serene, forgiving and thoughtful. But come a Saturday night that I'm not driving and hauling teenagers, I'm the All Mighty Queen. You got that?

All the loyal subjects in the land (my house) know that we Queen Mothers are entitled to a night off now and then. Sure, occasionally there's a case of sick kid, the interruption of a frightened child's bad dream, or someone begging to be retrieved from a slumber party. Still, we try for that perfect evening of decadent self-centered isolation, a royal rest. Hey, somebody get the phone! I'm off the clock.

Should the Queen snag a good Saturday night, it will be good for one and all. Sundays are lovely after a good Saturday night reign. There's no topping such a self-indulgent Queenly event. Spirits are lifted across the land. Waffles appear for Sunday brunch. Young Princess Dirty-Room is allowed to sleep well into the afternoon. When she wakes, the Princess is confused and skeptical. The Queen is gracious. Sincerity is running high. Princess Dirty-Room finds this a good time to tell her mother, Queen Still-Couldn't-Care-Less, that she has two term papers and an oatmeal map of Australia due the next day. All is calm. All is well.

Long live the Queen's Saturday night!

Sally Fingerett

Matinee Idol

Martha Gradisher

Temporary Song

I'm a temporary worker with a temporary job
And my temporary income isn't much.
But I'm happy for the moment in a temporary
    way
And for temporary reasons
That's enough.

I've got temporary colleagues and a temporary
    desk
And temporary duties to fulfill.
My superior she greets me with a temporary
    smile
'Cause I only have a temporary skill.

      There's nothing wrong with nine to five,
      It's just a way to stay alive.

I'm a temporary worker with a temporary job
And my temporary money's always spent.
But I'm happy for the moment in a temporary
    way
'Cause my temporary income
Pays my
Temporary
Rent.

Julie Gold

Tempests in a Tutu

B efore we get any further into hurricane season, someone
must speak out. I guess it will be me.

Hurricane names have got to be changed. Hurricanes are
huge, frightening, powerful storms, and the benign names the
U.S. Weather Bureau gives them are not only unsuitable, they
are unintentionally hurtful. My friend Andrew in Seattle still
winces when someone talks about the damage done by Andrew in Florida. Do you think anyone in North Carolina is
going to name a baby Dennis? Or Floyd?

It's time to STOP giving hurricanes nice human names.
They are not human. They are not nice. And yes, though this
next statement is politically incorrect, we must STOP giving
hurricanes male names. Hurricanes are female. Everyone
knows this.

If you take a picture of a hurricane from space it looks like
a giant, girly, swirling skirt gracefully dancing to and fro, capri-
cious in its nature, fickle when it comes to making landfall. If
you take a picture of a female ballet dancer from above, she
looks exactly the same.

Tornadoes, twisters—now they are male. Look at their
shape and construction, how quickly they appear; how quickly
they disappear—too quick to even get assigned a name. If
men want meteorological events named after them, let them
become storm chasers. Let us have our hurricanes back. After
all, it is HURricanes, not HIMacanes—didn't anyone notice
this?

I've thought up some new hurricane names that should
last us for the next three years. Here they are: scary, threaten-
ing, female, and giving hurricanes the kind of respect they
deserve:

Scary Hurricane Names for the Next Three Years

Agoneen	Jerkeen	Squasha
Aggravatia	Jackassally	Spoilisha
Anxieteeny	JudgeJudy	Scabretta
Blusteria	Kaboomboom	Tumora
Bloodeen	Kickboxia	Tuberculossa
Boiletta	Killjoyce	Thundrine
Catastrofifi	Legalisa	Undertowanda
Cadavra	Lawsuitia	Uglette
Cantankeruth	Lymphomally	Ulcerina
Demolisha	Malevolencia	Vomitrina
Deathretta	Mothra	Vandalina
Damnatia	Manslaughteria	Vagrantina
Explosia	Nastique	Worryanna
Exterminatia	Nooseen	Witchallah
Eczemally	Neuralgina	Wrathina
Frantique	Oucha	Xenophobette
Fatalia	Overbearinga	Xenaprincesswarria
Frighteneesha	Ogrette	Xfileen
Gargantuette	Punisha	Yodelilith
Gutsia	Palimonia	Yelpa
Guillotina	Pugnacia	Ytookay
Horriblette	Quarreleen	Zombibi
Hurtia	Quagmyra	Zythromaxim
Headachida	Queazinca	Zirconia
Ignoramissy	Revoltia	
Invincibleen	Rambunctia	
Insania	Riptideia	

Pick any name above, insert the word "Hurricane" before it, then say it out loud. Now these names telegraph the awful frightening power of deadly storms. Would anyone in North Carolina have sat complacently by and waited for Hurricane Damnatia? I think not.

I know a few of the names, though, have you perplexed. "Zythromaxim?" you are asking yourself, "a hurricane named for an antibiotic?"

Yes. Devastating storms often leave death and disease in their wake. Antibiotics are just what the doctor will order, but why wait for the aftermath when the drug companies can use the actual hurricane itself to promote its product? Every time the major networks report on the storm, it's money in the bank for shareholders.

"Hurricane Zirconia?" Yes. It will be sponsored by The Home Shopping Club! It's much too dangerous to leave the house! What better way to while away the hours indoors than shopping?

"Mothra" has you puzzled, but consider this: *Mothra* was one of the worst sci-fi films ever made. In the film, Mothra was a gigantic moth and its beating wings created such a cataclysmic wind that it destroyed building after building after building. The American Movie Classics or Turner Classic Movies channel could sponsor this hurricane; broadcasting *Mothra* at the same time the actual hurricane is carving its path of destruction. The giant film insect creates way more havoc than the actual real-life storm could ever do. In contrast, victims of Hurricane Mothra will feel grateful (assuming their cable TV hasn't been knocked out by the storm).

The corporate tie-ins will be plentiful, as will the snappy copy the local weather reporters will jump on: "Hurricane Punisha is living up to her name, punishing the Florida coast with gale force winds today, Taffy," is just one example. Another plus will be that no one out there gets their feelings hurt, unless by some unbelievable coincidence they happen to be named Damnatia or Uglette, but what are the odds of that?

In three years more scary hurricane names will be needed, and by then there can be a national contest in place: schoolchildren can create names, giving teachers a unique opportunity to combine language and science skills. I can even help them get started.

How does Hurricane Apocalypsa sound? I'm sure the bottled water and battery industry will love it.

Christine Lavin

Wicked Woman

I cross at the green and not in between
I don't tear the tags off my pillow.
I pay bills on time. I save every dime
And I won't shoot a rare armadillo.
From this one would think that I stand on the
　　brink
Of sainthood, but I must confide
My halo is starting to slide.

I want to be a wicked woman who plays her wicked
　　games,
Who sends cold-hearted heroes crashing into flames.
With a sultry look that smolders, and luscious lips
　　that burn,
One shrug of my shoulders is his point of no return.

I want to be a wicked woman, without a single
　　nerve.
Wear clothes that cling and linger round my every
　　wicked curve.
Make an entrance no one misses, make an exit—no
　　one moves.
I want a rotten reputation everybody disapproves.

A vixen or a gangster's moll,
A vamp, a tramp, a femme fatale.
I want to be a wicked woman, whom the neighbors all
　　deplore.
They would cry: Evict this woman! She is *not* the girl
　　next door.
I'd ignore my would-be jailors and just sing my siren
　　song
And lure a lot of sailors to the gal who'll do them
　　wrong.

I want dramatic hair so long that as it slithers past my
   cheek,
Its touch would make a weak man strong, and turn a
   strong man weak.
I'd always waken their desires and kiss them till they
   moan
Then laugh my Garbo laugh and say, "I vant to be alone.
   Hah!"

I would be a wicked woman, if I only *only* could
But I'm cursed with this insatiable compulsion to be
   good!
I do not want salvation, no—I pray for the reverse.
Being wicked may be wicked, but being *nice*—is worse!

Francesca Blumenthal

Non-Bridaled Passion

Non-Bridaled Passion

SCENE: *The bridal registry of a major department store. In the background we hear Elevator Chimes, Cash Registers, and Soft Muzak.*

ENTER: *A WOMAN in her thirties. She approaches the BRIDAL REGISTRY CONSULTANT, posted behind the counter.*

WOMAN: Excuse me, are you the registry consultant? Well I'm here to register. For gifts! This is a really big step for me; I'm very excited! I'll bet you hear that a lot, don't you?. . . When is the happy event? . . . Oh, you mean the *wedding* date. There isn't one. I'm not getting married. I'll probably never get married. But I need things, and I think registering is a good way for me to learn to receive. . . . Yes, I know this is the *bridal* registry and that you only register *brides*. Frankly I find that a bit discriminatory. I'm here to register and I really don't want any hassle. No, don't get the manager. I am not trying to cause trouble. Look, for months now I've been buying gifts for all of my friends who've been getting married. It's an epidemic. There's been a slew of weddings, not to mention showers, lately, and I've attended all of them, brought gifts to every event. It's not that I begrudge them their happiness—not at all—I'm a very supportive person. It's just that lately I've been feeling that something's a little out of whack, you know, sort of off-balance, and yesterday, while I was attaching tiny silver bells to a spice rack for my friends, Howie and Wendy, this voice inside my head started screaming at me. It said, "Schmuck. Why do you keep buying presents for people who have already found everything they want?" Or words to that effect. I don't remember exactly. I do recall that the voice sounded resentful. And I had to agree with it. I mean, isn't it enough that they were lucky and found each other? That they fell in love and made a commitment? That they'll be splitting the rent and filing jointly? My God, they've found someone who'll give them a *foot massage* whenever they want! They've already won the sweepstakes, why do they get the door prizes, too? Why do they get to register for things like . . . like . . . like a cookie jar shaped like a giant eggplant, or a set of "really good knives"? THEY'RE BECOMING A TWO-INCOME FAMILY, FOR CHRISTSAKE, WHY CAN'T THEY BUY THEIR OWN KNIVES???!!! Now, then. I need things. I am not getting married and I need things. I need better towels. Matching luggage. A pasta machine. And sterling silver candlesticks! Since I was five years old, my grandmother promised me hers the day I got married. Well, I didn't get married and last month they went to my cousin Marcy, who did. Why? Why do you only get family heirlooms if you wed? It's no damn fair. Candlesticks! Put me down for two pairs! Come on, just do it! You registered Ann and Deena, Lisa, Jane, and Cindy, I insist on registering too! . . . I know I'm single; I confront that fact every day of my life. It's fine! I accept it! But I'm not staying single without the same material goods as my married friends. My ship is coming in if I have to tow it myself! . . . Do you really want to know when the happy event is? It's a week from Saturday. I'm throwing a shower for myself, officially announcing a life of singlehood. And the beauty of it is, I won't have to return anything if it doesn't work out!

Kate Shein

85 Things Every Young Woman Should Know

A Guide to Getting a Grip

10 essential elements for a grown-up home:

- ◆ A bed lifted more than six inches off the ground.
- ◆ Enough wine glasses.
- ◆ Some evidence of personal style.
- ◆ A dictionary.
- ◆ An answering machine with a no-gimmick, no-music, no-mystery message.
- ◆ Enough toilet paper for tonight and tomorrow morning.
- ◆ A box of condoms.
- ◆ A toolbox.
- ◆ A casually displayed photograph of you looking your absolute best.
- ◆ A refrigerator whose contents do not require carbon dating.

5 signs it's a good day to go shopping:

- ◆ You aren't pre- or currently menstrual.
- ◆ You didn't fall in love last night and wake up convinced there's a romantic resort hotel in your near future.
- ◆ Debtors Anonymous hasn't advised you to cut up your credit cards.
- ◆ You have it on good authority that baby-doll dresses are definitely, finally, *out.*
- ◆ Your mom will not be coming along with you after all.

3 good-enough reasons to stay home on a Friday night:

- You're beat.
- You're cranky.
- You're in love.

4 ways to get a strange man to stop staring at you:

- Pick your nose.
- Bellow across the room, "Not getting any at home?"
- Nudge the person next to you and point.
- Remove the can of pepper spray from your purse and read the instructions aloud.

5 items to hide under the sink the first night he stays over:

- Mustache bleach.
- Bag Balm.
- Your retainer.
- Another man's razor.
- Prozac.

7 skills more useful than a Swiss army knife:

- CPR.
- How to knot a man's tie.
- How to measure for window shades.
- The basics of erotic massage.
- How to write a résumé that wildly exaggerates your gifts and achievements but never crosses the line into dishonesty.
- How to gracefully pick up the check.
- How to determine the relevance of the leggy blonde he just introduced to you without asking, "Who *is* she?"

4 numbers to know by heart:

- Your target heart rate.
- The percentage of your income that belongs to the IRS.

- The proper tip for the person who cuts your hair.
- Your own personal red zone for credit card debt.

6 reasonable expectations of someone else's wedding:

- Consecutive and sometimes overlapping rushes of happiness and sadness.
- A drunken man who gropes.
- At least one bridesmaid's ugly-dress-rebellion story.
- The opportunity to exercise your acute taste and dazzling judgment as a social critic.
- Poached salmon with that mysterious green sauce.
- A lengthy rendition of "The Wind Beneath My Wings."

1 unreasonable expectation:

- That the man you are destined to marry will appear and ask you to dance.

5 signs you're ready to fall in love again:

- You can't remember what you were wearing the night you broke up.
- *Dr. Quinn, Medicine Woman* just isn't the same anymore.
- You graduated from the Heartbreak Weight Loss Plan.
- You flirted right back.
- You finally found time to get your bikini line waxed.

5 things he thinks you don't know about him:

- Come-from-behind sports movies make him cry.
- Some of the things in the Victoria's Secret catalog scare him.
- He likes to read your *Glamour* when you're not home.
- Half the time when he says "What?" he knows exactly what you just said.
- He sleeps curled up around your pillow when you're out of town.

5 things that aren't worth their consequences:

- Extra mayonnaise.
- Telling off your boss.
- Unprotected sex.
- A deep, dark tan.
- Three-inch heels.

3 things that are:

- A stunningly gorgeous man.
- Coming clean.
- Birthday cake.

4 experiences that will strengthen your character:

- Getting audited.
- Getting fired.
- Waitressing.
- Vacationing with your three best friends.

5 overrated experiences:

- Sex in an airplane bathroom.
- Being the bride.
- Dating a very rich man.
- Shopping in Paris.
- Being the boss.

7 cures for what ails you:

- Two aspirin and as much water as you can drink.
- Black leggings and an oversized sweater.
- *Mary Tyler Moore* reruns.
- Calling home, collect.
- A tape of all the Brad Pitt scenes from *Thelma and Louise.*
- Anything caffeinated.
- A good cry in the ladies' room.

6 delusions to disabuse yourself of:

- "He'll change."
- "Just once can't hurt."
- "Oh, I don't need to have an orgasm every time."
- "Someday my prince will come."
- "Any fool could sell a screenplay."
- "I'll never make it in the real world."

Lesley Dormen

Decidophobia

I hate to make decisions. I've always hated to make decisions. I used to hyperventilate in our doorway when my mother said "in or out, in or out." And though analysts have tried to pin my decidophobia on two failed marriages and the trauma of having my first sexual experience in an Edsel, I'm pretty sure it all started with crayons.

When I was a kid I liked the box with only seven crayons. There was one brown, one green, one red, and anytime I wanted to color a tree it was a straightforward affair—brown bark, green leaves, red apples, no sweat. Then one afternoon my mother brought home that steroidal box of sixty-four crayons: the CRAYOLA colossus!

For many, this unabridged assortment of colors remains a cornerstone of childhood delight; for me, it reigns in memory as a gift from hell.

Staid colorer of trees that I was (what sunflowers were for Van Gogh, Norwegian pines were for me), I remember innocently opening the flip-up lid to look for my reliable dendrological shades only to find a Pandora's box of verdant choices, a Glocca Morra of green—lime, moss, shamrock, emerald, pea, avocado, olive (there might even have been a *fungus* green); in effect, enough greens to make even St. Patrick queasy and more than enough to set me up for the first of many forays into decision-anxiety.

No matter what shade of green I chose to top off a tree or bush there would inevitably be some friend who'd look at it and say, "Leaves aren't *that* color!" The implication clear as a slap: I had made the wrong choice, a bad decision—I had failed!

If my phobic dislike for decisions wasn't born then, it was certainly borne out when I made the transition from girlhood to womanhood. At that life juncture, I thought the only choice I had to make was between a pad and a tampon, right?

I couldn't have been more wrong if I had boiled sushi.

Suddenly I was faced with decisions that made Solomon's seem like choosing between vanilla and chocolate. Was it a "light day" or was it a "heavy day?" Did I want a regular or a super? A maxi or a mini? Looking back, though, those were the good old days; the choices escalated with each passing year. Periods were becoming profitable. A multibillion-dollar industry was soon thriving between women's legs by leaps and bounds and turning a simple shopping task into a mind-numbing nightmare! Today, I consider PMS a dawdle compared to outfitting myself for the main event.

Aisles in the supermarket literally tower with feminine hygiene products, and every month I find myself more and more in doubt about which is the right one for me! Do I want a slim maxi? A *thin* maxi? An ultra-thin maxi? A super-long, ultra-thin maxi? An extra-absorbent, super-long, ultra-thin maxi with *wings?* Straight, curved, or wraparound? An all-nighter! How about a weekender? I'm ready to just hitch up a mattress once a month and let it go at that! I know all women aren't created equal—but how different can we be?

Not all *that* different. Oh, sure, some of us might love too much or work too much or eat too much, but all of us are pretty much alike when it comes to sex chromosomes and preferring partners who bathe—which is why I think that, for the most part, distaste for decisions is a female thing.

Admittedly, it's an acquired distaste, but it's easy to understand why so many of us acquire it. Men make decisions easily; not correctly, necessarily, but easily. (Hey, it wasn't a woman who came up with "New Coke"!) For instance, a man will buy a dress shirt that is pinned and wrapped—totally sealed in cellophane, with only color, collar, and cuffs showing—and never give a second thought to doing it. For a woman, this is an unthinkable act, tantamount to meeting the ex-husband's new wife without makeup. A woman wouldn't buy herself an expensive blouse without trying it on. At least once! And, even then, chances are she'll still wonder if she's made the right choice when she gets home. Second thoughts are our genetic onus.

Women have to make more decisions in a single day than most men make in a month! Guys can go on date after date without ever having to consider whether they should wear a skirt or slacks, heels or flats, fake it or forget it. And then there are meals. In most instances, a woman has to decide not only what to cook for dinner (including what to serve before and after it) but what to wear for dinner, as well as what to wear *with* whatever it is she's wearing for dinner. This is known as accessory angst and is definitely a distaff difficulty; definitely, because women innately know that choosing the right accessories for an outfit is as important as the outfit itself, although deciding which accessories are "right" can often be more time consuming that choosing an outfit and preparing a meal combined! And dining out is no easier, not for women.

Men make reservations without reservation, at least with other men. ("Hi, Stan. How about Mexican tonight? Casa Rosa, seven o'clock." "Sounds great, Hal. See you at seven.") When a woman is involved it's a different story. And when more than one woman is involved, it's an ordeal in gustatory accommodation that can kill your appetite, like *that!*

Eight words that unfailingly put me in anxiety mode are: "What are you in the mood for tonight?" I have yet to have dinner with a female friend without this query surfacing like the dorsal fin of a Great White, creating an equivalent acceleration in heart rate. My usual response is, "I don't care, anything is okay," which is, of course, (a) untrue, (b) unsafe, and (c) unacceptable as an answer. What follows is a grilling that I wouldn't wish on a war criminal. It goes something like this:

"So, do you want to have Chinese?"

"That's fine," I say. (But is it?)

"Or how about Italian?"

"That's okay, too." (I think.)

"Do you like Mexican?"

"Sure." (I'm not sure at all.)

"Wait, what about sushi?"

"Sushi's good." (Maybe, maybe not.)

"How do you feel about Greek food?"

"Love it," I lie. (Or do I?)

"We haven't had Indian in a long time."

"Then let's." (Then again, let's not and say we did.)

"But you'd probably prefer French, right?"

"Right, French." (At this point, I'd prefer never having agreed to dinner in the first place).

"But it's so rich. What do you say to Spanish?"

"*Sí*," I say, hoping to truncate the volley before arrhythmia kicks in. "*Sí*, Spanish!"

And then, just when I think the inquisition is over, I'll hear: "So, do you want to go to that cute little cantina in the village or the place my sister told me about on the West Side? Or there's this new restaurant that the *Times* gave four stars . . . ?"

Generally, I make it a point to steer clear of Chinese restaurants and Greek diners; eateries that offer a choice of more than fifty entrees could seriously compromise my mental health. It's difficult enough for me to make decisions in restaurants, period. I'm always the last at the table to order, and, when I finally do, my sigh of relief is invariably premature. Just when I think that I've aced it, the waiter will ask if I want potato, pasta, or rice? If I say "potato," I'm suddenly on the spot again: "Baked, French fried, home style, or *au gratin?*" Then there's the salad dressing gauntlet: "French, Italian, Blue Cheese, Vinaigrette, or House?" I never even look at the wine list; it's enough that I make the choice between red and white without palpitations.

I'm all for options, but when they increase pyramidally on a daily basis, it's scary. I remember when choices at the conclusion of a meal—and standard offering on airlines—were coffee, tea, or milk. Now if you say "coffee," you have to, at the very least, specify regular or decaf. And if you're offered a selection of flavored blends, decidophobia can really start percolating. Where once there was merely the alternative mocha, today there's mocha-vanilla, mocha-almond, mocha-marshmallow, among mucho-mocha others. Say "tea" and you leave yourself open to facing the option of herbal brews, which come in a conundrum of combinations, none of which nature ever intended. Not even milk is just drinker-friendly "moo juice" anymore, not with choices of one percent, two percent, skim, soy, whole, long life, low-fat, no-fat, fat-free, to say nothing of chocolate and cherry-vanilla. All I have to do is look in the dairy case and I find myself craving a beer—a craving, needless to say, that disappears instantly when I reach that aisle!

The more things are supposed to simplify life, the more they complicate it. I remember when there was only one telephone company and I could make a call without thinking twice about whether or not the person I was phoning was in or out of my circle of friends. I've changed phone services more times than Liz Taylor has changed husbands, and, like Liz, I'm still not certain that I've made the right choice.

Packing for a trip, even a longed-for holiday, is a stress test for me. It doesn't matter whether it's three days or three weeks, deciding what—and what not—to take makes me feel as if I'm deciding the fate of a nation (or, at least, a vacation). I run every item through a scenario of permutations. (Hmmm. Evening dress. Okay, we will be whitewater rafting most of the time, but if we stop somewhere I *might* need it. I mean, you never know. I'd probably better pack a pair of heels, a couple of pairs of pantyhose, earrings, clutch bag, the beaded sweater, maybe my trench coat in case it rains . . .) And when it comes to first-aid equipment, I'm a traveling triage unit. All I have to do is say to myself, "You never know," and the whole medicine cabinet comes with me. My husband has often questioned the tourniquet, mustard plaster, and emetics—particularly when I'm just going to L.A. on a business trip—but it's less of an emotional strain to schlep them than to decide against them.

Some of my worst moments come at nail salons. The pressure of choosing a single polish from the enormous collocation of colors—in the space of an appointment—is enough to give me the bends (to say nothing of raising the specter of that old CRAYOLA colossus). In fact, it's endurable only because the alternative would be to select one polish for use on a permanent basis, a radical decisive move that I am not yet ready to make.

But I have decided (sort of) that I can keep my decidophobia at bay by cultivating a decidophobia-phobia, a fear-of-the-fear of making decisions, creating confidence by default.

This isn't easy, but then neither was learning the lyrics to "In-a-Gadda-da-Vida." Meanwhile, as I wait for the phobia-phobia to kick in, I don't even glance at multiple-choice quizzes in magazines; I avoid cineplexes: I restrict eye exams to when everything I read looks as if it's printed in Russian; I never ask for the remote control; I shun salad bars; I evade all either-or situations. And, of course, I keep myself as far away as possible from crayons.

Hester Mundis

Mood Swings

Mom thinks mood swings come from too much caffeine, but I am pretty sure mine come from life.

The man on TV said that humankind is over 3 point 7 million years old. When I think of all I have gone through in my short life, frankly, I do not know how humankind has stood it—just think, all those billions and billions of mood swings.

Jane Wagner

One Cranky Customer

Paige Braddock

Life 102

A book called *Life 101: Everything We Wish We Had Learned About Life in School—but Didn't* made the bestseller lists a while ago. Having read it, I think that much of its appeal was the enticing title, because it seems to me that the authors ignored a lot of the stuff I wish I had learned from someone. Thus my motivation for writing the following tips. These are lessons it has taken me a lifetime to learn.

Being a Woman

Finding "the makeup shade that's just right for your skin tone!" or "the haircut that's perfect for your face shape" or even learning all "ten terrific new ways to tighten your tummy" will still not help you look even a little bit more like the girls in the diet-cola ads. This is because the girls in the diet-cola ads are often *13 years old*. Even *they* are not going to look like the girls in the diet-cola ads in a couple of months. And so the only way to deal with your female vanity in our society is to remember this important truth: *Mirrors lie. You are much better looking than that in 3-D.*

Men

Men are completely nuts. Women can't understand their behavior because men themselves have no clue as to what they are doing or why. However, there is one incredibly important thing to watch for in the early stages of getting to know a man that will give you all the real information you will need. Men almost always feel compelled to announce their personal deficiencies. The mistake that women make is *we don't believe them.* Learning to listen for a man's usually accurate self-assessment can save a woman a great deal of time and guesswork. If a man tells you that he is a jerk and he doesn't think he is ready to make a real commitment, *believe him.* Spending a couple of months with you is not going to be the magical catalyst that will change him. And he almost definitely is not going to go into therapy. Men, as a general rule, shy away from therapy because there is no obvious way to keep score. Other danger signals are:

Excessive charm.   Men who have a lot of charm have it in place of something real that you are eventually going to want from them and find that they do not have. It is wise to remember that quite a few of our recent mass murderers have been cute guys. Somewhere, some stupid woman probably called up her friend and said, "Ted Bundy hasn't called me in two days. Do you think *I* should call *him?*"

Fast walking.   I don't mean fast walking. I mean walking half a block ahead of you, no matter how fast you walk, and never slowing down to accommodate you. An informal poll I have been taking for quite a number of years has convinced me that these fast-walking guys also have terrible tempers and commitment problems. If you don't believe me, ask a friend of yours who is seeing someone with a terrible temper and a history of cheating whether or not her man walks half a block ahead of her and prepare to be amazed.

Dating

Because of what we learned earlier about the essential nature of the universe, it only stands to reason that the more you prepare for a date, the more disappointing the date will turn out to be. In fact, the surest way to make a date cancel or disappear entirely is to go out and buy yourself some sexy, expensive new underwear. And while we're on the topic, it is wise to remember that although many of those underwear get-ups look fetching on the models in the catalog, most of them have the potential to make an otherwise fit and attractive female human suddenly turn into someone who looks like one of the dancing ballerina hippos from *Fantasia*.

One last bit of warning: there is a definite correlation between a man's gift giving and the longevity of the relationship. The more impressive the quantity and quality of gift items early on, the less impressive the chances for the future of the relationship. It's like the guys with the charm. Men who supplement early dating with a lot of swell gifts and prizes are generally distracting you from the stuff they are never going to give you.

Eating

There are four basic food groups: salad, hors d'oeuvres, pasta, and diet drinks. It is appropriate to eat from two of these groups per meal. If you are the sort of person who always thinks she needs to go on a diet, realize this: *everything will always make you fat for the rest of your life.* This is especially true if you live with someone who never gains weight. It is due to a little-known phenomenon called Secondary-Weight Gain, which operates in the same manner as Secondary-Smoke Inhalation. In other words, calories are calories and they have to go somewhere—meaning that *you* will somehow assimilate and convert into fat all the calories that are going unassimilated by perpetually thin people. You get your calories and their calories, thus causing you to mysteriously gain weight even when you eat only carrots.

Merrill Markoe

Trudy the Bag Lady

See, the human mind is kind of like . . .
a piñata. When it breaks open,
there's a lot of surprises inside. Once you get the
   piñata
perspective, you see that losing your mind
can be a peak experience.
I was not always a bag lady, you know.
I used to be a designer and creative consultant.
For big companies!
Who do you think thought up the color scheme
for Howard Johnson's?
At the time, nobody was using
orange and aqua in the same room together.
With fried clams.
Laugh tracks:
I gave TV sitcoms the idea for canned laughter.
I got the idea, one day I heard voices
and no one was there.
Who do you think had the idea to package panty
   hose
in a plastic goose egg?

Jane Wagner

Over My Dead Wet Body

This reporter never thought she would refer to herself as "this reporter." But this reporter has noticed that others writing columns go by that name. And peer pressure is the operative force on this reporter.

This reporter is upstairs in the house she lives in, quiet as a mouse, waiting for the two men who have offices downstairs to go home.

This reporter has come to realize how tedious the "this reporter" gimmick can be.

As I wait for the men downstairs to leave for the day, I indulge in one of my favorite activities: browsing through annual reports from King's College, Cambridge, where I went to graduate school. The reports contain lengthy obituaries of college members who died that year. The obituaries are usually quirky and catty, even by the petty standards of the English. To illustrate the point, a few excerpts:

"He was very tall (hence the stooping head), dark, with pronounced features, vaguely dinosaurian."

"Already . . . markedly fat, he showed an abundance of the geniality associated with fatness."

" . . . [He] was born on 19 May, 1931, and educated at Berkhamsted school where he was remembered for jumping through a window in a blue smock as St. Joan."

"Both his parents were doctors and Eric read natural science and medicine, perhaps more to act out parental assumptions than to fulfill a natural inclination. . . . Failed examinations came to his rescue and he left King's without a degree, but with friendships, some of them lifelong, originating in the Boat Club and other social activities."

"He was also much teased over his apparent reluctance to relate to women."

"He had become devoted to the College and it sometimes seemed that his membership of it had freed him from a long-standing feeling of insecurity, grounded perhaps in his Jewish origins and early difficulty in education and in choosing a career."

CHAPTER 7

Rereading these obituaries put me in mind of my one brush with death, which took place five floors below, when, one day, years before the two men worked downstairs, I stepped into the elevator and heard water dripping down below. Actually, it sounded more like the Hoover Dam breaking than water dripping. And so (like an idiot), I pressed the button to the basement, expecting to investigate.

When the elevator reached the basement, it did not stop. It descended about six inches farther before coming to an abrupt halt. There was a loud humming sound. As filthy water infused with cigarette butts and cockroaches rushed into the elevator, I tried without success to open the elevator or make it move.

Luckily, there was a phone in the elevator. I called the police and talked to someone whose interest in my plight dropped markedly once she learned there was no assailant with me in the elevator. She promised to send someone over, anyway.

By the time I had hung up with the police, the water had leveled off at my thighs. Vanity set in. Or was it cheapness? I thought: "I can't believe I wore my new Emma Hope shoes that weren't even on sale!"

I called a friend who had keys to my house. He came over immediately, and informed me that the elevator ceiling was probably detachable. I maneuvered myself to the top of the elevator, as much to get out of the bilge as to assess the damage to my shoes. I flipped off the ceiling board and shimmied up the greasy wires, praying that the elevator would not remember that I had, only minutes before, frantically pushed every button. Electrocution was a concern, but at least I would become dry. I reached the first floor. The door was locked. (I had not yet seen *Die Hard,* so I did not know that there is a lever that unlocks the door.)

I settled back into the muck. Eventually, the police showed up. My friend pointed them in the direction of the basement. After pulling on the door for a few minutes, one of the police yelled to me, "The door's stuck!" The other added, "And the elevator won't move!"

They called the emergency squad. While we waited, I listened to the police chat gaily with my friend. I felt left out and, frankly, resentful. The mood, I thought, should have been more funereal. I decided to make some phone calls and ended up leaving several messages on machines, all variations of "Guess where I am?" My friend told me later that the police, who did not realize there was a phone in the elevator, heard me babbling and thought I had lost my mind. Finally, the emergency squad arrived.

The next day, a plumber drained six feet of water from the elevator shaft. The elevator has never been fixed. The melodramatic hand prints left when I clawed my way to the top of the elevator are still vivid. The flood seems to have been the result of a water main break caused by Con Edison, which must have a training site on the street outside my house, given how much time they spend digging holes out there.

"You were lucky the elevator stopped where it did," the plumber told me. I'll say. The King's College Annual Report might have read:

> "Suffering from delusions of grandeur, she sometimes called herself 'this alumna,' and lived far beyond her means in a large house. In fact, she was probably the poorest person in New York to have a room exclusively for her shoes. She led us to believe she was on her way up, but a police report revealed that she died on her way down."

Patricia Marx

Just Say "Purl"

E very so often, I get what my mother calls "a bug up my ass"
about something. Take what happened when I learned
how to knit last fall. It started innocently enough. I was restless.
I was frustrated. I wasn't having sex, and I had to do something
with my hands (even masturbation gets old after a while). I figured I needed a hobby, so I enrolled in one of those Learning
Annex classes where you learn everything you'll ever need to
know in four sessions for about forty dollars. Sounds harmless
enough, right? Absolutely *wrong*.

The first class was relatively uneventful. We chose our
yarn, we got our needles, we made cute little swatches. Then,
in the second class, our instructor Brenda—a woman so calm
she makes Buddha look like a jumpy neurotic—handed out the
pattern for our first project, a sleeveless sweater top. I cast on
my ninety stitches in a desultory fashion and started to knit.
Suddenly, I realized this thing was growing. I swear I'd never
seen anything like it in my life. I was gone. I was possessed.
Working, dating, breathing, eating—nothing, repeat, *nothing*,
was as important as creating another teal-blue inch of sweater.

Knitting also turned out to be the perfect hobby for a compulsive shopper like me. There are so many wonderful little
doodads you need: row counters, stitch holders, cable needles,
swatch gauges, and on and on. Ecstatically, I swooped into yarn
stores and bought everything I could lay my hands on. Store
owners broke out party horns when they saw me coming.

My mother was the first to notice the telltale signs. The
poor woman already suffers from latent hysteria because I'm
thirty-something and there's not a potential husband in sight.
When she called on Saturday night and found me home happily knitting away, she really began to panic. "You're, um . . .
you're not giving up your social life to knit, are you?" she'd
ask, desperately trying to sound casual. "Of course not,
Mother," I'd lie, guiltily remembering the party at Tavern on
the Green I'd skipped because I wanted to finish my armholes.

But mothers know everything, and when mine started referring to me as "my daughter, the knitting spinster," I recklessly decided to show her that I had my habit under control. So I went out on a date.

Mike was a perfectly nice guy. A stockbroker with a co-op, he might even be called a catch. We went to a movie, where I busied myself trying to figure out the cable patterns on the sweaters of fellow audience members. At dinner after the movie, Mike told me what he was up to, and I pretended to listen. "Uh-huh," I nodded, wondering how many extra stitches I'd have to cast on to make a double moss Aran panel in a medium-weight cotton.

"So what's going on in your life," he asked, finally snapping me out of my reverie. "Oh," I said, trying to clear my brain. "Well . . . I've been asked to write a book, and I have two plays being published, and I just interviewed Shirley MacLaine, Geraldine Ferraro, and Ivana Trump all on the same day, but the *big* news is I've learned how to knit. Let me tell you about it . . ."

Several hours later, as a bleary-eyed Mike knocked back another scotch, I wound up my saga. Sadly, he didn't know a doctor who could cure me of my wool allergy, thus enabling me to knit in something besides cotton (no self-respecting knitter *ever* uses acrylic), so I didn't see much point in continuing the relationship. Oddly enough, Mike seemed to feel the same way. When I called him the next day to get his feedback on a men's sweater pattern, he muttered something about having to wash his hair and hung up so quickly my telephone rang back.

Things rapidly went downhill from there. On New Year's Eve, I was dying to stay home and start a new sweater, but my roommate talked me into going out. I knit on the subway as I traveled from one party to another. Stumped by a rib stitch pattern I was working on, I cornered revelers at each affair, sticking my swatch under their noses and demanding their opinions. I perfunctorily joined the New Year countdown, then beat a faster retreat than Cinderella when she fled from the ball. Home at long last, I breathed a sigh of relief and ushered in the New Year with four inches of ribbing.

I was fast reaching the point where a month at the Betty Ford Clinic weaning myself from my knitting needles seemed a real possibility. Then I tried on my sweater. Unfortunately, it turned out that I'd accidentally cast on eighty stitches instead of ninety, and the top fit like a slightly loose tourniquet. Staring at myself in the mirror glumly, I began mentally adding the costs involved in achieving this fashion disaster. There was the price of the course, the forty dollars I'd spent on yarn, the umpteen dollars I'd spent on various knitting accessories. Winding up my calculations, I realized that it had cost me about $150 to make a sweater I wouldn't have paid twenty bucks for in a store.

That cold blast of reality quickly helped break my knitting addiction. But have I given up the habit? Hardly. I just bought some great red yarn and a huge kit of needles. At the end of the day, my roommate usually finds me sitting in the old rocker, shawl over my shoulders, granny glasses atop my nose, knitting and purling to my heart's content. I've spent hours in therapy warding off the fear that I would eventually turn into my mother. Whoever thought that I'd actually turn into my *grandmother?!*

Ellen Byron

Remote Control

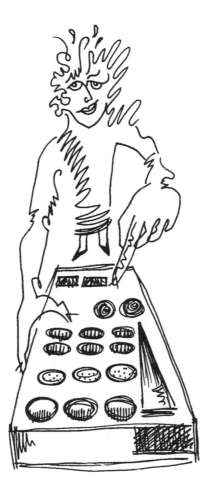

I've got a Remote for my TV
so I can see Remote broadcasts of Remote news.
I order catalog items from Remote places with my Remote
phone.
Why I've even got a boyfriend with Remote emotions.
I feel like such a modern woman.
I'm not in control . . . I'm in Remote control.

Flash Rosenberg

CHAPTER 7

Six Pretty Good Things to Do with the 90 Percent of Your Brain That You Don't Use

Que Cerebrum, Cerebrum

Since science and watching reruns of *Gidget* show us that we're only using 10 percent—imagine that!—of our brains, here are some useful and entertaining ways to get mileage out of that lazybone of yours. Pick one, or combine them as your enthusiasm dictates:

1. Time Share.   Let other people into the back of your head. After all, a little company isn't a bad thing and neighborliness is almost next to godliness. And if you time share now, you have a built-in retirement plan for when you decide to leave that part of the brain that you're in. When you advertise your time share, just remember the realtor's rule of thumb here: LOCA-TION-LOCATION-LOCATION. Your functional brain is awfully nice to be next to. You enjoy tennis, water sports, and are a fabulous Scrabble player. If that doesn't do it, promise Sony Walkmans just for visiting.

2. Add Post-It Notes.   Face it, that adhesive on those Post-it notes is going to be in our atmosphere forever. So instead of trying to recycle, use that empty 90 percent of brain up there to attach little bits of information to the big stuff you have going on in the other 10 percent. For example, your functional brain knows, "I have to take the dog out for a walk at 9:15 tomorrow morning."
   You then add to that:
   ◆ 9:15 is when that cute guy next door comes out for his morning paper
   ◆ doesn't he work?
   ◆ call Gloria who lives in 2F and see if she knows what he does for a living

♦ and be sure to pick up a half liter of soda while you're out because you want to be prepared in case he gets your bill again for the ungainly sum you promised to PBS during "The Three Tenors, Live at Disney World" and he brings it over in the afternoon.

3. Decorate. Any good interior designer will tell you this can make even an uninhabitable place livable. Of course, these are people who would sell couches to Tarzan if they had half the chance. But if chintz seems too patently busy, think space . . . think open . . . think

CHRISTO!

The empty 90 percent of your brain is THE PERFECT project for you and Christo. Not gauze . . . he's already done umbrellas . . . Why, he could Venetian blind the hell out of your head; and how symbolic, and so perfect for summer! Just imagine, a state-of-the-art *son et lumiere* (sound and light) show every evening. We hear strains of "Evita" as lights play off strategically placed blinds opening and closing, like so many petals of a flower, like so many borders in the Ukraine, like so many doors on refrigerators everywhere. Art is truly universal, and it's being created in your very own brain, not to mention the great kickbacks you'll get from selling souvenirs. And getting decorated is like buying a new outfit—it puts you in a new frame of mind which is, after all, what we're going for here.

4. Install Astroturf. The Olympics are never that far away, and why shouldn't 90 percent of your brain be the host? The biggest problem is housing facilities but, hey, you're providing the rest of it, so visiting countries can find their own lousy place to stay. Just remember to keep the opening ceremonies as simple and plebian as possible—say a few tarantellas from Aunt Ethel's Tap and Dance School, maybe even throw in some baton twirling in squirrel outfits—and the Olympics should go on without a hitch. And just think, you'll have front row seats!

5. Order Out. Have a phone installed in that cavernous brainspace and hook it up to your central nervous system.

Voila! The minute you're hungry, you've already speed-dialed an appropriate restaurant with delivery service. If you're really ready to take the plunge, you can have their itemized entrées also programmed so there's no more hemming and hawing over what to get or dealing with itinerant order takers who never really seem to know whether garlic macaroni and cheese is on the menu as an entrée or a side dish. WHO CARES? Your order is quickly taken over the fax machine, with no one to fax but fax itself.

6. Rewrite Your Favorite Books, Movies, and TV Shows. This time give yourself the starring role. You can also create fashion houses, governments, even famous family histories with you in them. It's *Mutiny on the Bounty* starring who? Why, YOU! . . . It's none other than Guess Who as Tina Turner, but it's only Tina-in-the-Good-Years (you know, post-Ike). Okay, or you could be a Kennedy in Tina Turner's body . . . whatever strikes your fancy. Be publicized . . . anglicized . . . immortalized . . . Go on and alter your ego. Mix and match. After all, you have plenty of space to get it right in your very own "Playhouse 90 Percent."

Laura Kuritzky Pedegana

Caroline's Cremation

It's *Caroline's Cremation*
And we hope to see you there
We're on five nights a week
Plus Sunday matinee—with prayer
It's Off-Off Broadway's newest
Biggest latest hottest show
Come help send up dear Caroline
As she'd have liked to go

It's *Caroline's Cremation*
A bonanza family treat
John Simon gave it three thumbs up,
One finger, and both feet
So come on down and mourn with us
And please do not be late
You know how crazy Caroline gets
When people make her wait

Shake hands with her ex-lover
And his madly jealous wife
And Caroline's dear spouse
To whom she would have owed her life
If when he'd seen her face turn green
He hadn't lost his head
And fled the scene while she lay
Limp and twitching on the bed

Meet kindly Doctor Harris
Whose certificate of death
Was signed before dear Caroline
Had drawn her final breath
And Oscar the mortician
Who with admirable haste
Made all the preparations
In impeccable good taste

You'll hug all nine of Caroline's
Distraughtly weeping heirs
Who held the dear departed's life
More dear to them than theirs:
They'll prove they never planned
To push her wheelchair down the stairs

At last—the act climaxes
As the coffin disappears
And Caroline goes up in smoke
With all of us in tears . . .

Now intermission opens with
A long and moving sermon
And solos by the pastor's wife—
Who looks like Ethel Merman

While waiting to reclaim
The former contents of the casket
We're served a catered wake
With home-baked chicken-in-the-basket
Then we pick the dear departed up
At window number four
And as the house lights dim again
We're headed toward the shore

The second act moves quickly
As the mourners gather round
And scatter dear old Caroline
Across Long Island Sound
We hate to say good-bye
But time, alas, is kind of tight:
We must break in a fresh new corpse
From Equity
By eight o'clock
Tomorrow night . . .

. . . For *Caroline's Cremation*
And we hope to see you there
We're on five nights a week
Plus Sunday matinee—with prayer
It's Off-Off Broadway's newest
Biggest latest hottest show
Come help send up dear Caroline
As she'd have liked to go

June Sigler Siegel

Scam

> My ex-husband left this morning for Bermuda to play in a
> tennis tournament, leaving me his dog, who is too big for
> my house, our kids, and instructions on how to get into
> his house through a second-story window in case of an
> emergency.

Here's a sure-fire money maker: a story in less than fifty words. Written on index cards, stories like that could hang from the rear-view mirror in a car for something to think about during traffic jams. Or against the Lavoris at the dentist's office to work from during drillings. Or on the bathroom mirror for flossing time.

Well, look: from this one you know a lot about her. You know she's divorced and has kids. If you're paying attention, you know she shares custody because otherwise he wouldn't have left the kids with her, he would have just left.

You know her ex is rich. Relatively. I mean you don't exactly know that some weeks she doesn't have enough money to do the laundry, but you know she has a small house, and he's got a big one plus airplane tickets, and you could surmise that he survived the divorce nicely. You could assume he's got old money, since Bermuda's a place for preppies. And you'd be right.

You know he's an athlete. I mean he's old enough to have kids and he's still gallivanting off to play tennis. From the bit about the second-story window you could assume that she's an athlete, too. Or that he's too much of a schmuck to have made a second key.

If you're still at it, you could wonder whether she always falls for preppies. Whether she's remarried or has a lover. You could wonder about the kids—sex, age, smarts. Are they preppies? Not without constant clean laundry.

But you know that she's a respectable person, because he doesn't expect her to steal stuff from his house or read his diary or anything.

Actually, he's an idiot. Because that's exactly what I'm going to do. There's probably some great material for my index cards up there.

Taffy Field

Unsolved Mysteries

Heather McAdams

Looking Back and Commenting on Stuff

I hung out with a pretty depressed crowd in high school. On Friday nights we'd pile into a car and go joyless riding. I was suicidal at the time, but I didn't believe in violence and was a bit of a health nut. One night I decided to end it all by drinking gallons and gallons of Sleepytime Tea. The doctors said I lived only because it hadn't steeped enough. To this day I have bladder trouble.

My high school days have been on my mind lately because I recently received a letter from my old guidance counselor. That dedicated woman tracked me down after all these years because she discovered that a mistake had been made with my aptitude test results, and it turns out I wasn't gifted after all. In fact, my potential is much, much lower than originally assessed, and she wanted to let me know. I'm still not sure how I feel about this—I've spent years in therapy thinking I'm an underachiever—and now it turns out I'm an overachiever. My analyst pointed out that I was now free to address other issues. So I signed up for a class on self-love through the Learning Annex. It was called "How to Win Your Own Heart." And I did everything they said. I bought myself flowers. And candy. *Lots* of candy. I took long walks in the park. I held hands. After awhile, though, I sensed that it wasn't going anywhere, that there was no real commitment on my part, so I broke it off. I didn't have the guts to do it face to face, though—I called and left a message on my answering machine. I said, "Look, it's nothing personal, I just don't have room for you in my life right now . . . Okay, the *truth* is I was only in it for the sex—*which*, by the way, was *terrific!*" I was hoping I could still be friends, but at this point I'm too angry. I feel used.

Despite everything you may have heard, not all of us have a "child within." I, for instance, have a convicted felon within. I want him out. He won't leave. I've taken steps to have him evicted. He's formed a tenant's association. They're taking me to court. If I lose, I can't go co-op.

I've got this book on obsessive behavior! Couldn't put it down! It said, if you want to avoid obsessive thought patterns, place a rubber band around your wrist. Whenever you catch yourself obsessing, snap the band. It will hurt, and eventually those obsessive thoughts will cease. So I did it. For a while. I did it until my wrists became bloody and desensitized, at which point I decided that it would be wiser to go back to inflicting emotional pain on myself. So I started dating. I had just seen *Beauty and the Beast* for the seventh time, and felt myself strongly attracted to the Beast. I vowed to pay closer attention to cloven-hoofed animals in the future—just the wealthy, literate ones, of course, who lived in castles and dressed well. Certain that there was a Beast out there just for me ("a lid for every pot," as the saying goes), I answered some personal ads. I tried to curb my tendency to project too much onto the other person but I had so much hope that I just couldn't. At last, though, sitting across the table from me one evening was a guy who also projected! He assumed, based on my demeanor, that I had a tragic past, and he was intrigued. Looking deeply into my eyes he said, "Ah, mysterious, sorrowful Kate. Talk to me. Tell me about the great love of your life. The one who kicked your heart out and left you crushed, broken, without a shred of dignity." And I looked right back at him, faith shining in my eyes, and said, "I'm hoping it's you!"

Kate Shein

Contributors

SYBIL ADELMANN (131) is an established television writer, recipient of the Writers Guild of America Award, and was nominated for an Emmy for "Lily" (a Lily Tomlin special). A resident of New York City, she collaborates with her husband, Martin Sage.

JANETTE BARBER (115) is the four-time Emmy Award winning supervising producer of *The Rosie O'Donnell Show.* Janette came to TV by way of twelve years of stand-up comedy. After taking the job on *Rosie,* she wrote a best-selling book, *Breaking the Rules, Last Ditch Tactics for Landing the Man of Your Dreams,* and currently writes humor for the magazine *Rosie.* Janette volunteers with the private relief organization AmeriCares, based in New Canaan, Connecticut, and has participated in relief missions to Albania, Kosovo and The Republic of Congo.

JENNIFER BERMAN (50, 109, 201), developer of the self-syndicated cartoon "Berman," can be seen in the *Chicago Reader, Funny Times, East Bay Monthly, Pacific Sun,* and many other choice publications around the country. She is the owner of Humerus Cartoons, a postcard company that features her work. Jennifer has published four books of cartoons, including *Why Dogs Are Better Than Men,* and *Why Dogs Are Better Than Kids.* She lives in rural Ohio with four dogs, three cats, two Sicilian donkeys and one husband.

JENNY BICKS (23) has written on staff for numerous network sitcoms. For the past four years she has written and co-executive-produced *Sex and The City,* for which she has earned two Golden Globes, an Emmy, and a Writer's Guild nomination for Best Episode ("Four Women and a Funeral"). A native New Yorker, Bicks now lives in Los Angeles.

FRANCESCA BLUMENTHAL (259) won a schoolbag at the age of 7 for her story in a local newspaper. All grown up, she collected many gold and silver awards for ads and TV commercials for Fisher-Price, Perrier, and Guerlain perfumes. Later, as lyricist-composer, Francesca won MAC, Dramalogue and Bistro Awards for her musical revue, *Life Is Not Like the Movies.* Her ballad, *Lies of Handsome Men,* has been recorded by 14 singers, and formed the romantic climax of a CBS Movie-Of-The-Week.

ERMA BOMBECK (167), born, raised, and educated in Dayton, Ohio, became the author of more than a dozen books, her columns syndicated in over 700 newspapers. She began her writing career as a "copy girl" for the *Dayton Journal Herald,* where she found her career niche. She raised three children, and until her death, she and her husband lived in Arizona. Her best-selling books include, *The Grass is Always Greener Over the Septic Tank, I Want to Go Home, I Want to Grow Hair, I Want to Go to Boise,* and her last book, *All I Know About Animal Behavior I Learned in Loehmann's Dressing Room.*

PAIGE BRADDOCK (81, 274) is a graduate of the University of Tennessee with a degree in Fine Arts. After working at the *Chicago Tribune* as a staff artist, she moved to Atlanta where she is Graphics Editor for the *Atlanta Journal-Constitution*. She is a full member of the National Cartoonist Society and creator of the cartoon series "See Jane."

MICHELE BROURMAN (114, 204), singer/songwriter, is a winner of the Johnny Mercer Award for Emerging American Songwriters. Her songs have been recorded by Olivia Newton-John, Rita Coolidge, Cleo Laine, Sheena Easton, and Margaret Whiting, as well as by Amanda McBroom and Michael Feinstein. Together with McBroom, she has written the songs for ten animated features for Universal Studios. She is currently at work on several new theatrical musicals. Michele has two sons, Noah and Luke.

BULBUL (14) is the pen name for freelance cartoonist Genny Guracar. Her cartoons appear in labor, feminist, senior, environmental, and alternative publications as well as in many books. After 30 years, she is still going strong. The name Bulbul, in Middle Eastern poetry, is a bird of protest. She lives and works in Mountain View, California.

BRENDA BURBANK (141) has, since 1970, sold thousands of cartoons to a variety of publications, including the *National Enquirer,* the *Wall Street Journal,* and *Medical Economics*. She lives on five acres near Alvin, Texas, with her husband, Bob, three horses, three loud geese, and an amazing number of barn cats.

DALE BURG (143) most recently co-authored *Mary Ellen's Guide to Good Enough Housekeeping* (St. Martin's, 2002) and wrote *Sloth* (Red Rock Press, 2001). She has written 18 books and many articles as a columnist for *Woman's Day, Family Circle,* and the *Star,* and has taught comedy writing. She has not yet adopted a hedgehog or a ferret.

ELLEN BYRON (282) has written for television, theatre and dozens of magazines. Her plays have been produced at prominent theaters such as The Actors Theatre of Louisville and The Ensemble Studio Theatre, and include the award-winning *Graceland, Asleep on the Wind* and *Old Sins, Long Shadows*. Most recently, she was Co-Executive Producer on the critically acclaimed TV Series, *Maybe It's Me*. She is the proud and incredibly exhausted mother of two-year-old Eliza Molly Remillong.

MARTHA CAMPBELL (27, 151) is a syndicated cartoonist. A graduate of Washington University School of Fine Arts, she has written and designed for Hallmark Cards and illustrated 19 books. During her 27 years as a freelance artist, Campbell has had more than 15,000 cartoons published. She lives in Harrison, Arkansas.

FRAN CAPO (42) is a stand-up comic, freelance writer, voice-over artist, adventurist, motivational speaker and the *Guinness Book of World Records*

Fastest Talking Female. She has been on over 250 radio and 150 TV shows. She is also an author of four books, including *It Happened in New York* (Falcon Press 2000), *Almost a Wise Guy,* and *Adrenaline Adventures: Dream It, Read It, Do It!* You can find out more about Fran at her Website: http://www.francapo.com/ and read the complete adventures of *The Estrogen Files* at www.theestrogenfiles.net. Fran is also a single mom of the world's youngest comedian, Spencer Patterson, and proud of it.

ESTELLE CAROL AND BOB SIMPSON (40, 48, 233) have been doing cartoons for the labor movement for 15 years under the name Carol*Simpson. Estelle is a professional graphic artist and illustrator. She was cofounder of the Chicago Women's Graphics Collective, which distributed thousands of feminist posters worldwide from 1970-1983. Bob taught history in Chicago's inner-city schools for over 20 years before joining Estelle's graphic design business in 1998. You may view their labor cartoons at http://www.cartoonwork.com. They sincerely hope their work offends politicians and CEOs everywhere.

ROZ CHAST (184), syndicated cartoonist, has been a regular contributor to *The New Yorker* since 1978, and has published collections of her work, including *Proof of Life on Earth,* and she illustrated *Now Everybody Really Hates Me.* She lives in Connecticut with her husband and two children, and is currently working on a collection of cartoons about families.

CINDY CHUPACK (110) is a writer/executive producer on HBO's Golden Globe-winning series, *Sex and the City.* Episodes she penned have been nominated for WGA and Emmy awards. Prior to working on *Sex and the City,* she spent two seasons writing the Emmy-nominated series, *Everybody Loves Raymond,* and before that she wrote for *Coach,* and before that she wrote for a bunch of failed series only her parents would watch. Cindy has written many essays about dating and relationships for *Glamour, Harper's Bazaar,* and *Allure,* and she was recently given her own monthly column for single gals in *Glamour.* She looks forward to not being single eventually, but fears it will end her career.

ANNA COLLINS (42) is a stand-up comic, writer, humor columnist, voice-over talent, actress, and author of the best-selling parody *Women Are from Bras, Men Are from Penus.* She is also a Kodak and Photographer's Forum award-winning photographer. Ms. Collins resides in Ft. Lauderdale, Florida, where she exercises regularly. Visit her at her Website: http://www.annacollins.com/ and read the complete adventures of *The Estrogen Files* at www.theestrogenfiles.net

CATHY CRIMMINS (180) has authored nineteen books, including *When My Parents Were My Age, They Were Old* (Simon & Schuster), *Curse of the Mommy* (Putnam), and *Newt Gingrich's Bedtime Stories for Orphans* (Dove Books). Her book about her husband's traumatic brain injury, *Where is the Mango Princess?* (Knopf 2000, Vintage 2001), won the Outstanding Book Award from the American Society of Journalists and Authors (ASJA). Her articles have appeared in *The Village Voice, Redbook, Parents' Digest, Success, Hysteria, Glamour, Working Woman, Funny Times, Philadelphia Magazine, Working Mother,* and many other publications.

CATHY N. DAVIDSON (14) is the author or editor of over a dozen books, including her most recent works: *Closing: The Life and Death of an American Factory* (with photographer Bill Bamberger)(Norton, 1998) and *No More Separate Spheres!* (with Jessamyn Hatcher) (Duke University Press, 2002) She is Vice Provost for Interdisciplinary Studies at Duke University in Durham, North Carolina.

ELISA DECARLO (154) is a playwright and performer based in New York. Her most recent solo show, "Toasted," was performed at the American Living Room Festival at HERE, and at the 2001 San Francisco Fringe Festival. Elisa's other solo shows are "I Love Drugs" (Chopin Theater, Chicago; "Best of the San Francisco Fringe" 1995); "Cervix With A Smile," and a comic autobiography with original songs, "Size Matters" (Westbeth Theater Center). Her play *Buddy n' Janice* was produced off-off-Broadway in June, 2000. Elisa has written two award-winning novels, *The Devil You Say* and *Strong Spirits,* as well as many magazine and newspaper articles.

LIZA DONNELLY (107) has been contributing cartoons to *The New Yorker* magazine since 1979. Her work has been in numerous collections, and she is the editor of *Mothers and Daughters,* a book of cartoons. She lives in Rhinebeck, New York, with her husband and two daughters.

LESLEY DORMEN'S (264) short stories, essays and articles have been published in *The Atlantic Monthly, Five Points, Elle, O, Glamour,* and many other magazines. She is the co-author of *The Secret Life of Girls* and *The Grownup Girl's Guide to Boys.* Dormen teaches at the Writers Studio in New York and is working on a collection of short stories.

KELLI "TUGBOAT" DUNHAM (35) is a Vice-Versa award-winning writer, activist, and nurse living in Philadelphia. Her first book, *How to Survive and Maybe Even Love Nursing School,* was recently released by FA Davis Company. You can read more about Kelli's life as an ex-nun on the run at www.kellidunham.com.

JAN ELIOT (99, 113, 118, 127), syndicated cartoonist, has been published in several humor collections including *Women's Glibber, Mothers!,* and *Men are from Detroit, Women are from Paris.* Her comic, "Stone Soup," runs in over 135 markets and there are two book collections in print: *Stone Soup the Comic Strip.* and *You Can't Say Boobs On Sunday,* both from Four Panel Press. They can be viewed at www.stonesoupcartoons.com.

DELIA EPHRON (141) is an author and screenwriter. Her most recent novels include *Big City Eyes* and *Hanging Up* (for which she was also the co-screenwriter and producer of the film.) She has written many other books for adults and children. Two of these, *How to Eat Like a Child* and *Teenage Romance,* were best sellers. She is the co-screenwriter (with Nora Ephron) of *This Is My Life* and *Mixed Nuts, Michael,* and *You've Got Mail,* for which she also served as executive producer. She was the associate producer of *Sleepless In Seattle.* She began her writing career as a journalist for *New York* magazine. Her work has also been published in the *New York Times Magazine,* the *New York Times Book Review, Esquire,* and *Vogue* among others. She lives with her husband, Jerome Kass, in New York.

DEBBIE FARMER (88) is an award-winning, nationally syndicated humor columnist. Her column "Family Daze" is distributed by Oasis Newsfeatures Syndicate. Her essays have appeared in *Reader's Digest, Family Fun Magazine, the Christian Science Monitor,* and hundreds of parenting magazines in the U.S., Canada and Australia. She is a contributor to *Chicken Soup for the Gardener's Soul, Chicken Soup for the Mother's Soul II,* and *Chocolate for the Woman's Soul.* Her book, *Life in the Fast-Food Lane: Surviving the Chaos of Parenting,* is available on her Website: http://www.familydaze.com

TAFFY FIELD (291) has taught creative writing since 1971. Almost a hundred of her essays have been heard on public radio, on the broadcast edition of the *Christian Science Monitor* and for Maine Public Radio. *Short Skirts,* a collection of her fiction, was published in 1989. Her fiction has also been included in two previous anthologies of women's humor, *Women's Glib* and *Women's Glibber,* and her non-fiction in *The Journal of Family Life.* She lives in mid-coast Maine.

SALLY FINGERETT (222, 233, 252) was born a poor white Jewish child on the South Side of Chicago. She went to a respectable college, married and divorced a respectable man, lives as a respectable single mother of a struggling-to-be-respectable teenage daughter, in respectable Ohio. As a performer, Sally is one of the founding/touring members of the musical revue the Four Bitchin' Babes. She also tours her one-woman show, *Mental Yentl,* celebrating the quirks of her generation of Jewish Mothers. With five "Babe" CDs and four solo CDs to her credit, Sally is a winner of the Kerrville New Folk Award for Songwriting. She has joined the National Touring Company of the *Vagina Monologues* for its Columbus, Ohio, run. Her radio appearances include the nationally syndicated NPR shows *Mountain Stage, World Cafe,* and Michael Feldman's *Whad'ya Know?* You can find Sally on the Web at www.sallyfingerett.com or www.fourbitchinbabes.com

ANNE GIBBONS' (8, 136, 193) cartoons have appeared in many national publications, including *Reader's Digest, Glamour* and *Redbook.* Her greeting cards have been published by Recycled Paper Greetings for over ten years while Marion Heath Greeting Cards and Pictura USA have recently introduced lines of her cards as well. Anne was the recipient of the National Cartoonists Society's prestigious Reuben Award for Greeting cards in 2000. Anne's cartoons appear weekly on the Web at CartoonLink.com, in a feature called *Women At Work* and she has her own Website at www.annegibbons.com. Anne lives in New York City with her husband.

JULIE GOLD (199, 255) is a songwriter who lives in Greenwich Village. She is best known for her song "From A Distance"; Bette Midler's version won the Grammy for Song of the Year in 1991. She has written songs for everyone from Jewel to Kathie Lee Gifford to Patti LaBelle to Patti LuPone. She performs regularly around the country singing and/or giving motivational speeches. As the daughter of a Russian immigrant, she is happy to proclaim that her life truly is The American Dream.

MARTHA GRADISHER (34, 254), syndicated cartoonist, has an endless list of accomplishments but keeps forgetting where she put it. In her twentieth year of waiting to be discovered overnight, she has amused herself by collecting minor awards for her hideously underappreciated cartoons. Gradisher takes pride in the fact that she has never resorted to using the word "tampon" for a cheap laugh. Her work has appeared in *Ms., Glamour, Business Week, PC Magazine,* and publications of ABC News, NBC Radio Entertainment, and Chembank. She lives in South Nyack, New York, with her husband, two boys, a puppy, and a garage full of sporting equipment.

CATHY GUISEWITE (23, 74), creator of the comic strip "Cathy" ™, was born in Dayton, Ohio. A former advertising copywriter, she began her career in comics by doodling her daily life traumas in letters to her mother. Since then, "Cathy" ™, has grown to become syndicated in 1300 newspapers worldwide, with an audience of over 70 million readers. Currently, she lives in Los Angeles, California, with her sub-teen daughter. In 1992, she became the second winner, since 1946, of the National Cartoonist Society's Reuben Award.

JULIE HALSTON (148) is one of today's premier comic voices in clubs, and in theater, film, and on TV. Best known for her enormously popular solo shows in NY, she has also performed sold-out engagements around the country. She appears often on television as a commentator on such shows as *This Evening with Judith Regan, Good Day New York* and *CNN News.* Well known to theater audiences, she has appeared in many Broadway and Off-Broadway productions, and performed a stint in Eve Ensler's *The Vagina Monologues.* Her hilarious takes on contemporary life have been read in such magazines as *Harper's Bazaar, Woman's Day,* and *Notorious.* She resides in New York City with her husband, 1010 WINS radio anchorman, Ralph Howard.

MARIAN HENLEY (119, 240) shares attitude with "Maxine!," which has appeared weekly in newspapers since 1981. Marian's comics have also been included in *Ms., Glamour, New Age Journal, MAD, Heavy Metal,* and numerous textbooks, humor anthologies, self-help books, and wacko newsletters. A "Maxine!" anthology titled *Laughing Gas* will be released mid-2002. Be sure to visit www.maxine.net for all the latest.

GEORGIA BOGARDUS HOLOF (6) was a songwriter who contributed to *A . . . My Name is Alice, A . . . My Name is Still Alice,* and *Skirting the Issues.* She was the lyricist for Ray Bradbury's musical version of *Fahrenheit 451* and lyricist/bookwriter for *Internal Combustion.* Her work, *Taking Care of Mrs. Carroll,* based on a novel by Paul Monette, was produced in Chicago. Before she passed away, she lived in New York City with her husband. Georgia was the mother of Seattle comedienne Amy Alpine.

MOLLY IVINS (123) is a nationally-syndicated political columnist who remains cheerful despite Texas politics. She became an independent journalist in 2001 and also in that year won the William Allen White Award from the University of Kansas, the Smith Medal from Smith College and was elected to the National Academy of Arts and Sciences. Her freelance work has appeared in *GQ, Esquire, Atlantic, Harper's, TV Guide,* and many other publications. She is also known for her essays on the Lehrer News Hour and NPR, as well as four best-selling books, the most recent being *Shrub; The Short but Happy Political Life of George W. Bush.* Ivins is active in the journalism network of Amnesty International, supports the Reports Committee for Freedom of the Press and the ACLU, and often writes about First Amendment issues. Ivins counts as her highest honors that the Minneapolis police force named its mascot pig after her, and she was once banned from the campus of Texas A&M.

LYNN JOHNSTON (189), award-winning cartoonist and creator of the syndicated comic "For Better or For Worse," was born in Ontario, Canada, where she continues to reside with her husband and children. According to Johnston, the source of much of the humor of her famous comic strip is "life." There have been 20 collections and seven special editions to date of "For Better or For Worse." Her comic strip currently appears in over 2000 publications worldwide and is printed in eight languages.

MADELEINE BEGUN KANE (164) writes about work, cars, computers, the Net, marriage, and other topics. She has received many awards, including one from the National Society of Newspaper Columnists. Her satirical Dubya's Dayly Diary at http://www.madkane.com/bush.html was named USA Today Hot Site of the Day and USA Today Fun Site of the Week and was awarded an About.com Bushie for Best Bush Parody on the Web. She has been published in the *New York Times,* the *Philadelphia Inquirer,* the *Chicago Tribune, Family Circle,* the *Miami Herald,* and has been featured by the *Los Angeles Times* Syndicate, Knight-Ridder/Tribune, and TheCarConnection.com. To read more of her humor, visit http://www.madkane.com

NURIT KARLIN (91) is a cartoonist and illustrator whose work is frequently seen in the *New York Times,* the *Washington Post,* the *Wall Street Journal,* and a variety of magazines. She is also the author and illustrator of several children's books. Karlin lives in New York City.

MARTA KAUFFMAN (137) is one of the authors of *A . . . My Name is Alice* and is the creator of the television comedy *Friends.* She lives in Los Angeles, California.

MARGO KAUFMAN (100) was the author of *1-800-Am I Nuts?,* a collection of humorous essays about life's little annoyances, published by Random House, and *This Damn House!,* an amusing look at remodeling, published by Villard. Her work appeared in publications including the *New York Times, Los Angeles Times, Good Housekeeping,* and *Redbook,* and she was the Hollywood correspondent for *Pug Talk Magazine.* She was heard weekly on the *Ken and Barkley Company,* KABC Talkradio, where she was their official "Gripe Lady." Before she passed away, she lived in Venice, California.

LAURA KURITZKY PEDEGANA (286), a freelance writer, is an alumna of the Warner Bros. TV Comedy Writers' Workshop, and has been involved in television development and production for ten years. She lives in Westlake Village, California, with her husband and her two mini-muses, Amy and Andrew.

LIEBE LAMSTEIN (75, 203) is a cartoonist whose work has appeared in the *National Enquirer, Good Housekeeping, Cosmopolitan,* and *Reader's Digest,* among other publications. Her cartoons were included in Avis Lang Rosenberg's international exhibition, Pork Roast, and are presently distributed through Jerry Robinson's Cartoonists and Writers Syndicate. Liebe lives in Brooklyn, New York.

CHRISTINE LAVIN (216, 241, 256) is a singer/songwriter/guitarist who has recorded 13 solo albums of original material and continues to perform concerts all over the world. She has written stories for the *St. Petersburg Times,* the *Washington Post,* and more. In 2001 *Backstage Magazine* named her "Outstanding Singer/Songwriter of the Year." She is the occasional guest host of *Cityfolk Sunday Breakfast,* a radio program on WFUV, public radio from Fordham University. Visit her award-winning Website at www.christinelavin.com to see what she's up to.

MARY LAWTON'S (13, 249) cartoons appear in a wide variety of publications, including *Utne Reader, Ms., San Francisco Chronicle, Hippocrates, Funny Times,* and *Comic Relief.* Her work has also appeared in several collections including *Getting in Touch With Your Inner Bitch, The Best Contemporary Women's Humor, Men Are from Detroit, Women Are from Paris,* and *Pandemonium, Or Life With Kids.* Her cartoons have been on exhibition in Boston, Berkeley, and at the Cartoon Art Museum in San Francisco. A native New Yorker, Lawton now lives in Houston, Texas.

CONTRIBUTORS

LISSA LEVIN (38) has been a writer and producer of television for sixteen years. Her credits include *WKRP in Cincinnati, Cheers, Family Ties,* Showtime's *Brothers* (which garnered her a CableAce Award nomination), Fox's *Women in Prison, Married People, Live Shot* and *Mad About You.* Her first musical, *Twist of Fate,* (for which she was librettist/lyricist) won two L.A. Drama Critics Circle Awards, *L.A. Weekly's* Musical of the Year, an Ovation nomination for Musical of the Year, and the Kleban Award for her libretto. She lives in Chatsworth, California, with her husband, television writer/producer Dan Gunzelman, and is the mother of two wonderful children.

GAIL MACHLIS' (95, 159, 206) syndicated cartoon, "Quality Time," was distributed by Chronicle Features Syndicate and later Universal Press Syndicate. She is the author of *Quality Time and Other Quandaries* (Chronicle Books). Her work has also appeared in *Ms., Cosmopolitan, New Woman, The Artist's Magazine, Road and Track,* and *The Writer* magazine. She is currently doing freelance illustration, and writing and illustrating children's books.

MERRILL MARKOE (9, 275), has written for *Rolling Stone,* the *New York Times, Time, US, U.S. News and World Report,* the *Los Angeles Times, L.A. Weekly, New Woman, New York Woman* and numerous other magazines and television shows. She also won five Emmys for writing on "Late Night with David Letterman." Her fifth book, and first novel, *It's My F...ing Birthday,* was published by Villard. She is currently writing a pilot for HBO.

JANE READ MARTIN (53) began her career at *Saturday Night Live* and was Woody Allen's assistant on nine films and Associate Producer of his film *Alice.* In addition to "Rosebud," which was selected for the 1992 Edinburgh Film Festival, she has written two children's books, *Now Everybody Really Hates Me* and *Now I'll Never Leave the Dinner Table* (both co-authored by Patricia Marx and published by HarperCollins). Born and raised in Princeton, New Jersey, and a graduate of Denison University, she resides in New York City with her husband, screenwriter/director Douglas McGrath, and their son.

PATRICIA MARX (279) was the first woman to write for the *Harvard Lampoon* and has since published in the *New Yorker, Atlantic,* the *New York Times, Vogue,* and *Spy.* She was a staff writer for *Saturday Night Live* and has written for many other TV shows. She has also written several screenplays and a number of books, including *How To Regain Your Virginity* and *Now Everybody Really Hates Me* (the latter co-authored with Jane Read Martin). She teaches comedy writing at New York University.

HEATHER McADAMS (37, 292) is a Chicago-based cartoonist, illustrator, and filmmaker whose work has appeared in the *Chicago Reader, Chicago Tribune,* the *New York Times, Nickelodeon, Mademoiselle* and the *New York*

Press. She is the author of *Cartoon Girl,* published by Longstreet Press. McAdams has made numerous 16mm films (available for rent through Filmmaker Co-op, New York City, and Canyon Cinema, San Francisco). Currently, she and her husband, Chris Ligon, are doing animation for MTV.

AMANDA MCBROOM (191, 194) is an actress/singer/songwriter, and a heck of a nice girl. She is best known as the composer of Bette Midler's Grammy-winning hit song, "The Rose." Currently, she has six albums and an interesting concert career. She lives in Ojai, California, with her absolutely perfect husband, George Ball. For all the latest on Amanda, visit www.amcbroom.com.

LISA MCCORMICK (214), alternative folk/rocker, is known for her outstanding songwriting and engaging live performances. She is characterized by daring and sophisticated lyrics, infectious guitar rhythms, and a powerful singing voice. Her debut CD, *Right Now,* received three preliminary Grammy nominations and its title song took the Grand Prize in the USA Songwriting Contest. Boston's *New England Performer* magazine calls Lisa McCormick ". . . an absolute genius. She is funny, sexy, smart, literate, sardonic, witty, and sings with all the power of a rock diva." Additional information is available at www.LisaMcCormick.com.

THERESA MCCRACKEN (185), struggles daily to meet the humor needs of the nation, creating cartoons and writing humorous article for hundreds of magazines and newspapers ranging from the *Saturday Evening Post* to the *Oregonian* to small trade journals. She lives in the woods outside of Waldport, OR with a bunch of stray animals. To see some of her cartoons, go to www.pioneer.net/~mchumor or contact her at mchumor@pioneer.net.

MEGON MCDONOUGH (221) is from Chicago and is the mother of a school-aged son. She has ten recording projects to her credit, including her latest Shanachie release, *My One And Only Love,* a collection of jazz standards. Her voice has been heard all over television—singing the theme for an HBO Olympic ice-skating special (which won her a cable TV ACE award) and enlivening a Danielle Steel made-for-TV movie. Megon's musical theater career has really taken flight in recent years. Her credits include productions of *Pump Boys And Dinettes, Beehive,* and her box office record-breaking portrayal of Patsy Cline in *Always Patsy Cline* (that performance garnered her a Joseph Jefferson Award nomination). She released a CD in August 2001 of Patsy Cline songs sung to jazz guitar arrangements/performances by Don Stiernberg called *The Patsy Project.* Her latest one-woman show, *An Interesting Bunch of Gals,* delighted audiences nationwide. Visit www.MegonMcDonough.com for all the latest.

CONTRIBUTORS

HESTER MUNDIS (269) is a humorist, a four-time Emmy nominee, and the author of twenty-two books, including *101 Ways to Avoid Reincarnation or Getting it Right the First Time*. She is the mother of two only sons and a chimpanzee.

ROBIN BROURMAN MUNSON (114) is a licensed Marriage and Family counselor, but writing has been her lifelong passion. Her songs have been performed by several distinguished artists and showcased on Nostalgia Television's *Live at The Russian Tea Room* series. She lives in Kingston Springs, Tennessee, with her husband, Art Munson.

SUSAN MURRAY (159) is an actor, writer, and comedian. The *Daily News* called her "One of the funniest improvisation comedians in New York City." Susan has performed Off-Broadway with Chicago City Limits and in London and Los Angeles with TheatreSports. After years of thinking fast on her feet, Susan finally decided she could write sitting down. She is the author of two plays: *The View from Relative Obscurity* and *The Mommy Show (If It's Not One Thing It's Your Mother)*, both of which premiered in New York City. She recently completed a musical for children entitled *Sandy Land!* which was commissioned by the PGT Theater.

KATHY NAJIMY (48) is an award-winning actress, writer, producer, and director. She was co-creator and star of *The Kathy and Mo Show*, an off-Broadway show for which she won an Obie as well as an American Comedy Award Nomination. Her two HBO specials based on that show garnered a total of four Ace Awards and an American Comedy Award nomination for Kathy. She is most widely known for her work in such films as *Sister Act* (American Comedy Award for Best Supporting Actress), *The Fisher King, Soapdish, The Wedding Planner, Rat Race* and several others. Television credits include a starring role in TNT's *In Search of Dr. Seuss*, and for three seasons she appeared as Olive on NBC's *Veronica's Closet*. Ms. Najimy is currently starring in FOX's Emmy Award winning *King of the Hill* as Peggy Hill, a role for which she won an Annie (animation award) for best actress. She is an activist for AIDS, Women's Rights and Choice. She lives in LA with her husband, rock musician Dan Finnerty, their daughter Samia, and two dogs, Blondie and Happy.

LYNN NOTTAGE (31) is a playwright from Brookyln, New York. Her plays include *'Po'Knockers, Crumbs From the Table of Joy, Las Meninas,* and *Poof*. A contributor to *A . . . My Name is Still Alice*, she is the recipient of playwriting fellowships from New Dramatists, the New York Foundation for the Arts, and Manhattan Theatre Club. Nottage is a graduate of Brown University and The Yale School of Drama.

ELLEN ORLEANS (156, 170) lives, writes and teaches in Boulder, CO. Her latest book, *The Inflatable Butch*, was nominated for a 2002 Lambda

Literary Award. Her other titles include *Can't Keep A Straight Face, Who Cares If It's a Choice,* and 1995 Lammy Award winner, *The Butches of Madison County.* She holds an MFA from Goddard College and an Honorable Mention in Ben and Jerry's 1994 "Yo! I'm Your CEO" contest.

MARY JO PEHL (207) is a former writer and actor for *Mystery Science Theater 3000,* nominated for two Emmy Awards and winner of a Peabody Award. Her commentaries have been featured on *All Things Considered* on NPR, *The Savvy Traveler* on Public Radio International and *Almanac,* a regional PBS news program. She is also co-author of the book, *Mystery Science Theater 3000 Amazing Colossal Guide,* and her work has appeared in publications like *Funny Times* and the *Minneapolis Star Tribune,* as well as many on-line magazines.

ANNA QUINDLEN (82, 151) has been called the "laureate of real life" and "the most eloquent voice" of her generation. Her *New York Times* column, "Public and Private," won the Pulitzer Prize in 1992 and was anthologized as *Thinking Out Loud.* Many of her "Life in the Thirties" columns are included in the collection *Living Out Loud.* Ms. Quindlen's novels, *Object Lessons* and *One True Thing* were both bestsellers. She lives in northern New Jersey.

ELIZABETH RAPOPORT (229) is a freelance writer and editor whose essays and articles have appeared in the *New York Times, Salon, Sky Magazine, Redbook* and many other magazines. Her work has also been anthologized in *Mothers Who Think: Tales of Real-Life Parenthood.* She lives in Westchester with her husband and two children.

KAREN RIZZO (20) is in her eighth year of a month-long trip to Los Angeles. Her essays have appeared in the *Los Angeles Times, Salon.com,* and several women's magazines. She and her two small children can usually be found in a South Pasadena coffee shop weekdays at 4.

FLASH ROSENBERG (1, 30, 41, 87, 103, 129, 162, 173, 179, 213, 261, 285) is an observer who researches the curiosities of life for everyone's amusement. She draws, writes, performs, sews, photographs, and makes films. Her cartoons, illustrations, and essays have appeared in the *New York Times, Wall Street Journal, Forward, Funny Times,* and *Lilith,* where she was awarded the 1999 American Jewish Press Association Award for Best Illustration in a Jewish Magazine. Her one-woman comic slide performance, *Camping in the Bewilderness* has been staged internationally. Flash also actively works as a freelance photographer. She can be reached at Flashberg@aol.com.

AMY KROUSE ROSENTHAL (19, 183) is the author of *The Book of Eleven: An Itemized Collection of Brain Lint, The Mother's Guide to the Meaning of Life: What I've Learned On My Neverending Quest to Become a Dalai Mama,* and *The Same*

Phrase Describes My Marriage and My Breasts: Before the Kids They Used To Be Such A Cute Couple. Her work has appeared in the *New York Times, Utne Reader,* and on National Public Radio. Her humor column "15 Megabytes of Fame" runs weekly at www.mommymommy.com. She is the founding editor of *Writers' Block Party: An Audio Magazine,* a CD showcasing writers and musicians coast to coast (www.writersblockparty.com). She is best known for never leaving the house with an umbrella.

CATHLEEN SCHINE (210) grew up in Westport, Connecticut. She attended Sarah Lawrence College, Barnard College, and the University of Chicago. The author of four novels, *Alice in Bed, To the Birdhouse, Rameau's Niece,* and *The Love Letter,* Schine is a regular contributor to the "Endpaper" column of the *New York Times Magazine.* She has also written for the *New York Times Book Review, New York Review of Books,* and the *New Yorker.* She lives in New York City with her husband, David Denby, and their two sons.

MINDY SCHNEIDER (221) is a comedy writer whose television credits include *Kate & Allie* and the *Tom Arnold Show.* Originally from New Jersey, she now lives in Los Angeles, California. She is still five-feet-four.

KATE SHEIN (262, 293) is a writer, comedian and actress—usually in that order. As a stand-up comedian, she won the "Funniest Person in Manhattan" contest. She has had her work published in *One on One: The Best Women's Monologues for the Nineties* and featured in *A . . . My Name Is Still Alice* as well as *A . . . My Name Will Always Be Alice.* She resides in California with her husband, author Garrett Soden, and a bunch of cats.

SHERRIE SHEPHERD (220) is a cartoonist who lives in North Little Rock, Arkansas.

JUNE SIGLER SIEGEL (2, 108, 288) has written lyrics for the *A . . . My Name is Alice* cycle, *The Housewives' Cantata, That's Life!* and other Off-Broadway musicals. Her staged theatre pieces and monologues have been anthologized in *Facing Forward* (Broadway Play Publishing) and Random House's *Crème De La Femme.* She is still working on the kaleidoscopic project begun at AMAS Musical Theatre, *Lipstick Politics: Women's Lives in the New Millennium.* The good news? It's almost finished. The bad news? It's not yet funded. And that's all the news right now from New Rochelle.

YVETTE JEAN SILVER, (147, 198) is a cartoonist/caricaturist/humorist of note. As The Strolling Caricaturist, she has drawn over 15,000 faces at trade shows and special events. She has published two books, *To Work Is Human, but Retirement Is Divine* and *Grandparents Run in the Family.* Yvette's animation storyboard won third place in Hanna-Barbera's national competition. Yvette lives in New York City with her husband, Marc, and their two sons, Lance and David. You can visit Yvette at her Website www.yvettesilver.com.

CONTRIBUTORS

CATHERINE SIRACUSA (123) is a writer, cartoonist, and illustrator. Her humorous drawings and cartoons have appeared in many books, newspapers and magazines, including *Cosmopolitan* and the *New York Times*. Among her published books are *Beef Stew, No Mail for Mitchell, The Peanut Butter Gang, The Parrot Problem,* and *Banana Split from Outerspace*. She lives and works in New York City with her husband, author-illustrator Sidney Levitt.

DEBI SMITH (232, 250) is a contemporary singer/songwriter/instrumentalist. Her media appearances include repeat performances on CMT (Country Music Television), *A Prairie Home Companion,* and *All Things Considered* She tours and performs as a soloist and as a member of The Smith Sisters and The Four Bitchin' Babes. She has won a half-dozen Wammies—Washington Area Music Awards—including Best Female Vocalist, Best Contemporary Folk Album (*More Than Once,* Shanachie), and Best New Artist. Her third solo album on Shanachie records is entitled *Redbird*. You can find her on the Web at www.DebiSmith.com.

JANET SMITH (65) is a retired performer and songwriter, now running her music publishing company, Bella Roma Music, in Berkeley, California. Working with Ann Draffkorn Kilmer at UC Berkeley, she creates background music for museums displaying the "Treasures from the Royal Tombs of Ur" exhibit, using samples of a replicated lyre and other acoustic type sounds on a synthesizer. Her upcoming CD will be soon available in museums and on her Website at joyinsharing.com. Parties interested in ancient lyre tunings and notation can e-mail Janet at jcsmith8@pacbell.net.

YEARDLEY SMITH (75) has appeared on Broadway, television and films. She played Marlene, the crabby secretary, on *Dharma & Greg* and she has been the voice of Lisa Simpson on *The Simpsons* since it began. She is working on publishing her first collection of short stories.

MARCIA STEIL (92) was born in Glenview, Illinois, into a normal, happy family except "we probably laughed more than most families." She later taught English at Evanston Township High School and taught history in a middle school in Los Angeles, where she currently writes and lives with her husband (who still can't find anything in the refrigerator).

GLORIA STEINEM (104) is a writer, editor, and feminist organizer, who co-founded *Ms.* magazine (in 1972), the National Women's Political Caucus (in 1971), and such other expressions of the modern Women's Movement as Voters for Choice and the Ms. Foundation for Women. She has published numerous articles and books, including *Revolution from Within* and *Moving Beyond Words*. She lives in New York City.

CARRIE ST. MICHEL (51, 196) is a contributing editor at *Good Housekeeping*, and a frequent contributor to other national women's magazines including *Parents, Working Mother* and *Family Circle*. She previously wrote a weekly syndicated humor column for the *Los Angeles Times*.

JUDITH STONE (96, 119, 186) was a contributing editor at *Discover, Health*, and *Glamour* magazines before becoming arts and features editor of *Mirabella*. She was formerly articles editor of *McCall's*, and of *Science Digest*. "Light Elements," the humor column she wrote for *Discover*, won a 1989 National Headliner Award. She is the author of *Light Elements: Essays on Science from Gravity to Levity* (Ballantine, 1991) and co-author, with Nicole Gregory, of *Healing Your Inner Dog: A Self-Whelp Book* (Times Books, 1993), a parody of the inner child movement. Her work has appeared in the *New York Times Magazine, Village Voice, Newsday, Elle, Vogue, Self, Ms., American Health*, and other publications. She was a member of the touring company of The Second City, the improvisational theater troupe.

M. SWEENEY LAWLESS (67, 235) was born in St. Louis, Missouri, and later attained her present height. She is a founding member of comedy troupes like Euphobia and The Central Fungus and was a member of the Chicago City Limits national touring company. Her work appears in Thurber House's *Mirth of a Nation II: The Best Contemporary Humor* (HarperCollins). Meg is a founding member of Young Survival Coalition (www.youngsurvival.org), an organization for women in their 20s and 30s who have survived breast cancer. She can hide up to five bees secretly in her mouth.

JACKIE TICE (219) won the prestigious Kerrville New Folk Award for Emerging Songwriters in 1996. Jackie tours the eastern half of the country as a performing singer/songwriter and has two CDs available from www.jackietice.com. Jackie is currently writing music for a film project and is in preproduction for her next album, *Second Skin*. A mother of preteens, she has become very adept at deciphering code language, and, incidentally, is fortunate enough to be in the care of two of the greatest kids on the planet!

MARTHA TRACHTENBERG (202) has had an interesting life, and she wears many hats—milliners take note! Back at the dawn of time, roughly 1973, she was a founding member of the Buffalo Gals, the first all-woman bluegrass band. She has spent most of the years since then as a working musician, largely—and happily—avoiding "real" jobs. *It's About Time*, her first solo CD, was released on Mom and Pop Records at the end of 1999; read all about it (and listen!) at www.momandpoprecords.com. Her first book, *Anne McCaffrey: Science Fiction Storyteller*, was published by Enslow Publishing, Inc., in May 2001, and while it was being written, she copyedited two of Anne's books. Martha and her erstwhile vegetarian husband are still married, and have a splendid, omnivorous son.

JUDITH VIORST (80) is a poet, nonfiction writer, novelist, playwright, and lecturer. She is the author of numerous works of both poetry and prose, among them *Necessary Losses, Forever Fifty and Other Negotiations, When Did I Stop Being 20 and Other Injustices,* as well as sixteen children's books. She resides in Washington, D.C., with her husband Milton, who is the author of several critically acclaimed political books. They have three sons, Anthony, Nicholas, and Alexander, and, so far, four grandchildren.

PATRICIA VOLK (174) is the author of the novel *White Light,* and two short story collections, *The Yellow Banana* and *All It Takes.* Ms. Volk's work has been published in the *New York Times Magazine, The New Yorker, New York, Playboy, GQ, Redbook, Mirabella, Allure, Good Housekeeping, Cosmopolitan,* and *Family Circle, among others.* A New York writer, Volk wrote the "Cityscape" column for *New York Newsday.* Her new book, *Stuffed: Adventures of a Restaurant Family,* (Knopf) has been short-listed for the James Beard Award and the Borders Award and is being made into a major motion picture.

JANE WAGNER (274, 278) has received four Emmys, a Writer's Guild Award, and Peabody for her work in television. She is the author of *Edith Ann, My Life, So Far* and the Tony Award-winning *The Search for Intelligent Life in the Universe.* She lives in Los Angeles, California.

WENDY WASSERSTEIN (85, 130, 163) is a contributor to *Harper's Bazaar, The New Yorker,* the *New York Times* and other publications. She is the Pulitzer Prize-winning author of *The Heidi Chronicles* and *The Sisters Rosensweig* and the essay collection, *Shiksa Goddess.*

RIGGIN WAUGH (28) was born during the Eisenhower administration and lives in Takoma Park, Maryland. She is the editor of two anthologies: *Dykes With Baggage: The Lighter Side of Lesbians and Therapy* (Alyson Books, 2000) and *Ex-Lover Weird Shit: A Collection of Short Fiction, Poetry, and Cartoons for Lesbians and Gay Men* (Two Out of Three Sisters Press [TOOTS], 1995).

CAMILLE WEST (226, 238), songwriter, diva extraordinaire, and chocoholic, has been delivering musical humor to audiences for the past 13 years. Since 1997, Camille has been a member of the national touring group The Four Bitchin' Babes. She was honored by the Kennedy Center in 1996. Most recently, Camille's song "Viagra® in the Waters" was named Song of the Year 2000 by the nationally syndicated *Dr. Demento* radio program. Camille lives in upstate New York with her husband, Scott, and two sons. Visit Camille's Website, www.camillewest.com, or www.fourbitchinbabes.com.

CONTRIBUTORS

CHERYL WHEELER (244, 247), New England resident and well-known singer/songwriter, is equally well known as a raconteur. The story that leads up to a performance of one of her songs is often as important to her fans as the song itself. Having learned that control over comedic timing is ceded once it is recorded, Wheeler normally saves her choicest moments for live appearances. Occasionally however, righteous indignation gets the better of her, she puts pen to paper in a diatribe on some utterly familiar topic, and somehow reveals to us the ridiculous. Visit her Website, www.cherylwheeler.com.

SIGNE WILKINSON (143) is an internationally syndicated cartoonist whose work appears regularly in *USA Today* and the *Philadelphia Inquirer.* A cartoonist for the *Philadelphia Daily News* since 1985, Wilkinson, in 1992, became the only female ever to win the Pulitzer Prize for Editorial Cartooning. A graduate of Denver University, she studied at the Philadelphia College of Art and the Pennsylvania Academy of Fine Arts. She has served as a museum art director, and written commentary and book reviews. A collection of her work, *Abortion Cartoons on Demand,* was published in 1992. A past president of the Association of American Editorial Cartoonists, she creates special cartoons for *Working Woman* and *Organic Gardening.*

Notes on the Charities

American Foundation for AIDS Research

National Alliance of Breast Cancer Organizations

National Coalition Against Domestic Violence

amfAR™

AIDS RESEARCH

The American Foundation for AIDS Research (amfAR) is the nation's leading nonprofit organization dedicated to the support of HIV/AIDS research, AIDS prevention, treatment education, and the advocacy of sound AIDS-related public policy. Funded by voluntary contributions from individuals, foundations, and corporations, amfAR has invested nearly $190 million in support of its mission since 1985 and awarded grants to over 1900 research teams worldwide.

amfAR is currently funding efforts to design a safe and effective AIDS vaccine that could prevent HIV infection worldwide; develop topical microbicides that could block the sexual transmission of HIV, particularly among women; and discover improved treatments and methods of restoring immune function for people now living with HIV/AIDS.

Since 1986, amfAR has published the respected *HIV/AIDS Treatment Directory*, a comprehensive, up-to-date guide to treatments and clinical trials that is available as a searchable online database at www.amfar.org/td. In addition, amfAR sponsors a variety of educational programs, including continuing medical education courses, community forums, and conferences.

As it has since the start of the epidemic, amfAR remains at the forefront of efforts to protect the human rights of all people affected by HIV/AIDS and to ensure the adoption of rational and compassionate AIDS-related public policy. The foundation advocates necessary increases in federal funding for HIV/AIDS research, expanded access to treatment and care, and a comprehensive national HIV/AIDS prevention strategy that includes making sterile syringes easily accessible to injection drug users.

For more information, please write to amfAR, 120 Wall Street, 13th Floor, New York, NY 10005-3902, or call (212) 806-1600, or visit amfAR online at www.amfar.org.

**NATIONAL ALLIANCE
OF BREAST CANCER
ORGANIZATIONS**

Founded in 1986, the National Alliance of Breast Cancer Organizations® (NABCO®) is the leading non-profit information and education resource on breast cancer. NABCO's programs educate the public and offer information, resources and referrals to patients and their families, medical professionals and their organizations, and the media. A national force in patient advocacy, NABCO works on the community, state and federal levels for regulatory change and legislation to benefit patients, survivors and women at risk. With public and corporate partners such as the Women's National Basketball Association, Lifetime Television and Sears, NABCO collaborates on educational and medical programs that are successful in reaching a national audience, heightening public awareness and connecting women with needed services. The *Within Our Reach* program, NABCO's national grantmaking and technical assistance fund, extends breast cancer education, screening and diagnosis to underserved women in their communities. NABCO's network of over 400 member organizations and supportive providers, agencies, professional associations and corporations provide detection and diagnosis, treatment and care, advocacy and research throughout the breast cancer community in the United States. All services are provided free of charge.

Reach NABCO at
www.nabco.org,
or toll-free at
1-888-80-NABCO.

NATIONAL
COALITION
AGAINST
DOMESTIC
VIOLENCE

Every Home A Safe Home

The National Coalition Against Domestic Violence (NCADV) was formed in 1978 to provide a national network for over 2,000 local programs and state coalitions serving battered women and their children.

NCADV provides general information and referrals, technical assistance, community awareness campaigns, public policy advocacy and sponsors a national conference every two years.

NCADV's work includes efforts to:

- Eliminate Domestic Violence
- Empower Survivors of Domestic Violence
- Promote and Unify Direct Services for Survivors of Domestic Violence
- Alert and Educate the Public
- Promote Partnerships with Organizations and Corporations

In addition, NCADV actively strives to expand the body of information on the impact of violence in the lives of children and youth, and to encourage society's effective response to that impact.

To learn more about domestic violence or NCADV, contact us at:

NCADV
P. O. Box 18749
Denver, CO 80218
303-839-1852
303-831-9251 Fax
www.ncadv.org

Credits and Permissions

Sybil Adelman's "Nanny Tyrannica" first appeared in *Child* magazine.

The cartoons from *Adult Children of Normal Parents* are reprinted by permission of Pocket Books, a division of Simon & Schuster. Copyright © 1994 by Jennifer Berman.

Excerpt from *A Marriage Made in Heaven* by Erma Bombeck, © 1993, reprinted with the permission of the Aaron Priest Literary Agency.

Ellen Byron's "Just Say 'Purl'" was originally printed in *Playgirl* magazine, June 1989. Reprinted by permission.

Cindy Chupack's "The End" originally appeared in *Glamour*.

The excerpt from *When My Parents Were My Age They Were Old* is reprinted with the permission of Simon & Schuster. Copyright © by Cathy Crimmins.

"Typical Japanese Woman," an excerpt from *36 Views of Mount Fuji: On Finding Myself in Japan*, by Cathy N. Davidson. © 1993 by Cathy N. Davidson. Used by permission of Dutton Signet, a division of Penguin Books USA Inc.

Leslie Dormen's "85 Things Every Young Woman Should Know" originally appeared in *Glamour*.

"How to Talk to Your Stepmother," an excerpt from *Funny Sauce* by Delia Ephron, © 1983, 1986, by Delia Ephron. Used by permission of Viking Penguin, a division of Penguin Books USA, Inc.

Sally Fingerett's "Tonight's Menu" originally appeared in song form as "Take Me Out To Eat" on *Buy Me, Bring Me, Take Me, Don't Mess My Hair, Life According to Four Bitchin' Babes Vol. 2*, Rounder Records (starring Christine Lavin, Julie Gold, Sally Fingerett, and Megon McDonough).

"Ida Mae Cole Takes a Stance" originally appeared in *A . . . My Name Is Still Alice*, conceived by Joan Micklin Silver and Julianne Boyd.

"Good Morning Fort Worth" from *Nothin' But Good Times Ahead* by Molly Ivins. Copyright © 1993 by Molly Ivins. Reprinted by permission of Random House, Inc.

FOR BETTER OR FOR WORSE © 1993 Lynn Johnston Prod. Inc. Reprinted with permission of Universal Press Syndicate.

"Welcome to Kindergarten Mrs. Johnson" originally appeared in *A . . . My Name Is Alice*, conceived by Joan Micklin Silver and Julianne Boyd.

"Parental Proposal" © Madeleine Begun Kane, first published by AOL.

"The Silent Partner" from *1-800-Am I Nuts?* by Margo Kaufman. Copyright © 1993 Margo Kaufman. Reprinted by permission of Random House, Inc., and the author.